Acclaim for
Identity Envy—Wanting to Be W
Creative Nonfiction by Que

"In a culture that often gives short shrift to the complexities of identity, this
book offers up a collection of truly fresh, inspiring, and revelatory explorations
of those shifting sands that make up the unsure ground of who we think we are
and what others assume us to be. A fascinating exploration of the formation of
identity, *Identity Envy* does what all great books do—it asks its readers to examine its subject matter as it pertains to themselves, encouraging all of us to not
only reflect on our own projections and struggles with self-acceptance, but beyond that, it invites us to examine the dynamics of our very sexuality and how it
aids us in integrating those parts of ourselves we perceive as 'other'. . . contains
testimonial after testimonial to the redemptive power of knowing oneself. . . .
A wonderful treatment of a very topical and misunderstood issue, an inspirational compendium of the power of the individual to not only integrate different
aspects of his or her identity, but to move beyond socially-imposed identities,
whether they be dictated by religion, ethnicity, gender, class, place—or even
sexual orientation vis-à-vis the dominant gay and lesbian culture which can op-
press as well as liberate. This book plumbs the depths of identity formation, examining all aspects of the issue, from externally-imposed identities to the
freedom and fluidity of creating our own internal identities. Ultimately it celebrates the courage of queer folk to assert their unique identities in the face of oppression and social stigma. . . . Deals with serious social and psychological issues
yet is filled with wonderful humor, inspiring tales of courage, and the enthusiasm and joy of self-realization and growth."

—Trebor Healey,
Author of *Through It Came Bright Colors*

"*Identity Envy* does what you always hope a good book will do—it takes you deep
into the lives of a group of fascinating, and in this case often startlingly honest,
people. You become so engrossed in their stories, full of hope and nostalgia, disappointment and courage, that you finish the book wishing you could know
each of them, even better, in person."

—Robert Taylor,
Author of *Whose Eye Is On Which Sparrow?* and *A Few Hints and Clews*

Identity Envy— Wanting to Be Who We Are Not

Creative Nonfiction by Queer Writers

Identity Envy— Wanting to Be Who We Are Not
Creative Nonfiction by Queer Writers

Jim Tushinski
Jim Van Buskirk
Editors

HPP

Harrington Park Press®
The Trade Division of The Haworth Press, Inc.
New York • London • Oxford

For more information on this book or to order, visit
http://www.haworthpress.com/store/product.asp?sku=5641

or call 1-800-HAWORTH (800-429-6784) in the United States and Canada
or (607) 722-5857 outside the United States and Canada

or contact orders@HaworthPress.com

Published by

Harrington Park Press®, the trade division of The Haworth Press, Inc., 10 Alice Street,
Binghamton, NY 13904-1580.

PUBLISHER'S NOTE
The development, preparation, and publication of this work has been undertaken with great care.
However, the Publisher, employees, editors, and agents of The Haworth Press are not responsible
for any errors contained herein or for consequences that may ensue from use of materials or information contained in this work. The Haworth Press is committed to the dissemination of ideas and information according to the highest standards of intellectual freedom and the free exchange of ideas.
Statements made and opinions expressed in this publication do not necessarily reflect the views of
the Publisher, Directors, management, or staff of The Haworth Press, Inc., or an endorsement by
them.

Cover design by Marylouise E. Doyle.

Library of Congress Cataloging-in-Publication Data

Identity envy : wanting to be who we are not : creative nonfiction by queer writers / [edited by] Jim
Tushinski [and] Jim Van Buskirk.
    p. cm.
    ISBN-13: 978-1-56023-586-6 (alk. paper)
    ISBN-10: 1-56023-586-1 (alk. paper)
    ISBN-13: 978-1-56023-587-3 (pbk. : alk. paper)
    ISBN-10: 1-56023-587-X (pbk. : alk. paper)
    1. American prose literature—21st century. 2. Gays' writings, American. 3. Bisexuals' writings,
American. 4. Transsexuals' writings, American. 5. Sexual minorities—Identity. 6. Identity
(Psychology) 7. Difference (Psychology) 8. Autobiography. I. Tushinski, Jim. II. Van Buskirk, Jim.

PS647.G39I34 2006
810.9'352664—dc22

                                                                        2006022948

CONTENTS

Introduction

Jim Tushinski
Jim Van Buskirk

So there we were, having lunch one day in San Francisco. We talked about a lot of things, but somehow that day we ended up revealing to each other that though raised in Christian homes, we had each developed a desire to be Jewish. We laughed about the odd coincidence of it, but wondered: Was this "identity envy" common? Of course, not every Christian-raised queer kid wanted to be Jewish, but surely other people had desires like this. Was it related to the universal childish fantasy that your parents weren't your real parents, that instead you were adopted royalty? If so, why did this feeling sometimes persist into adulthood? Surely it wasn't just some elaborate sexual fetish. We had no clear answers, but the idea intrigued us, and we set about asking friends if they had experienced something similar. The affirmative reactions we got, the number of variations, and the eagerness with which people launched into their own "identity envy" stories convinced us that we were on to something.

We cast our net, calling on queer writers to explore their own identity envies in personal essays, memoirs, and other works of creative nonfiction. We had no idea what to expect, and what we got surprised and delighted us.

Queers—including lesbians, gay men, bisexuals, transgendered, intersex, and other sexual minorities—often feel marginalized by mainstream culture. Considered as the "Other," their sexual orientation and/or gender identification render them strangers in a strange land. Many times this feeling comes early to queer kids. In other cases, it shows up later and lingers into adulthood. Along with this feeling of not belonging to the culture at large comes an intense need to belong *somewhere,* to claim some group as one's own. This isn't particularly unique to queer folks. But certainly the two of us felt that

Identity Envy—Wanting to Be Who We Are Not
Published by The Haworth Press, Inc., 2007. All rights reserved.
doi:10.1300/5641_01

somehow our desire to be "other" and our marginalization were inexorably intertwined. We wanted to find out if other queer people felt that way too and how it influenced their lives.

So what is "identity envy"? What causes it? Who has it? This anthology offers no answers to these excellent questions; instead it seeks to provoke an exploration of the many possibilities. The approaches, as you will see, are myriad and multivalent, humorous and hard-hitting, poignant and provocative. In many of the pieces we chose, the identities envied are readily apparent; in others the issue is dealt with more conceptually. At the risk of abusing our prerogative as editors, it seemed only natural to include our own takes on the issue.

Some of the pieces take popular culture as a point of departure. Max Pierce explains how his fantasy of being a "Child Star" helped him through a troubled family life, while Will McNamara references an unlikely media icon in "Tania, Sometimes." Gerard Wozek's *Kung Fu*–infused "Chasing the Grasshopper" and Jim Tushinski's ode to *Lost in Space* in "The Perfect Space Family" show the effects of mainstream television on not-so-mainstream identities.

Other authors look at the interplay between class and geography. Jeff Mann's "Plantation Fantasies" describes his rejection of and ultimate reconciliation with his Southern "hillbilly" roots. Frederic B. Tate travels to Ireland in his desperate attempt to "Escape from the Appalachians," while D. Travers Scott complicates his rejection of Texas and his embracing of Europe (and vice versa) to ultimately identify with an amalgamation: "EuroTex." Mike McGinty is able to see the humor in his city slickness as he is befriended by a "cattle folk" boy in "You Picked a Fine Time to Leave Me, Helen."

Sometimes, the "identity envy" crosses national borders. In "Acting American," Robert Boulanger renounces his French-Canadian heritage as he admits his attraction for all things American. Al Cho, the son of Korean immigrants to Illinois, describes his unlikely identification with Laura Ingalls Wilder characters as he reinvents the metaphor of gardening in "Farmer Boy." Daniel M. Jaffe explores the "Connections" between hiding his relatives' Jewish identity in the Soviet Union and hiding his gayness in the United States.

Race and ethnicity are explored in intriguing ways by several of the contributors. In "Italian-American Boys," John Gilgun explores why he preferred the emotionally involved Italian-American families to his own cold Irish-American roots. In other cases, such as Jay Blotcher's "The Day My Past Came Calling," the romance of adoption and discovering one's true roots doesn't always provide the answers one expects. As a "gay black man with locks," JDGuilford revisits his childhood harassment to confront homophobia in "Pimp Juice."

Perhaps not surprisingly, several of the writers wrestle with gender. In "Thieves, Pimps, and Holy Prostitutes—My World" Renate Stendahl looks at the development of her sexual identity and how it was bound up with her intense identification with gay men. Margaret Cleaver confronts the question of "Who Am I?" by revisiting her childhood identification as Native American and male. In "When I Was a Girl/1966," Deborah La Garbanza confesses that she "always wanted to grow up and be a guy with a white undershirt and large sweat stains under the armpits." Andrew Ramer's "Tales of a Male Lesbian" reveals his woman-identified involvement in literature and politics while living in Brooklyn's Park Slope.

Perry Brass, who grew up Jewish in the Deep South, envies both a different religion and gender in "A Serene Invisibility." Religion rears its head again as Lori Horvitz initially disavows her Judaism, preferring to identify with the unknown Aryan model in a framed photograph, the "Shiksa in My Living Room." Joan Annsfire similarly rejects her Jewish outsider identity in "The Promise of Redemption," chronicling her days as "Corinne O'Donnell," a tough Catholic girl. Goyisher Jim Van Buskirk goes the other direction, as he experiences a mysterious meltdown "At the Museum of Jewish Heritage."

Sometimes the identities envied are multidimensional. Rosebud Ben-Oni teases out the complexities of the linguistic genders of Hebrew and Arabic as she negotiates the Israeli/Palestinian and out/closeted divide in "*Mishmumken:* For Those Who Cannot Choose." Larry Connolly's series of "Primary Wishes" chronicles his education at the hands of Catholic nuns and the confusion that engendered, while Keguro Macharia offers multiple myths in an attempt to navigate the complicated art of "Living Mythically" as a same-sex-loving Nigerian in gay America. Robert Labelle's visits to "Nanna's Room" establish an early and profound connection to more than the elderly lady down the hall. Darin Beasley's dreamlike descriptions of two best friends and their complicated desires belies the power of "Treasure Chest." And in "Wanting," Cheryl Schoonmaker's account of her hospitalizations may provide haunting clues to her parents' problems.

In the tradition of the best anthologies we have included familiar names, alongside newer voices. Some of the contributors are writers by trade and others are not, but each had an interesting story to tell and told it with energy, candor, and a unique, yet universal, voice. And lest we be criticized for giving more space to male voices over female ones, we should note that our first criteria was always quality over any quota system and that, coincidentally, the anthology reflects the same percentage of female to male authors that the submissions as a whole did.

We think the resulting collection is adequately provocative to encourage readers to consider their relationship to identity—to their own identity and to those of others. It seems that as we make sense of our individual journeys, our similarities outweigh our differences. As we all seek to belong, we learn that in fact we do belong, to ourselves and to each other.

Primary Wishes

Larry Connolly

Agnes Antoniso sits next to me and cries all through class because she wants to be at home and Sister Mary Joseph scolds her to STOP THAT YOUNG LADY YOU'RE IN FIRST GRADE NOW and OUR LORD NEVER CRIED and LOOK AT THAT BOY SITTING NEXT TO YOU HE'S NOT CRYING IS HE? Then, because I'm that boy, I throw up my lunch, which had been chicken noodle soup from a thermos. All the noodles are swimming on top of my desk and Agnes's desk, too, and now she is really screaming and Sister Mary Joseph is screaming, but I am fascinated by the sight of all those noodles because this is the first time I realize what I eat is waiting in my stomach just like the wolf's stomach in *Peter and the Wolf.*

I wish I lived alone in the forest. Life would be much better.

Broadway Babies' volunteers clearly have an inside road into Sister Mary Frank's affections because whenever someone puts up their hand to volunteer for a particular section of our second grade talent show she smiles and says GOOD BOY or GOOD GIRL, depending, and laughs and clasps her hands to her heart because she has a class with so much talent for everything. So I raise my hand for every section and she laughs and clasps her hands about me and is very overjoyed because she DIDN'T REALIZE YOU SANG! and she DIDN'T REALIZE YOU DANCED! and YOU'RE A STORY TELLER AS WELL? and YOU'RE GOING TO DRAW SOMETHING ON THE BOARD FOR US, TOO? I really like the attention Sister is giving me and how my classmates are finding more things to talk with me about. It's too bad the Broadway Babies day comes and I'm so scared that I just stand in front of the class

Identity Envy—Wanting to Be Who We Are Not
Published by The Haworth Press, Inc., 2007. All rights reserved.
doi:10.1300/5641_02

in silence and won't make a sound and won't look down from the ceiling. ALL RIGHT THEN WE'LL JUST LET YOU STAND UP HERE IN FRONT UNTIL YOU DO THE THINGS YOU VOLUNTEERED FOR. WE CAN SIT HERE IN SILENCE UNTIL YOU SHOW US YOUR TALENT, NO RECESS NO LUNCH NO DISMISSAL UNTIL YOU DEMONSTRATE YOUR TALENT.

I wish I had the talent to make myself invisible.

CATHOLICISM IS A PERSECUTED RELIGION, Sister Mary Frank says, what with the Communists starving us to death and closing down our printing presses and driving us out of their countries and the Protestants burning our buildings and taking over our churches and the indigenous peoples of the world boiling our priests and cutting off their limbs and things and Americans not wanting to elect us to public office because we do whatever the Pope tells us—as though he would ever tell us to do anything wrong.

I wish I were in Public School, with science class instead of religion.

Dennis Wilburt is the only kid in third grade who is worse off than I am. He's really strange and ugly to boot, whereas I'm just a sissy. He follows me like a dog. I'm so pleased I finally have someone to treat badly.

I wish I were very popular; I'd treat everyone like dirt.

EISENHOWER! PRESIDENT EISENHOWER, shouts everyone, answering Sister Mary Bartholomew's question about the man in the painting on the wall. I have no idea who Eisenhower is. I'm probably the only kid in class who didn't learn this at home. My home isn't like theirs. Nothing about me is the same as them. Third grade is all about rewarding regular people from regular families.

I wish I were the boy sitting next to me. Having the right answer makes everyone think more of you.

Filippo's family is from Greece, and he has curly hair and is a real boy boy, tanned and always playing with balls. Whenever Filippo or I are the host of Treat Time we offer each other the first choice. I don't know Eisenhower, but out of all the third grade, Filippo likes me best.

I wish I were Filippo's Siamese twin. I'd never leave his side.

Geography is my absolute favorite fourth grade class because I love maps, which are now all over the walls and throughout the textbook on my desk. Especially, I like the historical atlases because the changing boundaries of the countries fascinate me and give me a sense that nothing has to stay the way it is.

I wish I lived in another century. Nothing too dirty or rough, though.

Homosexual is an extremely negative thing. I know because other kids spit it as the ultimate no-no. I finally looked up the word in the dictionary and had to slam the book shut before anyone else could see me there on the page.

I wish I were like the other boys in class, the ones who actually want to throw balls around.

Icarus is my favorite mythological character. I've been reading mythology, and that's not just Greek myths—it's Roman and Norse and Russian and whatever the others are. I love Icarus because his picture reminds me of Filippo, only in a short, short chiton with sandals strapped way up his muscled calves. Not just because of Filippo, though, but also because he gets to fly, which is something I've always wanted to do. You're free and you can travel anytime you want and you can look down at the earth and it all looks like some big map without the boundaries drawn, which are temporary anyway.

I wish I lived with people like Icarus, with clothes like that.

JEWS DID NOT KILL JESUS NO MATTER WHAT ELSE THEY MAY HAVE DONE. Sister Mary Charles is lecturing all of us in fifth grade. EVERYBODY KILLED JESUS. YOU. HIM. ALL OF US ARE RESPONSIBLE FOR THIS, BUT NOT UNTIL YOU REACHED THE AGE OF SEVEN. THEN YOU BECAME GUILTY OF MURDERING OUR STAINLESS SAVIOUR, BUT NOT BEFORE.

I wish I were not responsible for everything.

Keeper Of The Bell is the most privileged position in grade school. The Principal herself, Sister Mary Thomas, selected me for this special appointment after my parents didn't come to Parent-Teacher Conference and she called home to find out why. I'm the youngest student ever given this honor. She leads me to the secret room next to her office where the magic freedom button lives and shows me how to ring for Angelus and how to ring for Five Minute Warning and for Get In Class Now and for Get Out Of Class Now. THIS IS A SERIOUS RESPONSIBILITY, YOUNG MAN and I must never, ever mess around or let anyone else see where the button is hidden. I'm very good with this new job, and I just know I look very important as I leave class early for the Angelus and Recess rings. I never ring it early, despite the fact that Filippo suggests I do so—and despite the fact that several eighth grade boys want to give me money for it—and despite the fact that some of them might think better of me if I did. Ultimately I get yanked off this job because one of the other nuns claims I rang it early, though I most certainly did not, and they decide to let a girl take over because boys are not to be trusted.

I wish I were a girl. They look the way I feel.

Library Time is new in sixth grade and it's my favorite hour. It doesn't matter whether we have to read plays or novels or poems, though poems *do* come in last. However, I'm noticing trouble. When something is assigned to read, I fall asleep as I'm reading it. Whereas, the minute the assignment is over, I can read the entire book just for my own enjoyment. Also, if I have to answer a question about something, I can't pay attention to it and my mind blanks out.

I still wish I lived in the forest since life in grade school is not working out.

Misbehaving in the form of needing to go to the bathroom when it wasn't bathroom time meant that I was demoted from Group One to Group Two in Math, so now I'm with all of the slow kids in class who are working on problems that I worked on last year. The good thing is that I like watching the Group Two slow boys chew on their pencil erasers when they try to fill in the worksheets.

I wish I were teaching. I could watch these boys all day.

NERVOUS BREAKDOWN! YOU GAVE HER A NERVOUS BREAK-DOWN! SISTER MARY PETER LOVED YOU SIXTH GRADERS AS THOUGH YOU WERE HER OWN AND THIS IS HOW YOU REPAY HER BY DRAWING THESE FILTHY DISGUSTING PICTURES OF I WON'T EVEN SAY WHAT OF! I HAVE NEVER EXPERIENCED THIS FROM A CLASS IN MY LIFE!! AND YOU OF ALL PEOPLE HOW COULD YOU PARTICPATE IN THIS FILTH? I'm responsible for my teachers. I have to take care of them because they're very fragile, which is an added pressure because I am also responsible for my family. At school and at home I sit and stare out the window all day long.

I wish I were dead. There's no responsibility.

Orgasm is the most useful thing I learned this year. My entire class is at the public library doing research JUST LIKE we'll DO IN HIGH SCHOOL and I look up Sex in the card catalog, which in turn sends me to the book *Boys And Sex: A How-To Manual For The Young Male.* I'm not sure I know exactly what masturbation is, but the descriptions of all the various ways a boy does this sort of thing are very, very interesting, so very, very interesting that I put the book into my pants, not that there's any room right now, and take it home to see if what I'm reading is true—and it is. I wonder if Filippo knows about this.

I wish I had more than one pair of hands: one pair to hold the book and one pair to follow instructions.

PENMENSHIP IS THE MARK OF CHARACTER. IF YOU WILL NOT IMPROVE YOUR PENMANSHIP YOU CANNOT ADVANCE IN THIS COUNTRY. YOU'LL NEVER GET AWAY WITH THIS IN HIGH SCHOOL. I know that my handwriting is going to be my downfall because every day I have to leave class and rewrite all of my papers, which is bad enough, but Sister Mary Andrew, our substitute teacher, makes me do it with one of the eighth grade girls who all have perfect penmanship. Mine never improves no matter how many times I have to redo it. I'm thinking it might improve a little bit if they sent one of the eighth grade boys down.

I wish I were Helen Keller. They'd be happy I wrote at all.

Quinn Keating, who sits behind me and spends all day drawing cartoons or poking me in the back with his cartridge pen, sassed Sister Mary Andrew. She came down the aisle to smack him, but something was really in him today, more than his ordinary evilness, and he swore at her and ran out of the room and out of the school into the field next door where the Queen of Heaven Grotto is. So Sister Mary

Andrew ran out of the classroom after him screaming, STOP IT QUINN KEATING and COME BACK HERE YOUNG MAN. I saw them both running around the Grotto, Quinn Keating being chased by Sister Mary Andrew with a yardstick in her hand, and then my whole class is looking out the window because suddenly all of the Sisters are out in the Queen of Heaven Grotto chasing Quinn Keating. Our principal Sister Mary Thomas is the one who catches him because she's the fastest, which is probably why she's principal, and they drag him inside. No one in the class is breathing because we're waiting for the world to end. Later Quinn Keating comes back to class and Sister Mary Andrew comes back to class and no one says anything about it. We pick right up where we left off.

I wish I were blind. I hate seeing home at school.

Recess used to be fun because I could jump rope and play games, but lately everything has changed and I don't like it. Girls play with girls, boys play with boys, and the older kids don't play with the younger kids. Boys only play games with balls; girls do all of the fun things that require real skill. The girls and boys are totally separate, but all they think about is each other and no one is who they were anymore. Even Filippo. I can see I'm not making whatever crossover is happening here. I can't imagine lasting through recess day after day.

I wish I were in the hospital where no one expects anything.

Slick is my nickname from all the black kids at the Public School Arts Outreach I'm going to this summer because my grade school doesn't have an arts program. They call me Slick because they say it means sneaky-with-class, which makes me proud, though the sneaky part doesn't sound too nice. I think I know exactly what they're talking about.

I wish I were black. They can be any way they want and it's just the way they are.

Touch football completely baffles me, except for the part where I'm in the locker room with the rest of the seventh grade boys. Everyone cares so much about it and I don't understand why. All I want to do is run away whenever we have to play. They make me a rusher, which they figure allows me to run away, only in the direction they say. Coaches are screaming at me and teammates are screaming at me and the nuns are screaming at me. It's all I can do not to let anyone notice I'm watching boy butts.

I wish I had polio. I could skip gym and be very touching.

Ursula Schopchen is the first non-nun I've ever had. Mrs. Schopchen looks so young and pretty for a teacher. She wears makeup and is nice to us most of the time, considering what we are like. Everyday she puts musicals on the record player and lets them play while we do silent reading, and this is fine with me because I like musicals, though I may be the only one. Today seems a little off because she's playing *The Sound of Music* and singing along on "I Have Confidence," standing by the open door with her fists on her hips screaming it so she's louder than Julie Andrews. It feels almost funny and a little strange. I was going to suggest she close the door, but I've learned from home not to open my mouth when people are screaming.

I wish I were standing next to her singing at the top of my lungs.

Va-Gee-Na is what I say in my head, since that's how I read it, but it's a good thing I never said it out loud . . . not that I'd have occasion to. Mary Ann Navachezky showed me hers in her bedroom when I was in kindergarten when we were playing Strip Show with some neighborhood kids. She was the only girl and when she showed hers my mouth dropped to the floor because I couldn't believe anyone was like that; I thought we were all the same. Later I asked if I could see for myself to make sure I saw what I saw. She showed me. I knelt down and was looking and poking and trying to see if maybe she was hiding something.

I wish I had a Va-Gee-Na. This is obviously what eighth grade boys are interested in.

WRITING A MUSICAL WAS NOT WHAT I ASKED YOU TO DO ON THE FINAL EXAM. I APPRECIATE THAT ALL OF THE CONTENT WAS CONTAINED IN THE SONGS AND DIALOGUE BUT THE INSTRUCTIONS SPECIFICALLY REQUESTED THAT YOU WRITE AN ESSAY. A MUSICAL IS NOT AN ESSAY. I'M FAILING YOU FOR YOUR OWN GOOD. AS AN EIGHTH GRADER YOU SHOULD KNOW THERE IS SUCH A THING AS INAPPROPRIATE CREATIVITY. YOU WON'T GET AWAY WITH THIS SORT OF THING IN HIGH SCHOOL.

I wish I were in finishing school. They reward this sort of effort.

X-ray visors are standard spy equipment, so I have to pretend I have them when we play Espionage during recess. The only reason I'm willing to play is because no one else in my class knows mythology and they were calling me names when I tried to be Icarus for them. Espionage isn't so bad, but I hate having to squint to show that I'm using my X-ray visor, though squinting is very helpful when Quinn Keating is jumping off a wall to take down an enemy agent and his shirt lifts up and I can look at his stomach. No one thinks anything about it because I'm using my X-ray visor.

I wish I did have an X-ray visor. I would go to the lavatory and watch.

Yancy Collins is the first black person in my school. He's just transferred into my eighth grade class for this one year and I'm thinking he is so out of it because he doesn't know all these kids who have

been in school together for years and years. What's the point of trans-
ferring in for one year anyway? On top of that, he's so strange because he says What A Spaz and Dickhead, which no one here has ever
said. Sister Mary Frank takes me aside and tells me YOU NEED TO
MAKE YANCY YOUR FRIEND BECAUSE HE NEEDS SOME CONNEC-
TIONS HERE. I can't believe I have to talk to him and be nice. We start
hanging around his house, which is pretty fancy because his dad's a
doctor, and we play games and wrestle around. He makes me play
football with him, but it's pretty fun because he explains all the plays
and we practice them. He doesn't throw the ball too hard and we always plan where I'll be when he throws it so I will catch it. He plays
all the parts with different voices: he's the broadcaster describing the
plays, he's the coach yelling instructions, he's the cheerleaders chanting, he's the fans jumping up and down and screaming when I catch
the ball. I've never caught a ball before. We have a deal that we'll play
football for a half hour than we'll feel each other up for a half hour,
and that's what we keep doing.

I wish I were Yancy's brother. We could sleep in the same bed and
feel anything anytime we wanted.

Zits are all over everybody in eighth grade and I keep praying that I
won't get any more than the one I've got by my chin. They are so grotesque. School is tough enough without that. Dennis Wilburt is Zit
City, which is another reason I'm not as awful as he is. The pathetic
thing is that he doesn't even know how dreadful he is. He just goes on
following Yancy and me around like he's normal and has every reason to be walking the earth. He should probably just give up and go
home and never come out again. Hasn't he learned anything?

I wish I went to a school without people like Dennis. I hate that
kind of ugliness.

The Promise of Redemption

Joan Annsfire

It wasn't that I wanted to worship Jesus or eat fish on Fridays. What I coveted most was that Catholic girl swagger, a presence that stated, "I'm here, you gonna try to make somethin' of it?" It was an essence that came through even in those nerdy plaid skirts and white blouses. Perhaps it was bred in Catholic girls' schools, which, I suspected, were subversive hotbeds of female bonding, a sort of Western version of a harem. All those women together in a religion where sin could be easily neutralized by confession was fertile soil for my fantasies.

The year was 1967, the Beatles had landed, and the hippies had emerged from the stifling cocoon of the 1950s. The phrase "women's liberation" had not yet been coined. I was an angst-ridden teenager with a nebulous sense of herself as "other." It was a nagging feeling without shape or dimension.

Being Jewish accounted for part of it. It denoted the status of an outsider. In the "real" Ohio, the word *Jew* was used mostly as a verb. But in my high school Jews made up about a third of the student body. A minority of them were artsy types, girls who wore big earrings and longhaired boys with a philosophical bent. But mostly the Jewish kids were really boring. They were what we called preppies, the college-bound, well-to-do crowd. Females with little gold bracelets, Villager dresses, and Pappagallo shoes. Males with a highly inflated sense of their own importance. Only a rare few were aspiring juvenile delinquents, my chosen identification. Those of us in the live-fast-die-young set were given the status of honorary Gentiles because we fell so far from the norm.

The second component of my "otherness" was something I couldn't quite put my finger on. My assessment was that I wanted deeper relationships, a more intense emotional connection with my girlfriends

Identity Envy—Wanting to Be Who We Are Not
Published by The Haworth Press, Inc., 2007. All rights reserved.
doi:10.1300/5641_03

than they were willing to provide. I hoped that this added dimension would lead to greater physical intimacy.

The flames of Catholic envy had been fanned in the women's bathroom at the local bowling alley. I recall watching with fear and admiration as the girls from St. Dominic's smoked their cigarettes and ratted their hair. It was a ritual that seemed methodical, sacred, almost holy. And they had some big hair. Rumor had it that they hid drugs, makeup, and razor blades in its depths. I visualized their coiffures as a cross between armories and cosmetic counters. This arsenal seemed unnecessary, because these chicks could probably take down a mad rapist with barely more than a withering holy-mother-of-God look.

Kathy Fabiani was a Catholic girl from my school I'd met while hanging out at the Coffee House. She had long, dark hair that was silky on the bottom and teased up on top. Her body was short and skinny, which gave her the look of an inverted broom, one that could definitely sweep me off my feet. Her eyes were huge and dark, reminiscent of the Keane paintings of bug-eyed children that were so popular back then. Her nose was chiseled and fine, her lips luscious and full, and she could fight like a tiger and swear like a sailor. We shared a similar outlook on life combined with the freedom that comes from having parents who were too consumed by their own problems to monitor our behavior.

I hung out with a motley group of about ten to fifteen kids from various backgrounds. A few were from the "real world," kids who had dropped out of high school and gone on to criminal activities. They were the big guns we could call in to guarantee access to drugs or help when we needed to break a lock open or solder it shut. At lunchtime we lurked in our own hallway, which was a dead end with a door leading outside. It was so private we could even smoke grass and spent many a lunch period wasted.

Kathy had studied judo and knew how to use another's superior size and strength to her advantage. Her martial arts practice provided her with moves she could perform flawlessly even when stoned, which was most of the time. She claimed she never slept but stayed awake nights flying on acid or mescaline and painting the surrealistic landscapes that covered her bedroom walls.

She spent much time complaining about the hypocrisies of Catholicism. One lunch hour she described in detail the last time her "devout" stepfather tried to grab at her breasts. I played the role of her stepfather as she demonstrated the way she pulled his foot forward and pushed his shoulder back. Just before I hit the floor, she grabbed me in her wiry arms. I felt the electric current of her touch as we both went down together in a heap, laughing.

Our descent into thievery started as a challenge, a way to outwit the gatekeepers of the "system." Soon small groups of us began making forays into downtown Cleveland that were actually shoplifting sprees. It was a way to "pick up a few things" and get a rush too, not unlike the drug experience. We would head downtown on the Rapid armed with shoplifting lists of "necessities" like record albums, clothing, makeup, and small items of jewelry.

Two or three of us would walk into the stores separately so as not to arouse suspicion. One of us would then begin looking at merchandise in a distracting and odd way, pawing through things, being noisy, or making a mess of the displays. This person was the decoy who would attract the attention of the store detectives as the designated pilferer discreetly selected items from the list.

This new pastime, coupled with the desire to get into clubs that we were too young to enter, made us realize that fake identification was imperative. The Terminal Tower had photo booths where we could make several attempts to capture just the right new look. After we had our photos taken, I began the project of typing up, pasting together, and laminating our new ID cards, trying for something that looked official. That's how my alter ego, my evil twin Corinne O'Donnell, was born. With my kinky red hair I was often mistaken for Irish, so I transformed myself into a Catholic girl in her senior year at St. Dominic's. I imagined her as someone who could do anything at all and get away with it.

Catholic identity was more than just being a tough cookie. It represented transcendence, an escape from the parts of my Jewish identity that I found overwhelming. Corinne O'Donnell was free from the suffocating burden of history, a life without the ghosts of the pogroms and the Holocaust constantly peering over her shoulder. Beyond the social stigma of Jewishness lay the gift of individual responsibility. In restaurants Corinne could talk and laugh as loudly as she wanted without having to worry about others finding her behavior "too Catholic" and giving her people a bad name.

I was so energized and inspired by my new persona that I learned to say Hail Marys just in case I was abducted by the enemy and had to prove my Catholic origins. At a flea market I bought a used rosary that one night almost brought me to my knees. It was white and looked like fake ivory, so I hadn't realized it was made of the kind of plastic that glowed an unearthly green color in the dark. I awoke deep in the night to witness what I thought to be the eerie presence of J.C. on my dresser.

Corinne reigned supreme in my life that year. As long as that ID card was in my pocket, I felt invincible. In our hallway, word began circulating about an "acid house" in East Cleveland that was really cool. Jeffrey, a hallway denizen, was friends with Pascal who lived there. We all made plans for a field trip to the place that the papers would later call "a hippie haunt in East Cleveland."

The morning of our journey was one of those crisp, sunny, autumn days. Six of us showed up for the adventure. We traveled by bus to the run-down, tree-lined streets of East Cleveland where the houses were old and interesting with big front porches on both the upstairs and downstairs levels. Pascal's pad was a big, funky farmhouse on an urban street. We rang the doorbell and an "older" woman, who looked either stoned or half-asleep, answered.

"Hey, hi Jeff," she said slowly, her eyes moving over our faces. "Come on in guys, take a load off. I'm Jean, Pascal's old lady."

"Where's the big P?" Jeff inquired.

"Out making sales."

Jean and Jeff continued their conversation as the rest of us put our stuff down and began to look around. The first thing I did was put on my jeans and take off my skirt. At that time girls were not yet permitted to come to school in pants. Once properly transformed, I stepped, like Alice, through the looking glass. The walls were covered with acid-inspired murals of huge flowers and winding vines. The furniture was overstuffed Victorian a la Salvation Army. In the middle of the living room there was a disconnected toilet that served as an ashtray. We had only been there ten minutes before Jean asked that magic, rhetorical question, "Do you guys want to get high?" She opened the door to a large closet with posters on the walls. It was equipped with a black light that made the colors glow bright neon in the dark. We piled in and she produced a pipe and some hashish from a secret compartment behind the wall.

Jean, who turned out to be all of twenty-three, was telling us about Pascal's tour of duty as we passed around the pipe. She was in the middle of a story about a Vietnamese child, whose leg had been blown off by a landmine, when we heard a knock on the kitchen door.

"Just ignore it," I said, mostly because I couldn't imagine being lucid enough to talk to anyone at that moment. A few others agreed, but Jean was determined to play hostess in her home. She left us shut in the smoky closet and answered the door. We heard men's voices and were suddenly aware that they had come inside. Did she let them in? Did they push past her? Was she too bombed to ask for a search warrant? They sounded like cops. We found the hole in the wall and hid the stuff. Then we all fell silent, holding our breath. The men were asking questions and searching the house. They found a guy who had been sleeping upstairs. Jean and the unknown man were denying the presence of high-school-aged people in the house. They were telling them to leave, saying they were alone, that they had done nothing wrong. I heard stuff falling as if being thrown in the kitchen.

"Who do these things belong to?" one of them asked. They had found our coats and packs, which we'd left strewn in the kitchen.

"There were some kids here, but they left." It was Jean's voice now.

"Well, evidently they'll be back," one of the pigs replied.

And then he opened our hideout door. Smoke poured out to greet him along with the sight of the six of us sitting three against each wall, our legs alternating and outstretched on the floor. We filed cooperatively out of the closet, blinking in the harsh daylight. The house had been ransacked. There were four no-nonsense-type Blue Meanies and one plain-clothes undercover guy directing the operation. They all looked the same to me, white guys with permanent sneers on their faces. I suddenly recalled the story in the *Cleveland Plain Dealer* saying members of the police department had been found wearing swastikas on their uniforms while on active duty. I hoped that these cops weren't the ones that had been described.

I was very stoned and scared as I stood in the kitchen wondering if my legs would give out beneath me. Kathy looked at me with terrified eyes. I touched her shoulder inconspicuously. She crossed herself and I followed suit. "It couldn't hurt," was all she said. The officers had us lined up, standing in the kitchen against the wall. Looking at that wall, I began to notice things I'd missed earlier. There was an American flag that the papers would later describe only as "desecrated." The form its desecration took was that all the five-pointed stars had been replaced with six-pointed, Jewish stars. In my gut, which was not really Corinne O'Donnell's, I knew that those stars implied that Jews controlled the country. It saddened me to realize that I wasn't as much a part of this devil-may-care group of troublemakers as I'd hoped. My true identity just kept slipping out of me at the point where I felt I had it most in check.

"Get them to the station," the fat cop with the red mustache instructed his cohorts, and they marched us outside and piled us into two squad cars. There were eight of us now counting Jean and the unidentified sleeping man whose name, we later found out, was Frank. All the girls were in one squad car, the boys in another. Kathy was pretty much on my lap, because four of us in the back seat of one car was a squeeze.

"They'll probably interrogate us and hold us till our parents come."

"Interrogate? Isn't that a bit overly dramatic?" That was Nancy, the intellectual.

"I can't deal with this, I really can't. My parents are going to kill me." Kathy was starting to cry. I stroked her hair, trying to comfort her.

"We'll be okay. Just don't say anything incriminating. Deny everything. Act like stupid teenage girls. They'll buy it. They always do." That was me trying to sound rational even though my heart was racing.

When we arrived at the police station, they unloaded us underage types into a corridor just outside the area where the cells were. They put Jean and Frank into their own separate cells because they were adults. At first we just stood in the hall as Jean and Frank called out to us and each other. We were then told to line up and produce identification. I was the first up and out came Corinne. The officer just looked at the card and chuckled.

"I mean produce real identification," he clarified. So much for all my dedicated forgery.

Kathy whispered that she had a headache and needed an aspirin. Her hands were shaking so much that when she opened the bottle all the pills spilled onto the floor. Cold pills and No-Doz and other colorful over-the-counter medications rolled to all corners of the station. The cops went wild with excitement, gathering samples of all the pills. "Take this to the lab," was a phrase they repeated like a mantra. None of us had drugs or contraband, aside from Kathy's legal medications, but the younger, slightly hip cop who searched our stuff was so fascinated by a hippie, underground newspaper called *The Buddhist Third-Class Junk-Mail Oracle* that I gave it to him.

Then we were returned to the corridor where we sat with our backs resting against the wall. Time was crawling by. It was midday and none of us had eaten anything. Jeffrey had a peanut butter-and-jelly sandwich with him that he passed around. We told our captors we had to pee and they led the girls into one cell and the boys into another to use the toilets.

It was at least three in the afternoon before they started calling us individually for our "depositions." I can't say I remember being read my Miranda rights, but nonetheless, a female officer escorted each of us, one at a time, to a room upstairs where a fatherly guy asked us questions and a court reporter typed our answers. Did I know there was hash and grass and acid in that house? Of course not! Had I ever cut school before? No, never! I signed my carefully worded deposition in which I took on the persona of a sweet, pampered Jewish girl bound for college and great things. And, as luck would have it, we all stuck to the same story. Later, our lawyer would inform us we'd lied more consistently than a group of professional criminals. It's something I take pride in to this day.

It was after 4:30 in the afternoon when they finally allowed us to phone home to inform our parents where we were. I could tell by my mom's voice that she'd already started on her evening Bloody Marys.

"I'm in the middle of something. I can't pick you up today," she responded after I told her I was at the police station. After I hung up, I had no idea whether or not she would show.

Everyone else had been picked up and had gone back with their families. I was sitting in a chair making conversation with an officer. A burly cop came in and began a monologue about D.H., the Cleveland Detention Home, my evening's destination if my mother didn't arrive soon. "There are big rats all over the place," he was saying, an idea you might use to frighten a ten-year-old. Cleanliness couldn't possibly be scarier than the specter of physical and psychological abuse. I reflected upon Eleanor Parker's descent into depravity in the movie *Caged*. Did I possess that spark of earnest naïveté that could be doused by the cold water of cruel experience? And more important, would they shave my head? I grabbed a handful of my waist-length frizzy hair and became lost in a scenario involving a wicked matron with a razor and another terrified but stunning inmate who looked a lot like Kathy. Her warm body was trembling as we held onto each other for dear life. At that critical juncture my mother appeared, looking angry yet amazingly sober.

A police officer took her aside and asked her point blank, "Did you realize that there were two Negroes with your daughter when she was arrested?" This was the last straw for my mother. The lasting image I have of her that day was with her mouth open yelling. "I'm a Jew, so don't try to pull any of your Nazi crap on me. If you think the race of my daughter's friends is the main issue here, then clearly you have shit for brains." Wow, that's my mom. Who else could threaten to abandon me to the prison system and on the same day bond with me against the world and its hateful prejudices.

I never used that ID card again. Looking back, I believe Corinne O'Donnell died that day. Both she and I proved to be less than invincible. I finally was forced to admit that, for better or for worse, I was a Jew and unable to turn my back on the many ways that shaped every aspect of my existence.

A couple months before we were to appear in court, Kathy was busted, at her mother's request, for the exclusively adolescent "crime" of incorrigibility. She was locked up for three weeks before she got someone to believe her stories about her pawing stepfather and place her in the custody of her aunt.

Upon her release from D.H., she looked reassuringly the same. After our long hello hug, I followed her eyes, alert for signs of trauma. All she would say was what a relief it was to be beyond that pervert's reach. At lunchtime in our hallway hang-out, we clamored to hear exactly what happened to her, how she fared in the "big house." In response to our questions, her face became introspective, far away. "There were lesbians there," was her only reply.

"Ooooh," we murmured in response to this profound and unanticipated summary of her incarceration experience. I mulled over this revelation, visualizing Kathy as the Blessed Virgin, dispensing a sacrament of compassionate love to wayward lesbians, the bare light bulb behind her head framing it with a radiant halo. For the first time since I embarked on my dissolute life of crime, I looked down the long, dark tunnel of my future and saw a faint glimmer of light.

EuroTex

D. Travers Scott

I am in Texas, dreaming of Europe.

In Europe, when I'm in seventh grade, and when the bonus word on our spelling test is "hollandaise," I am not the only student who spells it correctly. I am not the only student who knows what it is. I do not survey my classmates' limpid eyes and furrowed brows. I do not snap with supercilious exasperation, "It's what you put on artichokes!" To this, I do not encounter further bemusement. I do not futilely flog the issue: "Asparagus? Eggs Benedict?"

In Europe, this marks me as nether a big ol' 'mo, nor the progeny of aspiring middle-class foodies.

I inhabit a class system of clear demarcation. I know who I am and where I fit. No whiplash transitions from nibbling caviar poolside in Beverly Hills with a bestselling author to living in a sixteen-foot fishing trailer with no running water, using an empty paint bucket and trash bags as a toilet. My parents do what they're supposed to do. Their tastes are uniform, coordinated, and bereft of unsettling juxtapositions. Dad does not come home from working the loading dock to excitedly open this month's fragrant, gooey delivery from the Cheese-of-the-Month Club. My mom does not drag me to Charlie Daniels' Band concerts at the state fair one week, a Nicholas Roeg retrospective at the indie cinema the next. My stepmother does not prepare the aforementioned hollandaise with equal zest as her Velveeta-based queso dip.

Europe is stable, refined, steadfast, aligned. Tradition-bound and temperate. Consistent. Classy. Couth. Well-dressed polylingual aesthetes populate my dreamscape of piazzas, cafés, and cathedrals. The press is partisan, and everyone is bisexual. People imbibe an aperitif or digestif, and, although I'm not really certain of the difference be-

Identity Envy—Wanting to Be Who We Are Not
Published by The Haworth Press, Inc., 2007. All rights reserved.
doi:10.1300/5641_04

tween the two, I do know that absolutely no one drinks wine from a box.

School may be uniformed or even sex-segregated, but freckle-faced redneck boys do not drag me by my underwear across the gymnasium floor. Making a grand entrance into tenth grade sporting a new oversized Willie Smith black-and-white boucle-knit trenchcoat, my girlfriend does not point and squeal, "Bohemian Eurotrash!"

I have a history. One extending back centuries, one whose crowning glory is not a little over a decade of independent nationhood, secretly admitted to be less a golden era of sovereignty than an extended twiddling-of-thumbs waiting for admission into the Union. In my fantastic lineage, Romans and Vikings replace slaveholders and conquistadors. It makes a difference, I dream.

I dream of forgetting. Of losing knowledge: not knowing the secret for getting the most distance when pitching cowchips or for winning a greased pig contest. I haven't a clue how to change a septic line or pack the cupboards so nothing spills when you hitch up and move your mobile home.

I dream of the place I will go as soon as I am old enough to escape the place I am. I dream of the words I will no longer say, the syllables I will no longer stress improperly, the dipthongs I will no longer drawl. I dream that I have no need for a list of twenty-three idioms and pronunciations to avoid saying, lest I be mistaken for a rube.

I am in Europe, dreaming of Texas

I am in Europe. It's taken me a decade to get here. My fingers are thick from walking all day; still, a wisp of vertigo spins around my mind from the near heat-exhaustion of trekking through miles of Umbrian sunflower fields in mid-August. Collapsed on my cot, I see the cool and reassuring stone slabs of the floor, smooth bearers of centuries. Touching the temperate rock, I'm stunned by the bare fact that my pensionne is older than my nation.

Wow, I think, this is old. This is the Old World. As a moment of American-abroad profundity, my fever-thoughts are far from Jamesian.

I sink into sleep. I do not dream of the day's cafés and piazzas. Not the medieval mountaintop town or the tryst in the history museum's WC. Not the tearful breakdown before Donatello's Maddalena. Not the catacombs lined with skulls. Not the jellyfish attacks in an Ibizan alcove or the Moroccan pirate in the Basque gay bar sharing his hash with me.

In Europe, I dream of Texas. "The eyes of Texas are upon you, all the live-long day," we sing in grade school. "The eyes of Texas are upon you, you cannot get away." Mockingbirds trill the melody, scoring my dream from pecan branches. We pledge allegiance to the flag of the state of Texas. Armadillos scamper through bluebonnet fields. Homeland emblems embrace this weary traveler, a comforting clutch of kitsch.

I fly. Swirly Cinerama spectaculars surround me: the pine forests outside Texarkana, cement infinities of the Metroplex, Gulf Coast oil refineries flaming in green-orange a.m. glory. I survey El Paso desert rattlesnakes and naked hippies diving from rocks into frigid emerald springs outside Austin, citrus farmers hosing down orchards before a freeze in the Valley. It's a montage, a music-video falling-in-love sequence as the Holiday Parade of Lights, floating down San Antonio's Riverwalk, dissolves into dunes of dead Christmas trees on Padre Island's grey January beaches. But as Galveston's Spanish-mossed secret New Orleans cuts to the God-light of the Panhandle, then morphs into the ghost-lights of Marfa, is this storyboard the best part of a movie or a dramedy's lazy anticlimax?

My reveries grow savory. I do not dream of fried rabbit with calf brains, roasted cingale, or petite, discrete, and oh-so-chic gelato. My slumber binges center on Tex-Mex victuals, and I do not mean the anemic concoctions of California, New Mexico, or Oregon. I crave the real grub of carne guisada, pico de gallo, and chili con carne. On the pure Tex side: steak, steak fingers, and chicken-fried steak. Texas toast and endless iced tea. Frito Pie and Snickers Bar Cake. Drippings saved for gravy.

Why, when actually present in the land of my dreams, corporeal in the land after which I've lusted, envied, and coveted, do I dream of my dreaded homeland? Maybe those Texans at the Vatican infected me. The guide asked from what country everyone hailed, and they cheered, "Texas!" Maybe it was the subway graffiti in Rome that declared, "Texans go home!"

But as I sleep to the chimes of a church bell—a real forged one reverberating with a concrete clang, not the prerecorded tones our neighborhood congregation tolled—I am steeped in memories of a birthday rifle from a drunken grandfather, a birthday longhorn steer lounging under the kumquat tree. Reading comic books to illiterate older boys while their mom shot up in the other room. Family dramas of money, land, insurance, wills, secret bastard siblings, stolen children, and children left behind.

I am awake.

I wake up and am the norm. Everyone is EuroTex. Our cowboy president battles a Europhile challenger. The pre-emptive first lady can gaffe in seven languages, and positively exudes élan. Her opponent wears the tight-lipped smile and steely eyes of my every Vacation Bible School teacher. Austria rules California. Red and blue are no longer colors but teams, sides, sub-nations. Deadly serious meterosexuals don mullet wigs for tongue-in-cheek white-trash parties. Frito Pie no longer surprises friends; it's a mass-media punch line climbing the ladder up to comfort-food status, and I gave away my family's secret recipe to an AIDS benefit cookbook. My mechanic brother-in-law waxes his back, and *King of the Hill* steals all my jokes. The cool kids in my trendy neighborhood dress like the kids that beat up the cool kids in high school. The twangy tunes I fled now blare from every cable channel and awards show, only to be followed by vapid Europop club beats. Bob Wills & His Texas Playboys in a mash-up with DJ Tiesto? No longer outré, it's more like passé. Cynar, Campari, and Lillet lilt knowingly past my lips, but aren't they all just one degree from a margarita? And while I full well appreciate the irony of bringing a case of PBR to a coke party, I still don't have the taste for it.

It is years since I've lived in Texas, and I've become more Texan than I ever was living there. By all appearances I now have Texas envy. The snakeskin boots and belt, the black hat—never would I have deigned to look at, let alone own, such things when I was a resident of the state. On my office bulletin board, alongside snaps of Bilbao, Ouro Preto, Jamaica, and Melbourne, I have an official Native Texan birth certificate. My father warns me that it soon will be invalid: I'm approaching the point of having lived outside the state longer than I've lived in it, at which point, he tells me, one loses Native Texan status.

I lost my accent long ago. I taught myself not to talk "all Texin" while attending a fine Yankee institution of higher learning. Now I can't remember how. I wish I could. I envy my friends with accents intact. Now, thousands of miles from my source, a twang is a desirable commodity. Here I watch Southern men swagger their tongues for faster service at a bar and brighter light in the eyes of stalking men. Here a twenty-first century *Midnight Cowboy* is a good thing. A detriment becomes a fetish, even though, back in Texas, sodomites are no longer outlaws.

Integration is disconcerting. It's unclear upon what side to sit, for which team to cheer. Dreaming and awake, Texan and European, mongrel overlap throws desire askew. How can the grass be greener when I'm on both sides of the fence? Does EuroTex need some Cialis? Yes, waiter, I'll have the Exotica filet stuffed with sun-dried Quotidian, please. With my taste displaced, nothing tastes so sweet anymore. If nothing is more disappointing than a fantasy fulfilled, what are the ramifications of a dream embodied?

My Euro-envy is sated, my Tex-antipathy abated. I dream of both; I live in neither.

The Day My Past Came Calling: Adventures in Unexpected Multiethnicity

Jay Blotcher

For as long as I remember, I wanted to be white. I mean, I was born Caucasian. But that was not enough; I wanted to be tall and slim, with elegant wrists that suggested a blue-blood lineage rather than outright feyness. I wanted the type of body that looks perfect in a varsity jacket. I wanted piercing blue eyes and a shock of blond hair that would constantly fall over my high forehead into my eyes, requiring me to shake it back with a practiced insouciance.

From the start of first grade, at Margaret L. Donovan Elementary School in Randolph, Mass., I nursed an extreme case of WASP envy. Why not? Children have a simplistic notion of social justice: the good people are clearly the ones at the top. And from all I could divine from 1966 TV, magazines, and the classroom, WASPs ran the world. People liked them, coddled them, gave them extra candy at birthday parties. So why not become one of them?

But an unruly set of genes had undermined my simple quest. I was short, chubby, and olive-skinned. I had a prominent nose of Semitic character, not the aquiline type that, I was convinced, was a passport to a better world. My eyes were hazel, but thick glasses upstaged them. And then there was the hair: dark brown to the point of blackness, and as soft as barbed wire. It grew up and out in a tangle. At first, I felt I could retrain it. For months, I went to bed wearing a ski cap, praying that the constant pressure would force the hair to fall across my brow. My ploy failed.

When it came to my ethnic identity, I simply knew who I wasn't. Who I actually was became the tougher question. There weren't many clues. In 1961, at the age of one year and three weeks, I was liberated from a Jewish adoption agency in Scollay Square, Boston, and brought home to suburbia. My new parents possessed one single fact

Identity Envy—Wanting to Be Who We Are Not
Published by The Haworth Press, Inc., 2007. All rights reserved.
doi:10.1300/5641_05

about my heritage: I was born to a Jewish mother. Any other guesses relied on my physical appearance, the way one parses out the mixed breeding of a mongrel dog. Thanks to laws governing Bay State adoptions, my true racial background lay in a sealed file. But in our tribe, the Jewish classification suffices; everything else can be grafted on.

My new parents—Lolly and Sonny Blotcher—were both first-generation Americans, born to Jewish immigrants from Eastern Europe. And they worked to pass on that ethnic legacy, equal parts pride and shame. The shame came from the fact that American Jews are descended from a biblical line of people hounded, persecuted, and slaughtered for centuries. Under conditions like this, a suspicion of others becomes hardwired into the chromosomes. So does a sense of inferiority. The goyim may be nice to us, my mom would caution me, but they are not our friends. She was fully justified to say so; the Holocaust had been only sixteen years earlier.

So, I was trained well as a suburban Jew. From kindergarten on, my culture and religion were indivisible. I knew the score of *Fiddler on the Roof* better than any Beatles songs. At the time, we were mired in the great Jewish-American assimilation. East Coasters were shedding their *shtetl* mentalities and heading west to Los Angeles to transform their neuroses into popular sitcoms. Another bloc of Jews was discovering neo-conservatism as a means for advancement.

By age ten, I was regularly attending Saturday morning services, as much out of piety as loneliness. This chubby dweeb had no friends. Around this time, my WASP envy was tabled out of sheer genetic impracticality. (The yen would eventually transmute into simple desire; a favorite high school fantasy would be jocks in varsity jackets. After I came out, all subsequent boyfriends were quite white and sported impressive bone structure.) For now, I was coping with grade school socialization—and navigating badly, thanks to my appearance. In our simple town, Irish Catholics were the norm, and dark-skinned boys like me the exception.

Count on the inventive cruelty of children. Always. By first grade, I was being teased on the playground, in the cafeteria, after school. Kids are cruel, but hardly inventive; the easy targets were my glasses ("four-eyes!"), my whiffle haircut ("baldy!"), and my weight ("fatso!"). But when the bullies gave me grief about my skin color, I had no killer comebacks.

I was eight years old at summer camp when I first heard the word *nigger*. I didn't understand the word, but I knew it was meant to hurt. That was enough to bring me to tears and run to the office. However, the camp director, a brusque woman named Eve, dismissed my foolishness. "Those other kids are jealous because you have such a gorgeous tan," she explained. That tan would get me into numerous scrapes over the years.

Occasionally I'd think about my "real" mother and father. This usually happened after my mom swatted with "the strap,"—the worn-smooth remnant of a belt, its buckle removed, which hung in the broom closet for the frequent times I misbehaved. Left to sniffle in my bedroom, I would wonder who had given me up. And especially what they looked like. It would take several years before that curiosity receded. Before I made peace with myself, my Jewish neurosis, my swarthy looks, my wild card ethnicity, and with being queer. And only then, with ironic timing, did my past come calling.

It was 1988, and I was living in Long Island City, a freelance writer collecting puny sums interviewing rock musicians for one magazine and optometrists for another. I was dating Elliot, a manic-depressive who worked at New York University and drank too much. At age twenty-eight, I still confused dysfunction for adorable vulnerability, so I stayed with him. It was mid-March. There was a registered letter for me at the post office. When I walked over, the clerk handed me an envelope decorated with latticework, addressed in calligraphy a shade of brown that resembled dried blood. The front was stamped "personal and confidential." I casually pulled out the letter, written in the same corny penmanship. I began skimming when a line in the second paragraph stopped me: "I have held you in my heart since I gave birth to you on June 9, 1960...."

A few months short of my twenty-eighth birthday, I was holding a four-page letter from my birth mother. Valerie Bishop was a legal secretary living in Santa Monica. She had had me at age twenty in Boston and was forced to give me up. She vowed she would try to find me. In the days before routine Internet searches, she had spent two years searching Massachusetts public records. And now, a small, uninvited bombshell was sitting in my lap.

I hid the information for a month, as if it were a dirty secret. Mainly, I was afraid to tell my parents. Valerie's arrival would suggest a betrayal of Lolly and Sonny's love, even thought I hadn't conjured her. I finally called my parents and told them of the registered letter. My mom became hysterical. It was a primal reaction which had probably lodged itself there the first day she took me home: a fear that someday my birth mother would want me back. My father, who had a knack for practicality over emotion, had a simple question: What did Valerie want. I didn't know. For that matter, what did I want from Valerie?

A month passed before I got it together to write to Valerie. In a measured longhand, I apologized for the delay and assured her I held no lingering resentments for being given up. I was eager to speak. I sent the letter by Federal Express. That Sunday morning, Elliot and I were sleeping in when the phone rang about nine o'clock. I jumped up nude, thinking a friend was calling to suggest brunch. I never got a chance to put on my shorts. It was Valerie, calling from Santa Monica at 6 a.m. By listening to my side of the conversation, Elliot realized who it was. He slipped into the kitchen and sat behind me. For three hours, Valerie talked. And for three hours, Elliot sat silently, his arms wrapped around me. It seemed an appropriate scenario: for the first revived connection with my birth mother, I was as naked as when I had been born.

Valerie was a real talker. With a damned good story. Like many, Valerie had been a baseball fan as a teen. But while most collected baseball cards, she actually dated players when they came to town. On this occasion, a pitcher for the Baltimore Orioles named Arnie Portocarrero had come to Fenway Park for a game. He was a tall, olive-skinned, green-eyed man with a careless charm. After the game, Valerie and a girlfriend went out with Arnie and a pal. Many drinks later, Valerie and Arnie ended up in his room at the Kenmore Hotel. I was the product of a one-night stand between a second-generation American Jewess of Lithuanian ancestry and a first-generation American, born in Washington Heights, New York, to Puerto Rican parents. And I finally had the key to my indeterminate racial identity.

I learned that being hassled for my skin color had started long before grade school. Valerie sent me a copy of my hospital record. It had been a traumatic delivery; after twelve hours of labor, I emerged with the umbilical cord wrapped twice around my neck. I did not take my first breath until almost a minute later. But that did not deter Dick A.J. Brown, MD, from making a crucial notation on my record, which reads: "Addendum: There was considerably dark pigmentation of the scrotum which made the Obstetrician suspect that this was probably a negroid baby." Negroid? God bless Puritanical, bigoted Boston! Less than an hour old, I had been singled out for racial profiling.

By grade school, racial teasing was a daily occurrence. Since I was on the receiving end of such taunting, I ached to find a scapegoat to pass on the abuse. It finally happened in fourth grade. It was another recess at Martin E. Young Elementary School. I was standing by the jungle gym with my only friend, Howie, a chubby kid with a face splattered with freckles. We were watching a boy named Eric, who always wore a white shirt and tie to school. The ensemble drew our attention because the shirt contrasted sharply with Eric's dark brown skin.

After a few minutes, Howie elbowed me in the ribs. "I dare you." So I did. Eric's placid face grew pained. He walked over to Mrs. Parker, the playground monitor, to announce that I had just called him a nigger.

Eric and I were led to the principal's office for my first lesson in racial compassion. Mr. Dodero asked Eric and I to hold out our hands. What difference did it make, he asked gruffly, that Eric's skin was a deep brown and mine just a lighter shade of the same hue? Then he held out his own freckled hands to drive home the point. I was instructed to tell Eric that I was sorry, and I was grateful for the quick absolution. I did my best to stay out of his way for the rest of the school year.

There was certainly no moral imperative to speed black or Latino compassion in working-class Randolph. People of color literally lived on the other side of the tracks, the poorer south side of town. My parents could be accused, at worst, of suburban-caliber bigotry. When they spoke of black people, Mom and Dad would qualify the mention with "that nice black family" or "that nice Negro couple." This was to distinguish them, apparently, from the rest of them.

By college, I had shed my baby fat, found contact lenses, and was finally making peace with my homosexuality. I also distanced myself from Judaism and its entrenched homophobia. I no longer agonized over my ethnic identity. After all, my peers had matured and "nigger" was no longer part of their vocabulary. But a semester abroad in London brought the issue of ethnic identity back to the fore.

It was the winter of 1981, and Maggie Thatcher was ruling a fading empire. Economic despair always provides an irresistible soil for racial bigotry. In this case, South Asian immigrants were being blamed for job shortages and young nationalistic thugs were on a rampage in a new blood sport known as Paki-bashing. I was spared any physical violence. But my skin color made me the target of sneers and nasty comments by older British people, as I marketed in Queensway or strolled along Nottinghill Gate. I was considered a "wog," the preferred pejorative for Indians. Only once did this identity crisis yield unexpected humor. One afternoon, I was walking home from school down Westbourne Grove. I suddenly heard the sound of sandals slapping loudly on pavement. My body stiffened as I weighed my fight-or-flight alternatives. Quickly, I turned to see a young man in a turban at my shoulder. "Abdul, Abdul," he said breathlessly. "Don't you remember me? I'm Farhad. We met in Teheran."

When the semester ended, I shouldered a backpack and spent six weeks trekking across Europe. I was a twenty-year-old with a strong command of French and Spanish. But my dark looks exposed me to the European custom of racism. One afternoon in Paris, I was standing on a Metro platform near a group of Iranians. As we boarded the train, a pair of gendarmes approached us and swept me up in their round-up. When I produced my American passport, they released me, quickly but without apology. Another time, I was returning to France from Madrid and was crossing the border when I was pulled out of line. For fifteen minutes, I stood in a corner, my only company a short, frightened Arab man.

Even on the bar scene, there was an element of racism. I was newly out and made it a point to visit a gay bar in every city I visited. Whether in Geneva or Zurich or Munich, I'd prop myself up against a wall and try to look worldly. Inevitably, a man would glide up and coo in my face, "You're very sexy. I really love Italians (or Lebanese or Iranians or Greeks or Arabs). They are so passionate (or dangerous or dominant or passive or easy)." And then he would describe in lascivious detail the bedroom scenario ahead of us, based on facile ethnic stereotyping.

These incidents were annoying but hardly traumatic. When Valerie returned to my life, I learned she had faced a more palpable type of racism, because she had married a man of color. His name was Walter Bishop Jr., and he was a bebop pianist who had jammed with Charlie Parker and Miles Davis. She had met him in New York City, which is where she fled in 1961 after giving me up. Valerie had gravitated toward the jazz circles of Greenwich Village. This was second nature; her father, Harry Paul, had been a publicist for several jazz musicians over the years, many of them black. But when she fell in love with Bish, Harry's compassion was stretched to capacity. He refused to attend his only daughter's wedding. The pair relocated to Los Angeles where racial hassles, while somewhat mitigated, still existed. Valerie and Bish became part of a group of mixed-race jazz couples, which included Herbie Hancock and his German wife, Wayne Shorter and his Brazilian wife, and Austrian Joe Zawinul and his black wife. Valerie found work as a personal secretary, working a while for Ike and Tina Turner. It was Valerie who introduced Tina to Buddhism, a force that helped her leave her abusive husband.

Soon after we reunited, Valerie organized a family barbecue in Massachusetts and introduced me to a backyard full of uncles and cousins. It was a staggering contrast to my younger years. My adoptive family had always fit me like a tight pair of shoes. My restless, artistic personality was always clashing with my mother and father's pragmatic working-class personalities. They simply didn't know what to do with a boy who wanted to be a writer. A boy who had no time for sports. (Cruelly, my birth father's sports ability was not handed down, nor was his height of 6' 3".) Now, for the first time in my life, I was watching genetics at work. Here were people who mirrored me in so many ways: habits, thoughts, values, talents. And especially my appearance. Valerie and I shared various physical tics: a narrowing of the eyes in moments of skepticism. The timbre of our voices. My grandfather Harry had been a successful Boston publicist. At the time, I was currently handling publicity for ACT UP. And never underestimate a mother's intuition; Valerie knew I was gay before I even admitted it. She remains a cheerleader for gay offspring and adores my husband Brook.

In August of 1988, my mom Lolly Blotcher was diagnosed with pancreatic cancer. She was gone by late October. I was left emotionally dazed and psychically scarred. In the space of five months, I had gained a new mother and lost the only mother I had ever known. During the next few months, my boyfriend Elliot was unable to rouse me from a stifling depression. Wisely, Valerie kept her distance, or I would have surely lashed out at her in my grief. But in time, we grew closer. I made an effort to connect emotionally with Valerie, and to understand where she belonged in my life. Mother? She was barely two decades older. Surrogate sister? Friend?

In the fall of 1989, I traveled to Santa Monica to spend a week with my new mother. Valerie held a Sunday brunch at the home of her best girlfriend, Gigi, in the Hollywood Hills. I was shown off with a motherly pride. For three hours, I was hugged and kissed by a conga line of women just like Valerie: hip, New Agey, and just a bit neurotic. Halfway through the event, Gigi's husband emerged from his home recording studio, where he had been composing since five in the morning. Herbie Hancock grabbed my hand and drawled, "Man, have I heard a lot about you!"

I soon became close to several Paul family cousins: Leslie, Cathie, and Jen. They were artists and writers, with a command of language and a playfulness that my adoptive family lacked. I also bonded with my grandmother Gretchen. But I realized I only had one half of the story. The baseball player's family was out there. Actually, I already knew how to find them. Soon after Valerie found me, I called the sports desk of the Kansas City Star and requested newspaper clippings. Missouri had been Arnie's final home. Although Arnie was all-American, in every article about him, sportswriters emphasized his Puerto Rican background, an exotic quality at the time. Arnie had succumbed to heart disease in 1986, at age fifty-five. The obituary listed his surviving family, including my half-brother, half-sister, an uncle, and grandmother.

It wasn't until 1995 that I reached out to the Portocarrero family, spurred on by my friend Pegi. She was in the New York University film program and needed a subject for a documentary. Pegi, also adopted, was intrigued by my story. One afternoon, she filmed me as I retold the unlikely tale of Valerie's one-night stand after a Red Sox game. Pegi asked me on camera what I knew about the other side of the family. I didn't have an answer.

I thought about the gap. I convinced myself that the failure to contact the Portocarreros was simply diplomacy. How would they handle a bastard on their doorstep? Arnie's indiscretion made flesh? Or maybe I carried my own bit of racism. The only Puerto Ricans I knew, aside from some ACT UP comrades, were neighbors near me on the Lower East Side who held stoop parties in the summer with merengue blaring from on a boombox. What could I have in common with them? But I finally sat down to write a letter to my half-brother who lived in Phoenix.

I came home from work two days later to a greeting on my answering machine. "Jay Blotcher; this is Mario Portocarrero. Call me. It looks like we share a father." I spent two hours on the telephone with a candid, friendly man. He explained that our family came from Spain and were originally members of Columbus's expedition team bound for the New World. When I asked about the father I never knew, Mario was blunt: he knew Arnie little more than I did. When he was about four, his parents Arnie and Pati divorced. Arnie was eking out the last year of his baseball career and their mother, a former beauty queen, was alcoholic. So Mario and sister Marisa were sent to live with their maternal grandparents. (Marisa's birth may have been a guilt spasm; she was conceived in Kansas City less than two months after Arnie's night with Valerie.) Only after he'd been discharged from the army did Mario make contact with his absent father. "What happened, Dad?" he asked one day. The retired baseball player, now an insurance salesman, shrugged, "Life just sort of got away from me."

News of the new family member reached Arnie's mother, Julia, who was then eighty-five. "Oh no," she insisted, "my son would never do that; have a son and not take responsibility." To be fair, Valerie had never told him. A few months pregnant, she had visited Arnie during Spring Training in Florida, a raincoat hiding her family condition. When she learned he had a wife at home, she left without making her little speech.

Julia and I met in January of 1996. When I walked into her Long Island home, Julia saw her son's face in mine, stood up from the couch, and wrapped her arms around me. I was officially a member of the Portocarrero family. A flurry of loving female second cousins (Julia's many nieces) filled me with family gossip. I became closest to cousins Helen and Nancy. Although several years older, they shared my mischievous energy. Helen had married a Jewish man in the 1950s and converted; she spoke Yiddish as well as I did. When her husband died, this housewife and mother began dating a biker and rode with him across the country. Cousin Nancy had lived as a hippie in the 1960s, shacked up with Jimi Hendrix and attended Woodstock with him, tripping on acid backstage as he played. She had been a junkie for decades but had finally kicked it. Still, Nancy looks twenty years younger than her age. Faced with two new families, I was aware of some immediate truths: no matter what nationality or ethnicity, all families are alike in their rituals of loving and dysfunction. The Pauls were Eastern-European Jewish neurotics. The Portocarreros offered a Puerto Rican variation of the same. The Pauls were adept at observing everyday misfortunes and funerals; the Portocarreros were better skilled in raucous celebration. But both sides offered a generous supply of unconditional love.

I often wondered what Arnie would have made of me: a homosexual whose stint in Randolph's Little League lasted a mere two months. The only part of my father's heritage I could clearly trace was his legendary hedonism. My Jewish restraint had always been overshadowed by a gregarious nature I could now identify as Latino, which helped me accrue a list of sexual partners now closing in on four figures. Arnie might have questioned the gender of my partners, but he wouldn't be able to impugn the sheer number. I was clearly my father's son. (Years later, I learned that matriarch Julia had laid down the law. Her new grandson was gay, and if anyone dared to make me feel uncomfortable, they would have to answer to her.)

With new family members comes the joy of a wider expanse of love. But with the increased love comes the increased potential for loss. The past three years have been especially painful: I lost grandmothers Gretchen and Julia, but gratefully they were eighty-seven and ninety-four. More upsetting was the loss of cousin Leslie at age fifty and Helen at sixty-five. Within sixteen months, the four strongest women in my life were stolen away.

Having grown up in a Jewish family, I readily identify with the Blotchers and the Pauls. As for the Portocarreros, it seems disingenuous to boast a Puerto Rican lineage. There remains a gap between my genetic and cultural ethnicity. This gap is common among Latino Americans, I learned. Several times a month, I take a Harris Poll that arrives by e-mail. I report on shopping habits or political beliefs. At the end of every survey, they ask about demographics. A pair of questions that appear in this section suggests that my ethnic duality is common. The first question asks if the survey taker's nationality. I check Hispanic or Latino. However, the following question is: What do you consider yourself? I always check "Caucasian." In our increasingly overlapping world, new ethnic categories arise every day.

Once upon a time, I was a neurotic suburban Jew who longed to be a WASP. In the space of seven years, I learned I was an amalgam of generations of Lithuanian-American and Puerto. Rican-American life. When I graft that stupefying information onto my history as a Blotcher, I'm left with an indefinable collection of cultures, upbringing, and personal idiosyncrasies. Meeting the Pauls and Portocarreros changed my life forever. But in another way, it simply explained how I got to be who I was always meant to be. And why I could never coax that damned hair to tumble WASP-like into my eyes.

Chasing the Grasshopper

Gerard Wozeck

When I turned fifteen years old, I had a fierce desire to shave my head. Not because I was enthralled by the U.S. Marine commercials playing on television at the time or because I wanted to dance with the orange-robed Hare Krishnas handing out books at the entrance to Chicago's Union Station. The truth was that I wanted to take a razor to my unkempt blond shag because I ached to be a disciple of the Shaolin priesthood. It wasn't because I completely understood the strict discipline of those Buddhist precepts that made me want to give my life over to their religion. I was more enticed by the spirited male bonding I witnessed on the dramatized television series *Kung Fu* and the air of nonviolence that seemed to pervade their lives. Though I saw no proof of it, I was convinced of their covert but tangible male-to-male erotic love. And I wanted to find out for myself.

I wanted to take the hand of the grown-up version of the character Kwai Chang Caine and follow him into the next adventure-packed episode. I wanted to stand in front of that glowing incense burner in the temple I saw on television, drop to my knees, and kiss the rugged neck of that willowy Buddha-inspired hunk. I wanted to be the trail guide, the one who would help my fugitive protagonist escape from the American cowboys. At fifteen, I had become an enraptured devotee of David Carradine's soft-spoken and sensual pacifism. I adopted his mannerisms. His plainspoken phrasing. His gentle demeanor. I wanted to be just like Caine.

A couple of years before, I had abandoned my fantasies of getting lost in the Rockies with John Denver or guest starring on the Saturday morning *Monkees* television show in order to comb out the bangs of Davy Jones. I no longer pretended that I could play footsie underneath Mr. Kotter's classroom desks with John Travolta or start up a high school courtship with hunky Greg on *The Brady Bunch*. Even

Identity Envy—Wanting to Be Who We Are Not
Published by The Haworth Press, Inc., 2007. All rights reserved.
doi:10.1300/5641_06

my daydreams of shampooing David Cassidy in the shower began to wane when *The Partridge Family* series was cancelled. In fact, it seemed all my early *Teen Beat* infatuations lapsed as soon as I began to develop a more distinctive Adam's apple.

Then, when *Kung Fu* began its run in the early 1970s, I was instantly hooked on Caine's charm. The lanky, soft-spoken hero of the show was everything that Bobby Sherman on *Here Come the Brides* wasn't. Caine was compassionate yet stealthy; vibrant but humble; and always slow to use his skills in the martial arts. The Shaolin discipline taught that there were many ways to conquer an enemy besides fighting. Developing an alliance with your fellow human beings was critical to the devotees of the philosophy, and whenever I would see Caine's pouty lips puckered to drink from a cup or a forest stream, I imagined my own secret alliance with him, complete with kisses and a long, tender embrace.

Kung Fu told the story of Kwai Chang Caine, son of a Chinese woman and an American sailor. Caine, orphaned as a boy, was admitted as a student to the Shaolin temple in China. At some point, Caine killed the emperor's nephew and was forced to flee his homeland for fear of retaliation. The series followed the furtive, resourceful Caine as he journeyed through the pioneer days of America, searching for his half-brother, Danny, and fighting off the desperados and gun-toting ruffians that tried to knock him off course. The program juggled back and forth between the handsome older character, played by Carradine, and flashbacks of when he was a little boy named "Grasshopper." As a young student, the sweet-faced neophyte would glean prophetic insights as his Chinese masters patiently instructed him in self-defense and honor.

I tried to imagine a storyline for the series that would somehow feature Caine and myself in a deep abiding bond. I could almost see it, an episodic adventure between a willowy teenager mired in adolescent acne in the repressed outskirts of Chicago, in a long-distance love affair with Caine, a renegade roamer on an endless, winding Zen journey through nineteenth-century America. Perhaps with a little time traveling, we could both meet, I thought. Improbable, but it was the universe of television after all, and since there had been two "Darrens" on *Bewitched*, and horses like Mr. Ed that talked, I figured I could at least invent the story in my mind.

In another unique version I conjured up, I imagined that the grown-up Caine would have a compelling flashback to when he was a boy. In his vision, he would be lying awake all through a stormy night in the Shaolin temple in China. Dressed in embroidered silk robes, the adolescent Caine, or "Grasshopper" as he was affectionately known, would find himself unable to sleep. He'd tiptoe to the other side of the temple to locate none other than me, cast in the role of his best friend, and he'd challenge me to a wrestling match. As the two of us struggled to match each other's strength, a spontaneous but overwhelming tenderness would suddenly overtake us. Naturally, much of what followed in my mind would have been edited out of the final televised version, but in my mind I saw that in between our wet kisses and soft caressing, we would pledge our devotion to kindness and peace.

Still, it was the older version of the Caine character that truly intrigued me. He was so different from the men I saw around me. Clear-headed, industrious, and filled with Eastern wisdom, he was able to sustain himself in the world without the weary workaday routine that seemed to drain the life out of my father and uncles. He was steadfastly pledged to an ideal. His mission in life was to seek out truth and justice and show genuine concern for the moral well-being of all men, despite their indifference and sometimes hatred toward him.

All of this was gigantically appealing to me. Week after week I tuned in to see this amiable man overcome the brutish egos of his male adversaries. Caine would endure humiliation, ridicule, and oftentimes heinous physical torment. Cowboys would tie him up, call him names demeaning his Chinese ancestry, yet always Caine would walk away, triumphant and proud. He rarely turned to anger, but he also didn't deny that it was part of human nature either. His humility and wisdom, more than his physical presence, were what attracted me to him. Caine became my teacher.

I remember in one standout episode, the young "Grasshopper" received some gentle advice from one of his Masters: "In striving for an ideal, we do not seek rewards. Yet trust does sometimes bring with it a great reward, even greater than good."

Then the young Caine asked, "What is greater than good?"

In my mind I tried to latch on to what was good for me. Good was being able to cry and not have my father ridicule me. Good was being able to put my arm around the jocks I admired at school and feel like I could rest it there, without embarrassment or fear. Good was feeling

like I could openly sing the words to some of Karen Carpenter's
songs when everyone else was listening to Aerosmith and the Eagles.
Good was being able to recognize myself as someone worthy, someone who was really, deep down, pretty much okay.

Of course for the Chinese Master, harmonious love could be the
only thing that was greater than good. But to me that was some ab-
stract, unattainable theory; they were pretty words that had no real
meaning or tangibility in my world. Sure, I wanted to get closer to
that philosophic truth, and at fifteen I thought the best shortcut would
be to end up in a deep kiss with Caine. Naturally I wanted to learn
how my television hero was able to break through walls and split
rocks in half with his foot. But what I desired more than anything was
to be able to languish in some sutra-inspired meditation and swoon in
the swirls of licorice tea with just a campfire, a two-man pup tent, and
my glowing bodhisattva.

Still, it was the 1970s and nobody talked that much about men in
rapture with other men, and besides, I was just a grasshopper then
myself, without a Shaolin Temple Master or a flesh-and-blood men-
tor, without a shaved head or an ancient principled discipline to ad-
here to. I had to learn how to fight off my own adversaries. I had to
learn how to disguise my true self, hide my hard-ons for Caine under
my flannel bathrobe. I had to learn to play rough and learn the ways of
not provoking the brutes at high school who threw spitballs at the
back of my neck during geometry. Or the jocks who would shove me
into walls as I tried to walk unnoticed to class.

In my mind sometimes, I wanted to practice judo on those guys
who sat on the back of the bus and said the word *faggot* under their
breath every time I got on. Or the guys or who broke into my locker in
junior high, stole my books, only to return them with pee stains on
them. Or the time I was chased home after a sock hop with my assail-
ants yelling, "We're gonna kill you, queer boy."

I had to struggle with the idea that there could be something pure
and wholesome in being young and gay in semi-rural Illinois in the
mid-1970s. I had to discern that there was truly something noble in
loving other men. Feeling shamed and as though I had to hide my
erotic desire and power, I could relate to some of the misadventures
and problems that Caine encountered. But somehow, through my secret affair with him, watching him week after week defend his honor

and overcome his setbacks, I was able to learn patience and a kind of honor.

Over the month of July, the public library bookmobile would drive down the street, and neighbors would come out to gather up pulpy novels to read over the vacation months. I picked out a book on martial arts that discussed, in part, some of the Shaolin philosophy as it related to the skill of Kung Fu. I was intrigued by the idea of a student surrendering completely to the wisdom of a Master Teacher. One who would guide and inform the youthful adept at every step along the way. I was also inspired by the notion that one must be humble and have the ability to sense when one is off track or wrong, then make amends and be honorable and truthful to both oneself and the surrounding community.

This idea seemed liberating from my strict Catholic upbringing. There was no fearful dogma or guilt-ridden fears of burning in hell, or worse, lingering in purgatory in the hope that someone would pray for your soul to get out. There were no punitive nuns or terrifying confessionals to go into. No priest to scold me or make me do one hundred Hail Marys on a cramping kneeler. The idea of the Buddhist philosophy was to seek harmony in all things, to achieve a kind of balance with nature and become guardians of one's fellow man. It seemed I was on the brink of a kind of conversion.

I remember one summer night when *Barney Miller* had replaced reruns of *Kung Fu* and I wanted to feel closer to my heartthrob. I took my father's electric-charged razor and attempted to cut off all my hair. In the glow of a half moon and my flashlight, I managed a very uneven and hacked-up crew cut. I splashed on my father's limey Hai Karate aftershave, put my bathrobe on backward, and sat up in my backyard tent imagining my hero Caine would stumble onto me, his long-lost friend from the temple. Oh how I was ready for that passionate reunion.

But Caine never found me. There were only crickets that night, and the distant wail of a suburban train whistle, not the breathy words of my make-believe television stud brother or even a wise, bearded teacher who could tell me, "You're fine. The desire you feel for other boys is perfectly okay. And one day, even a little grasshopper like you will grow up to be a noble man after all."

It didn't matter. I kept my hair short that September when I went back to school. I walked a different walk down the hallways, and the more I read and meditated on this whole concept of harmony, the more I understood the fear of my antagonists. I didn't fight back when they taunted me. I thought of Caine and the bounty hunters who were after him with their guns. I tried to remain strong and fearless in the face of those red-faced football jocks cursing at me when I'd stumble on the volleyball court, and that seemed to be enough. Everyone at high school seemed to sense my resolve that autumn, because the jeers and threats subsided by the time our Homecoming football game came around. It was later, after the game, at the victory dance, that my Zen moment began to dissolve.

I didn't want to attend that year, but I was a member of the Forensic League, and the various participants had formed a fairly close alliance with one another. Since the bulk of the group was comprised of borderline or full-blown geeks, we decided that we could go as a group of just friends and dance on the gym floor in a kind of loose huddle. I agreed and told my cohorts that I would meet them in the lobby outside the gym at around seven. I arrived stag that night, paid my admission fee, and entered the hallway where couples were standing in line to get a photo taken.

"We don't allow queers in here." The bellowing voice from a nameless football jock silenced the line of gawkers.

"Yeah, fairies need to check their purses outside." Another voice, this one even more gravelly.

There were murmurs, some nervous laughter. Then someone came forward, striking his chest with his fist and shadowing my way into the dance. I knew I had the choice to turn around and flee from the building or to stand there and accept the blow that would most likely land on my quivering jaw.

But I remembered Caine. In his most dire moments he was always able to ask his opponent just the right question to avoid using his self-defense technique. The crushing blows from a Kung Fu discipline was always a last resort for Caine, since the object of harmony was to disarm your challenger by making him think more deeply about his anger. I had no martial arts skill, but I knew I wasn't going to run.

Something in me commanded a relaxed but solid stance. I looked at the faces of my peers. For a flash, I wondered if they felt sorry for me. Or if they felt completely removed from my situation, comfortable because they were on the arm of a well-dressed crush. Safe, because they could be completely themselves in the open, blending in, as they were, with the other attendees. I had no beau to take to this party, and if I did, I'm certain we wouldn't be welcome. But I was not going to leave and stand my fellow club members up.

"Excuse me, but I'm going in now." I couldn't believe I was saying the words, but there they were, quietly floating in the air with the kind of understated but solid phrasing that Caine might have used. The remark lingered in the air for minutes and seemed to hover above the astonished faces of the debutantes and their jocks.

"I'm part of this school and I'm expected here by my friends and I'm going to dance." My eyes were steady on his, and I didn't flinch for a moment. I was calm and faithful to the spirit of Caine. "I've come here to dance."

My assailant stood still. No one stepped up behind him to underscore his threat; no posse emerged to toss me out. As I quietly passed through the doorway into the dance, the fellow simply shrugged and muttered something under his breath as he stepped back into line.

I walked into the gymnasium that had been transformed with a festive garden theme; papier-mâché bluebells and strings of faux roses and daisies were streaming over the basketball hoops, and candied lily pads floated in cherry-red punch bowls. I chuckled to myself for a moment thinking that indeed the flower fairies had arrived and taken over my high school gymnasium. Couples softly embraced all around me as the band was doing a take on Gary Wright's radio hit, "Dreamweaver" and the urgent lyrics, "I believe we can make it through the night," strengthened my resolve. I stood for a moment, in the dimmed lights of the gym, amid the swaying twosomes, and folded my arms across my chest, and felt, just for a moment, I was coming home to myself.

I finished out my high school career as a boy struggling with self-acceptance in a world where there was little to affirm my desire and need for inclusion. There was no *Queer as Folk* on television back then or Oprah shows that dealt with the hurdles of "coming out" or even a Gay and Straight Alliance on campus. I walked around in kind of somnambulism, always mired in self-doubt and never fully present for the moment, too afraid to realize the full reality of my hostile environment.

But the notion of becoming a different kind of man—someone like Kwai Chang Caine—carried me through those arduous years. I followed him, trying to center my heart's clumsy logic on the path of the weaponless soldier, the little grasshopper making his way in a world that never seemed to validate his worth. But perhaps even that was okay. The notion that I tried so hard to wrap my mind around at fifteen, and still wrestle with at certain moments today, is that we are all connected to one another, even, amazingly, to our adversaries. With that in mind, every day, it's another little leap forward.

When I Was a Girl/1966

Deborah La Garbanza

I always wanted to grow up and be a guy with a white undershirt
and large sweat stains under the armpits. To not care how I looked,
have greasy hair, a powerful chest with bulging arms. To scratch my
crotch absentmindedly. I wasn't meant to be a girl. But a major reas-
signment sent everything that was outwards inside. Now at fourteen,
nothing was spontaneous and I became self-conscious, self-hating.
"Hypocrisy" became my favorite vocabulary word as I tried valiantly
to fit in, yet deplored the conformist I had become.

I sat in the last seat in the third row in Mrs. Kuznitz's English class,
stewing in my sweat, my mouth cracked, half-formed answers froth-
ing and dying on my lips. I was surrounded by girls, most of whom I
had known since the second grade. There was Lisa Fishgrund with
her little turned-up nose and ironed hair, looking like a princess. She
had endless pairs of soft and rounded Cappezio shoes in plum, per-
simmon, vermillion, puce, teal, and olive to match corresponding colors in her endless plaid kilts. Lisa wasn't pretty, but I didn't notice.
Her nose had been fixed and all her earrings matched her outfits. She
didn't seem to mind being a girl; in fact, she seemed to revel in it.

I had only recently and reluctantly become one. Due to my
mother's renewed efforts to break me of my tomboy ways, I succumbed to the pressures of girlhood. This involved corralling my
movement and feelings. I watched in horror as budding breasts grew
on my once-flat chest. They became the symbol of my new, restricted
landscape. No longer would I be roughhousing with the boys, playing
left field, fighting Eddie Lombardi for neighborhood domination. I
could kiss the undershirt good-bye.

Mrs. Kuznitz said that because it was the ninth grade, our performance counted and that meant participation as well as written work.
No longer would our grades be thrown in the educational garbage can

Identity Envy—Wanting to Be Who We Are Not
Published by The Haworth Press, Inc., 2007. All rights reserved.
doi:10.1300/5641_07

but instead college officials would peruse them. "Make no mistake about it," she said, pacing back and forth in the front of the classroom. She was married to Barry Kuznitz, the social studies teacher. He was a goofy, fun-loving guy and everyone wondered how the two of them could be married. Sweet and sour. Happy and mean. Relaxed and tight. It didn't make sense. He would pop his tousled head into our classroom and give her a boyish grin. One time he stuck his tongue out at her and the whole class laughed. A tiny smile appeared around the edges of Mrs. Kuznitz's mouth.

She was short, with shoulder-length auburn hair that was her crowning glory. Her face was a mask of beige foundation upon which a layer of powder was applied to create a flawless canvas. Rouge at the cheekbones was the final touch. When the chalk screeched across the blackboard and Mrs. Kuznitz's skirt inched up from behind, the boys guffawed and rolled their eyes, but none of the girls made a sound. Mrs. Kuznitz expected the room to be silent as a tomb. Once when I opened a hard candy under my desk, the noise of the crackling wrapper sent her searching until she found me with the offending candy. A brief nod of her puffed hair, a moment of recognition from her eyes and that tight smile told me I wouldn't be penalized this time.

Of course she'd never penalize the Davids. In all Jewish communities, there are many sons named David. In our class there were three: David Glassberg, David Silverman, and David Stern. All surely headed for Ivy League schools. Although she seemed to like all the boys better than the girls, Mrs. Kuznitz loved the Davids the most. They could do no wrong. David Glassberg was the most disgusting. There was always something brown or green stuck to his braces. Yet for him was reserved the kindest, most animated looks. She didn't even like Marilyn Gottlieb, the smartest girl in the class. Like every female teacher, she knew our fate. Wives, mothers, teachers, we would be consigned just like her to places of little power and status.

Unlike me, the Davids seemed to have no problem with participation. They rambled and roamed, jousted and debated, speculated and theorized. They did verbally what I did physically just a few short years ago. Their speech was like jazz, spontaneous and brilliant. They talked about Pip and Miss Haversham, Lenny and George, Montagues and Capulets, the Red Pony's crusty eyes and rheumy lungs. They said it all. By the time I started to raise my hand, the Davids had already made their point. I sat in the last seat, trying to pull down my polka-dotted miniskirt that was rising up past my garter snaps.

The Davids didn't have to think about making an outfit, matching the kilts to the knee socks. The earrings to the shoes. My mother suggested a panty girdle to help with the jiggle. As a girl, I would be wearing makeup and ironing my hair. I would wear a bra, a tight bandage constricting my chest, and mini- or maxi-skirts. The boys could still wear the same clothes. My mother thought since my own hair was so kinky and unmanageable, I should get a fall. I could throw it over my shoulder like Lisa Fishgrund. A soft and silky thing that some David could pet. I looked around at the other girls for clues. There was Frannie Lipschitz, who was so small and defenseless that she looked and acted like a baby doll. Peggy Dukakis, pale as a full moon with large buck teeth and a thick mane of chestnut hair. There was nothing to be gained from Peggy. She was lost in her horsey fantasies, always drawing pictures of the black stallion in her notebook. In her faraway eyes, she was permanently mounted on the big steed, galloping in the Arabian Desert. She'd rock back and forth at her desk, like a Hasid davening in prayer.

"Stop it, Peggy," Mrs. Kuznitz said in disgust. Peggy barely had to move for the teacher to know what she was doing. I tried it once, felt the pleasurable pressure in between my legs, and stopped instantly. Peggy was up to something disgusting and Mrs. Kuznitz knew it.

Then there was Marilyn Gottlieb, modestly covered with dresses that had ruffled bibs. Underneath, I could make out the outline of her already heavy, pendulous breasts. A gold chain with a Jewish star hung dead center. Her body was thick and maternal. She wasn't pretty in the way that Lisa Fishgrund tried to be, but that didn't matter to me. Marilyn played classical piano. I'd watch in fascination as her stretched fingers moved to the music in her head in silent rehearsal. Her hands were plump and rounded. Her fingers were beautiful, sensitive. She never raised her hand in class but still she created her own spell. Sometimes, when the Davids faltered for an answer, Mrs. Kuznitz would impatiently call on her.

I felt the strongest desire to impress Marilyn but also humiliate her. The urge for both these impulses was something I knew had to be kept secret. In truth, I wanted to kiss her. I had been standing in the stairwell alone when the thought overtook me. It was undeniable; I couldn't push it away. It was the most horrifying thought I'd ever had.

In my fantasy, Marilyn swayed backward, her mouth opened, and she
moaned with pleasure. A little moan, barely audible. I was lost for a
minute, gripping the handrail, enjoying the fantasy until the loneliness swept over me. I was going to have to guard this secret forever.
No one in the world had such a feeling. The telling of this desire was
the linchpin that would unravel my entire personality. I became even
more silent.

Meanwhile, the Davids spoke in topic sentences. They exhaled
supporting details. They wove subordinate clauses around their fingers. A line of sweat dripped from my crotch, from the sides of the
bulging sanitary pad I was wearing. At least I hoped it was sweat. It
slid down my leg beneath the tightly meshed confines of nylon stock-
ings. My hand went up and down, up and down. I didn't want to spoil
the discussion.

"Yes?" Mrs. Kuznitz asked coldly. I had yet to participate that year,
even after she had warned us that two times was the minimum if we
wanted to keep our grade up. "Do you have something to add?" she
asked. My mind went blank.

"Can I go to the bathroom?" I asked.

"Yes, you can go," she said. I could see her making a mental note of
how my inappropriate question sliced right through the Davids' spirited discourse of the foreshadowing in *Macbeth*. I rose up and attempted a regal pace down the third row to the door. Soon the boys
were guffawing, the Davids made special noises with braces glinting.
I could feel their pimples popping, blackheads oozing. I was walking
at a snail's pace. Even Peggy Dukakis came out of her reverie to offer
a small laugh. Lisa Fishgrund looked at her nails. Marilyn Gottlieb
got to enjoy it with her beautiful hand in front of her mouth. I had
drawn attention to myself. Everyone would know everything about
me. "Better speed up," Mrs. Kuznitz said with that tiny smile.

When I got back from the bathroom, Mrs. Kuznitz had assigned
the essay for *Macbeth*. I panicked. The edition of *Macbeth* we were
forced to read was in the English of its time. There was no translation
into its mid-twentieth-century equivalent on the opposite page. There
was no comic book. No movie. No Internet notes. This Macbeth
ranted and raved on his own terms. His wife compulsively washed her
hands. The witches spat out their confusing prophecies: "Fair is Foul,
and Foul is Fair" and "When Burnham Woods comes to Dunsaine." I
didn't understand paradox. The world seemed confusing enough for

someone clinging to adolescent absolutes. Mrs. Kŭznitz warned us. "No plagiarizing." That began the internal debate of what constituted plagiarism. Could I buy the yellow Cliff Notes from the local drugstore? After all, those authors were Shakespearian scholars. I was only in the ninth grade. Could I borrow their ideas but not their words? Could I change a "because" to a "perhaps" and still call it mine?

Mrs. Kuznitz wrote her expectations for the essay on the blackboard. It was an elaborate outline of main ideas and supporting detail, demanding cross references, quotations, and an understanding of the fine mesh of human psychology. She wanted our own ideas, that much was clear. I could feel the sweat pouring out of my armpits. I would never get into a good college. "Any questions?" she asked in a way that ensured no one would say yes. She turned back to the blackboard to add something more.

From the back row, I watched David Glassberg lean across the aisle toward Marilyn. He turned his head and made a face. I gasped. How dare he? Marilyn giggled. Mrs. Kuznitz whipped around at the sound. "Is something funny?" She gave Marilyn a wilting look.

David blurted out, "It's my fault. I made a joke." First he made her laugh and then he played the hero. Mrs. Kuznitz's face softened. She was imagining the romance, the one I would never have. When the bell rang, he offered to carry her books and she accepted. I plotted ways to humiliate Marilyn at the lunch table. I would ridicule her hair, her weight, her bosom, make her cry. And nobody would know the secret, excited feeling I would get from it. It was only a matter of time before Marilyn would be wearing David Glassberg's ID bracelet. I was overwhelmed with the feeling that had I been born a boy, my life would have had its promises fulfilled. I didn't even need the undershirt or the powerful chest. I could have been a Jewish boy. Instead of Marilyn, I wound up with a panty girdle, blood red Capezio shoes, and a mass of Dynel hair spreading out like an enemy fortress around my head, weighing down my shoulders.

Italian-American Boys

John Gilgun

I came of age sexually in an Irish-American/Italian-American working-class neighborhood in the blue-collar city of Malden, Massachusetts, in the 1940s. Yes, I had the fantasy that a mistake had been made in the hospital and that I was in fact the child of a rich couple who lived in another part of the city and would find me some day and take me to their thirty-room mansion and drive me around in their Buick Roadmaster. But I really wanted to be an Italian-American boy, living as part of an Italian family, with Italian brothers, cousins, and uncles.

I did not want to be Irish-American. Irish-Americans were hard, mean, aggressive, and spiteful. Irish-American boys rejected me before I could open my mouth to say something to them in a friendly way. Being friendly itself was suspect. What did I want out of them anyhow? Being friendly was queer stuff. Who needs it? It was always the Irish-American boys who picked me last and then complained about me when I struck out or dropped the ball during a softball game. "We don't want him. Why don't you take him?" always came from Irish-American boys. Italian-American boys were willing to give me at least half a chance. Irish-American boys gave me no chance at all. I was rejected by them as soon as I stepped into the city park across from the house we lived in. And if a fist hit me in the face it was always an Irish-American fist. No Italian would ever do that to me.

My father was a thin-lipped, angular, alcoholic who looked like Beckett. You know, the hard cheekbones, the intense dark eyes, the twisty lips. He had rejected me by the time I was five. Italian-American boys had fathers who never rejected them no matter what they did. These fathers seemed able to love. They were there for their kids. They weren't alcoholics.

Identity Envy—Wanting to Be Who We Are Not
Published by The Haworth Press, Inc., 2007. All rights reserved.
doi:10.1300/5641_08

You wouldn't find Italian-American fathers in the Irish bars where my father spent his afternoons. They were with their kids at a Red Sox game or at Revere Beach or at a lake in New Hampshire. I had an Italian-American boyfriend when I was twelve. He said, "I love my father." I was astonished. "I hate mine," I answered. I used to try to bond with the fathers of my Italian-American boyfriends. I wanted a father, but I wanted an Italian-American one. No Irish need apply.

The Italian-American boys were bonded together. In the schoolyard they played that numbers game with their fingers that no one could understand unless they were Italian-American. And once in the locker room in the seventh grade I heard one singing "O Sole Mio" and right away another Italian-American boy popped his head around a locker and said, "Hey, gumb-ahh! My aunt taught me that song too!" And they were linked up immediately because of that song. Imagine, daring to sing in the locker room? Irish-American boys would die first.

Then these Italian-American boys would get up on the stage with an accordion during an assembly and play "Spanish Eyes" and they didn't feel it was necessary to say to the other guys afterward, "Aw, my mother made me do. Fag stuff, playin' an instrument." They just did it and enjoyed it without guilt and without shuffling around later and saying, "Shit, I hate it. Doing it makes me feel like a queer. Fuckin' 'Spanish Eyes.' Gimme a break. It should be 'Spanish Fly.' Ha ha!"

There was a softness inside the Italian-American boys that was warm and comfortable. I found it dreamy. What they carried around with them in their minds wasn't all jagged and nervous and cruel like Irish-American boys. Italian-American boys weren't defensive about their masculinity. They didn't have to be. As for being a queer, Italians had a different idea about it. It didn't bother them all that much. While Irish-Americans, who seemed to hate sex anyway, were uptight about being queer. The faggot jokes came from Irish-Americans. They did not come from Italian-Americans.

These jokes came from people like my father who seemed to spend every day of his life protecting his threatened masculinity. He defended his manhood by drinking. Italians drank too, of course, red wine with dinner, but they didn't drink the way my father did. They didn't get drunk to blot out consciousness the way he did or fall on the bathroom floor in a stupor and pass out there. They drank wine around the supper table with relatives laughing and talking over good food. And the food was better, too. Not boiled potatoes and boiled carrots and frozen Birdseye peas and beef with all the flavor boiled out of it. But ravioli cooked with love. As I pressed my fork against my boiled potato, meal after meal, I imagined I was next door in the three-decker eating ravioli and laughing with the Italians.

I was eleven years old when I came for the first time. I was real early getting to that. It was a Memorial Day weekend and my mother and father had gone off on a three-day party, leaving me at home. They took my younger sister and brother with them, but I wouldn't go. I wouldn't go because I didn't want to be in the car with them when one of them drove drunk. I'd had an experience with that which was terrifying. So they left me behind.

I was in a blossoming apple tree behind a house across the street. I'd put a couple of boards up there, and I used to climb up to read comic books. The comic book I was reading was *The Flash*. He had a boyfriend whose name I can't recall. Little Flash? No. But I was staring at his flaming body, then at his crotch, and I began to fondle my dick, and then I came. I had no idea what had happened.

I had no idea what had happened because no one in my family ever mentioned sex to me. At eleven I didn't know how babies were conceived. I didn't know anything about female bodies. All right, I was only eleven. And that's the way it was in those repressed times. But I masturbated every day for the next nine months, and after all that time I still had no idea what it was about. Then I got my first Italian-American boyfriend and he told me. He told me though he hadn't himself achieved an orgasm. He told me because his Uncle Frankie had told him about it and then his cousins and his other uncles confirmed it for him. Meanwhile, in my Irish-American family, all lips were sealed. It was total lock-down in the Sing Sing prison of Irish-American sexuality.

This boyfriend's name was Coz—for Cosmo—and our relationship was totally sexual. We talked about nothing but sex, for instance. It was our secret knowledge. Well, secret from parents, secret from adults. At the age of twelve, really, what boy was talking about anything else? But we also had sex. Coz brought me off himself by groping me through my dungarees one day, after which I had to go home and put on a dry pair.

Coz had a friend, Joe Cippoli, who could blow himself. "It's all that spaghetti we Italians eat," he told me. "It makes us big." It was one more thing that turned me off the boiled potatoes.

I used to wake up in the morning imagining that I was Coz waking up in his house. I could imagine myself in his body, thinking his thoughts in his brain. I had already begun to keep a diary. Every entry was about Coz. I loved him. I might have known at the moment I turned into him on waking up that I was going to be a writer. What else does a writer do except transform himself into some other character, a character he loves? That character can take over entirely during the transformation. I'd walk around half the morning as Coz. In the afternoon I was with him. What bliss it was to be alive.

The friendship ended in time. But the need never left me. Twenty years later in graduate school, I fell in love with a twenty-eight-year-old Italian-American. He was straight but he was also like all the Italian-American boys I'd grown up with. He had that inner warmth. He knew how to laugh. He loved life. We were together every day, walking to class, sitting beside each other, studying together. I loved him in the same way I'd loved Coz when I was twelve. One afternoon I turned into him. I was walking across a parking lot and suddenly I was him—in his army clothes, in his big old combat boots from Vietnam, and in his mind. I was thinking his thoughts. When I reached the other end of the parking lot, I came back to who I was with a jerk as if I had been shocked.

"I don't want to be myself," I thought. "I want to be him."

His mother's name was Costa and she'd been born in Sicily. I'm sure she was a great cook and loved him to pieces. His father loved him, too. Used to take him to ball games back home in Baltimore, which was where he was from. Who wouldn't want to be him? Wasn't he Italian-American? Couldn't he laugh? And couldn't he love back? Bet your ass.

At the Museum of Jewish Heritage

Jim Van Buskirk

I had been looking forward to visiting the Museum of Jewish Heritage: A Living Memorial to the Holocaust since I read about it some months previously. As I approached this new museum with the cumbersome name in Manhattan's Battery Park, I noticed the unusual hexagonal-shaped structure with its six-tiered roof, and was reminded of the six points of the Star of David and the estimated 6 million who perished in the Holocaust. The first time I tried to enter, the museum was inexplicably closed, so a few days later I tried again.

I wound my way through the peculiarly circuitous security leading into the museum. Upon entering the first hall I heard music and followed it to the rotunda, where images were being projected onto walls all around the large room. Color and black-and-white, contemporary and archival, the still and moving images of the Jewish experience, traditional and modern, flooded and flowed across the walls. I watched as a bridegroom smashed the glass under the chuppa, as a fiddler played in a Polish shtlel, as well-dressed children danced and romped, as an old woman wrapped herself in a prayer shawl. Suddenly I began weeping. What was it, I wondered, that was affecting me so?

I am familiar with aspects of the Jewish tradition.

"Are you Jewish?" a visitor once asked, noticing the brass Menorah on my windowsill.

"No," I answered. "I've just had one too many Jewish boyfriends."

But I had to confess it is a question that has haunted me most of my life. In addition to having had several Jewish boyfriends, the preponderance of my women friends are Jewish. I have counted out the plagues at Passover Seders, eaten oily latkes at Hanukkah parties, been moved by the Kol Nidre at Yom Kippur services. I enjoy eating matzoh brie, blintzes, humatashen, challah bread, and gefilte fish.

Identity Envy—Wanting to Be Who We Are Not
Published by The Haworth Press, Inc., 2007. All rights reserved.
doi:10.1300/5641_09

Yiddishisms inadvertently sprinkle my speech. I light candles over the eight nights of Hanukkah and struggle through the prayer: *Baruch ata adonai, Eloheinu melech ha-olam . . .* I confess, I've been accused of being a "Macca-wanna-bee."

As a teenager I carefully copied Hebrew characters from the World Book Encyclopedia onto cardboard tablets to complete my Halloween persona as Moses, from Cecil B. DeMille's *The Ten Commandments.* Later I bought and played incessantly Elmer Bernstein's soundtrack from the film. My sympathies for the liberated Jews were matched by my attraction to the handsome Charlton Heston.

As I wept, watching these images from a tradition that was not mine, I realized that it was mostly the music that was moving me. I did not recognize any of the jubilant folk dances, lively folk songs, solemn hymns, or other traditional melodies as they were woven around each other. There was something inviting about the lushly orchestrated soundtrack, alternately joyous and melancholy. At times the melody was carried by a lone plaintive violin or a wailing flute. Feeling both haunted and held, I hoped that in the dark no one would notice the tears streaming down my face.

Eventually I eased myself from the room and into the remainder of the museum. I was impressed by the exhibits. I consider myself a connoisseur of such museums, having been many times to the Jewish Museums in New York and San Francisco, the U.S. Holocaust Memorial Museum in DC, and the Skirball Center and the Museum of Tolerance in Los Angeles. These exhibits were as informative and thoughtful as any I'd ever seen. I felt a connection that was mysteriously troubling.

Looking out from the upper-story windows, I saw the Statue of Liberty and Ellis Island in the harbor, and realized that this spot might mark where many Jewish immigrants first set foot onto the new world. I wandered through the museum's many vitrines and displays dedicated to preserving the history of lives lived and lost, of families and friends, of traditions and taboos.

In the museum's small gift shop I noticed among the too-many tchotchkes and books on Judaica, a CD titled "Heritage: The Symphonic Music of the Museum of Jewish Heritage." I had never heard of Michael Isaacson, who had composed and arranged the music, and was conducting the Israel Philharmonic Orchestra. I fondled the CD, wondering what it would sound like out of context. Would I really listen to it in my apartment back in San Francisco? I hemmed and hawed about adding yet another CD to a collection that includes many I rarely listen to. Finally I decided to take the risk: it might make a nice souvenir of my visit.

When I listened to the music at home, I was not as moved as I had been in the museum, but I found myself listening to it more often than I'd anticipated. Unaccompanied by the evocative images, the lively klezmer melodies and stirring symphonic strings felt familiar and comforting in my small, studio apartment. The disc stayed in my five-disc CD player for weeks. Once in a while I took it out to make room for something else, but then it would find its way back and I would again enjoy its mysterious magic.

One day I took it out of its jewel case and put it in the changer. I pressed the play button and the machine skipped right over it. Odd, I thought. So I tried again. Again the player refused to acknowledge it. I opened the player and moved the disk to another slot. Still no luck. How peculiar. It had played so many times. I tried another disk in the same slot. It played perfectly. So it wasn't the player, it must be the CD itself. Had it somehow gotten magnetized or demagnetized or...

I took it to my friend, Joan, who works with audiovisual formats, to see if she could figure out what was wrong. It worked fine on her player, she said, handing it back to me with a shrug.

I tried it again in each of the five slots on my machine. Still no recognition of its existence. Frustrated, I put the disk back into its box. From time to time I'd look at it, and sometimes even try it again. The player would skip right past it, as if it were not there. None of my other CDs were similarly affected.

Months passed, and I missed hearing the CD. I considered giving it away, or asking someone to make me a cassette tape of it, but I did neither.

This morning, I noticed the CD again, and without thinking took the disk from the case. I pushed the button to close the tray, pushed "play," and waited.

As the digital display clicked by I realized that music was coming from the speakers. The sounds of the disc, unheard for so many months, were reverberating through the apartment. What had happened? Why had it started playing now? Why had it refused to play before?

Immediately I thought about my brother, three and a half years younger. My only sibling, John and I have had a complicated relationship, one marked by different perspectives on the family dynamics. Our perceived closeness was then punctuated by my pulling away when the pain grew too intense. I have tried to talk to him about my feelings of years of betrayal, of his seeming inability to acknowledge me for who I really am (or even my birthdays), of me refusing to play the proscribed roles of son, or brother, or uncle. I have written letters, engaged in counseling sessions, made myself vulnerable, and had my feelings hurt repeatedly. Are my expectations too high? It is as if we are from different families, speak different languages. He seems to understand nothing of what I can articulate. Finally, sadly, I gave up. At this point we have not spoken in several years.

So I was surprised to receive a week ago, a two-page handwritten letter saying that he would like to renew our relationship. I read and reread the letter trying to discern what agendas might lurk between its lines. He made reference to the fact that we were both in our late forties, and reminding me that our father's first stroke came at age forty-nine. He talked about his sons, my nephews, Adam and Jacob, whose ages I'm not even sure of, who were curious about their estranged Uncle Jim.

John invoked our common Family of Origin, or "FOO" as he irreverently referred to it. But nothing he said seemed to dislodge me from my frightened, irrationally self-protective stance of not wanting to have anything to do with him, for fear of getting dragged back into the crazy, crazy-making vortex of our family dynamics. I couldn't explain why I was so resistant to consider responding, either to my therapist, and, especially, not to myself.

When I took the risk of putting in the disk, and finding that it played again after being silent for so long, I was flooded with feelings of hope. Hope that not everything necessarily stays as it once was. Perhaps my brother has changed; perhaps I have. Perhaps there is a chance that we can have some sort of relationship again. Perhaps we might be able to reminisce about the traditions and the history that is uniquely ours. Not religious perhaps, but over forty years of a biological connection that can be ignored but not erased. I have been in a quandary since I received the letter.

I sit down on the couch to think. Listening to the soaring music, I am swept away by its power and poignancy. When the music ends, I get up to push the button on the changer to listen to the CD again.

It fails to play.

Suddenly I realize I have my answer. The possibility of a miraculous reconciliation has dissipated. I feel my hopefulness quickly drain from me, as I stand in the middle of the now silent room. Again, I consider my inexplicable connections to Judaism.

One day as I was approaching adulthood, my father said he had something important to tell me. I waited, hesitantly. My father so rarely said anything of value to me.

"Your mother's family was Jewish."

"What?" I responded, incredulous.

Had I ever thought of my grandmother's maiden name, he asked. He reminded me that Simon (pronounced, in French, SEE-mon) was the name shared by Carly, Paul, and many other Jews.

My grandfather's name was Burns. But it had been, he suggested, Bernstein. Why had some of his relatives, the Jewish ones, changed their names to Branston. Why had my cousins, David and Gordon, had traditional Jewish weddings?

As the questions accumulated, they almost seemed like evidence. Things were falling into place. Some of my earliest memories involve raiding the refrigerator at my grandmother's and being allowed a thimbleful of Manoshewitz loganberry wine. I felt nice and glowy after sipping the sweet syrupy red liquid. I never thought to question why she stored a bottle of Jewish wine perpetually in her "frigidaire."

As I sought more examples from my father, my obvious pleasure seemed to stem his flow of information. I think he expected me to be horrified, that this revelation was to have been a wedge in the strong bond between me and my mother. It had, like so many of his efforts, backfired.

But it served to plant a seed. One which though it never really sprouted, certainly never died. Did it help explain my feelings at the Museum of Jewish Heritage? At Anne Frankhaus in Amsterdam? On Ellis Island, at Klezmer concerts, at the Jewish Film Festival? One of my favorite days was a December 25 some years ago, when I arrived in New York after a red-eye flight, had blintzes at Veselka's, toured the only open museum, the Jewish Museum, surrounded by New York Jews, and felt at home. The day ended with dinner at Carnegie

Deli and a Broadway show. I felt freed from the foreign celebration of Christmas.

I looked again at the date that my grandfather left Europe with my mother: September 1933. A few short months after the beginning of the boycott of Jews in Germany. A ruling that instigated the emigration of nearly 60,000 artists from Germany, before an estimated 6 million European Jews were murdered. My grandfather, a businessman and astute observer of current events, may have had pressing personal reasons for spiriting his daughter away from his wife, but there may have been extenuating political reasons as well.

I just read a memoir by Helen Fremont, titled *After Long Silence,* in which the author describes her uneasy feeling being raised Catholic in the midwestern United States. Slowly she and her sister uncover the family secret: their parents were Jews who had escaped the Holocaust. They assumed a new identity in the new land and lied to their friends and their daughters. The book spoke directly to me, and not just because the author had another secret of her own, her lesbianism.

None of this, I realize, means anything, really. But in some ways, my fascination with Judaism remains an intriguing mystery to me. As if it is somehow imbedded in my body. Is it in my brother's body too?

Sadly I remove the disc of Jewish music from the changer and press it into its case.

Maybe someday it will play again. Perhaps that is the day the secret will be revealed.

Pimp Juice

JDGuilford

As a child, I settled on words as a rail, all that stood between me and the abyss.

—Carolyn Ball, "Dear Family and Friends"

Pimpin' ain't dead. That's what I said. Pimpin' ain't dead. Hoes just skared.

—Anonymous (quoted by my uncle Frog, an O. G.)

I woke up this morning I was feeling kind of high. It was me, Jesus Christ and Halie Selassie I.

— Wyclef Jean, "Manifest"

He sat on the curb, wearing baggy sweats and a triple-X T-shirt. A mass of dreadlocks fell around his face and over his shoulders, framing his head like a pharaoh's nemes. I watched him talk emphatically, waving his hands and palming his fist. His two boys stood on either side of him like brothers from the Nation of Islam flanking Minister Farrakhan. Their red, black, and yellow bandanas announced that they were Rastafarian. As I approached, Pharaoh stopped midsentence. His eyes landed on me and I became aware, agonizingly aware, of my fitted jeans, my sparkly bracelets, and my French-cuffed shirt, which was pulled corset-tight across my chest. Walking through Crown Heights—a hip-hop haven, a black thug Mecca—I stood out like a pink pumpkin, dressed as I was like some 1970s homo-pimp. Pharaoh's eyes grimaced and something inside me shivered. My clothes, my bracelets, and the swivel of my walk took Pharaoh aback. But what most caught his attention was my dreadlocked hair.

Identity Envy—Wanting to Be Who We Are Not
Published by The Haworth Press, Inc., 2007. All rights reserved.
doi:10.1300/5641_10

Stemming from Marcus Garvey's 1920s prophesy that an African King would be crowned, which was evidenced with the coronation of Haile Selassie I as Emperor of Ethiopia, dreadlocks originated as a radical political statement. Emperor Selassie I, formerly Ras Tafari Makonnen, garnered the moniker "The Conquering Lion of Zion," Selassie being the Lion and colonized black Africa being the Zion he would reclaim. Many black people who believed Ras Tafari to be the messiah began growing locks, a lion's mane of sorts, as a symbol of black strength and unity. At its inception, dreadlocked hair was more than mere fashion flair. It came about as a refutation of colonization, the establishment, and Eurocentric standards of beauty. Those conscious of its origin considered locked hair the ultimate assertion of militant black politics. Unfortunately, homosexuality had no place in Rasta doctrine. In fact, many dreadheads posit homosexuality a disease, a by-product of slavery and European colonization, an infestation, like typhoid fever.

In my ten years as a gay black man with locks, I have noticed the shaking of heads and clicking of tongues issued to me by other dreads. "Another black man lost," a Rasta woman once commented. It was as if I were a crack-addicted uncle who, despite all efforts at rehabilitation, continued to smoke his life away; as if I were a lunatic covered in puss-filled sores, wandering the streets, babbling to myself. This same look of reproach shadowed Pharaoh's face.

Pharaoh glared. I walked. Pharaoh scowled and I continued toward him, determined in my stride. We were desperados facing off at high noon. We were drunken frat boys speeding toward each other in a deadly game of chicken. My throat tightened and my knees quivered beneath me. Somehow I knew my trek to the subway would end in tragedy. Nevertheless, I willed myself forward. I had come too far, figuratively and literally, to acquiesce to Pharaoh.

"Oh shit," Pharaoh said to his boys, pointing at me as I approached. Immediately, fear made jelly of my limbs. I was snatched back in time. I was in sixth grade again, boxed in my seat, being smacked around by Ray-Ray Jenkins while the entire middle school looked on and laughed.

✳

"Top cabinet." With my eyes locked tight, I whispered these words to myself. Though the school bus was less than one block away from my stop, it felt as if I had a thousand miles to travel before I would get home. "Top cabinet, second shelf," I repeated, attempting to drown out Ray-Ray's insults and the tidal wave of laughter swirling around me. I pressed my head against the vinyl seat and held strong to my tears. Sixth grade proved the most horrendous year of my childhood life.

"Faggot ass bitch." Ray-Ray yelled, smacking me in the mouth. He had boxed me into my seat. There I sat, shaking like a wind-torn sapling. "Faggot ass!" Ray-Ray's words were ant pincers pricking my skin. "Faggot ass, with them cheap ass, bitch ass pants on."

This was not my first time in the throes of humiliation. I had been subject to bullying since second grade. Though all the incidents centered on my homosexuality, the actual insults differed depending on the bully. My third grade tormenter dubbed me *Strawberry Short Cake* after the popular polka-dotted cartoon character. My forth grade bully, partial to alliteration, used *Sweet Sugar* or *Bootie Buddy,* depending on his mood. In fifth grade, I graduated to the status of *pussy,* joining the ranks of four other sheepish, lispy-tongued boys. Ray-Ray, my sixth grade nemesis, was the least imaginative of my tormentors. He relinquished his creative license, opting for the tried-and-true *faggot.*

Every week, at least once a week, I suffered the wrath of Ray-Ray. On this particular day, he began my persecution by tugging at my too-tight jeans (handed down to me by a distant cousin) while I boarded the bus. During the ten-million-hour ride through East Atlanta to my stop, Ray-Ray profaned my father, my mother, and several of my aunts and uncles before working his way to me and my "faggot ass pants." By the ride's end, Ray-Ray loomed over me, a dark angry cloud, spitting insults and jabbing his finger into my forehead.

Finally, the bus hissed to a stop. I scooted past Ray-Ray into the aisle. He dismissed me with a slap across the face. "Bye, bitch ass."

"Good-bye," I said mechanically, my voice small and crackly. I was, if nothing else, a Southern gentleman. I walked blindly down the aisle, barely aware of the spitballs pelting me in the back of the head.

"Top cabinet," I mumbled to myself, stumbling down the narrow steps of the bus. My shoestrings caught in the closing doors and I tripped, of course, skinning the palms of my hands on the sidewalk. Tears streamed down my face in salty rivulets.

"Top cabinet." My words came in stutters. "Second shelf . . . on the left." I was deep inside myself, picturing the bathroom, the medicine cabinet, and the half-empty box of Gillette razors, my final means of escape.

The house was empty when I arrived. Momma was at work and my sisters had skirted off to the park around the corner to smoke cigarettes and kiss boys. I walked through the living room, dusty in the midday light, straight to the bathroom. Years of hiding and lying and lamenting to God Almighty to excise me of my homosexual demons had yielded no results. In fact, the older I grew, the more detectable my softness became, until, by sixth grade, faggotness wafted off my skin like a skunk's stench. I knew I was trapped. Despite my best attempts at manliness, I would never pass for straight. So, I decided to end it all. Two quick nicks and I would be on my way. To where? Hell, perhaps. Purgatory, if I were lucky. It didn't matter though, as long as it was far away from Ray-Ray and his successors.

I knew about the warm water from an episode of *The Facts of Life* where Tootie had attempted suicide. Or maybe I had learned it from Vanessa on *The Cosby Show.* Either way, I knew warm water was a necessary part of the process. So I ran a bath, stripped nude, and slide inside. Submerged to my neck in tepid water, I held my wrist out, preparing to make the cut. Then I pictured Momma finding my body. Committing the act would be difficult enough for me. But to have Momma walk in on me dead *and* naked? Even in the bowels of hell I would shudder with embarrassment. So I hopped out of the tub, dressed in faded jeans and a torn T-shirt, and lowered myself into the water a second time. Then, I was halted by another thought: The letter! I had to leave a letter. After all, Tootie (or Vanessa) had left one. Besides, inquiring minds would want to know. So, I slipped out of the tub, pattered across the living room, and rummaged through my backpack for pen and paper. But damnit, I had misplaced the razors. Where the hell were they? This suicide thing was more involved than I thought.

By the time I found the razors, composed my Nobel-Prize-winning epistle, and dried my wet footprints—Momma was serious about her floors—I no longer possessed the necessary angst to kill myself. Standing in a bathroom, fully dressed, sopping wet, shaking a dead Bic ballpoint to life and debating the phrase *a dark and discouraging den of despair* (had I earned this cliché?) would take the fire out of even the most determined of suicides. Needless to say, I got my wits about myself and cleaned up before Momma arrived. Later that day, I decided on a less involved way of escaping Ray-Ray. I would transfer to a different school.

During my first day in my new sixth-grade classroom, I happened upon a valuable discovery: I could use words to thwart would-be bullies. The unfortunate victim in my discovery process was none other than Michael "Big Mike" Dodson, a five foot eleven, one hundred seventy-five pound mass of middle school fury. I had noticed Big Mike sizing me up as I entered fourth hour social studies class. Years of training had taught me to locate the enemy like a soldier in guerilla warfare. Unlike a soldier, though, I was totally unprepared for combat. Big Mike approached as soon as I took a seat.

"Hey! Stupid!" Big Mike said this loud enough to alert the table of the pending spectacle. "This my damn seat!"

Shell-shocked as I was from the Ray-Ray incident—it had only been a week prior—I sat mute with fear.

"Hey," Big Mike yelled, and more heads turned. "I said get up."

The Strawberry Short Cake in me retreated, but another part of me advanced: a twelve-year-old, fire-mouthed snap queen who had had enough. As if I had channeled a spirit, as if I were indeed possessed by a sassy, sissified demon, my mouth opened reflexively and I spat out a response.

"Go to fuck, stupid you!"

Okay, so it wasn't the most eloquent of insults. In fact, my retort was down right pathetic. Still, my words clipped Big Mike midstride. There was nothing he could do. Mike had counted on my peaceful surrender. I should have buckled under the sheer weight of his intimidation. Thanks to my gay demon, I didn't. Of course, Mike could have slapped me, but to do so would have been an admission of defeat, an admission that his brawn failed to evoke the necessary fear.

Mike faltered, and in that moment I saw him for what he was: a stupid, mean animal, a bored dog locked behind a fence, barking at passersby for his own amusement.

Mike shrugged his shoulders and tried to feign indifference. "Aw forget it," he said to no one in particular and shuffled to the back of the class.

Later that week, I walked down the halls amid looks of awe. I had become the Go-To-Fuck Boy, no pun intended. No one so much as shot a spitball at me. The fact that I—the new kid on the block, a kid who obviously had a little too much sugar in his tea (I had worn my famous too-tight jeans that day)—had stood up to Big Mike earned me asylum from Mike and all other bullies. Wow, I thought. Five little words, not even grammatically correct, five words had garnered me a bully-free school year. Mrs. Henderson, my fourth grade English teacher, was right. Words *were* power.

I used the next two years at my new school to sharpen my verbiage into a flaming sword of fury. After graduation, I blazed through high school like a samurai avenging the death of his master, cutting would-be bullies off at the knees. In college I employed words more constructively. Instead of slicing and dicing tormenters like Mike, I sharpened my blade with essays and poems and opinionated editorials in the university paper. I wrote a volume of journals in which I sorted through a gallimaufry of issues, from my irrational phobia of toes to my overwhelming obsession with Otis Spunkmeyer orange-poppyseed muffins. Most important, though, I embraced my Strawberry Short Cake lineage. I journaled my way out of the closet.

My coming out was not as dramatic or as tear-filled as I had hoped. When I told my roommate, he sat before me blinking like a bored cat then asked a few questions about cross-dressing. He hoped I would avoid the downward spiral into thick-rouged drag-queendom he had seen take the lives of several other homosexuals. Besides that, he was fine.

My closest female friend listened to my confession, shrugged, and then asked me if her foundation matched her complexion.

"You're not shocked?" I asked, flustered by her lack of astonishment.

"I knew when I first met you." She checked her teeth for lipstick in the rearview mirror.

"You *knew*!" My voice was shrill with indignation. "How did you know?"

"Your pants," she said through bared teeth. "You wear them too tight."

Momma's response was even more laissez-faire.

"I'm gay," I said with my head in my hands, summoning up the necessary shame. This was Momma—Pentecostal Bible thumper, Holiness Sanctified, Lamb of the Lord. In Momma's circles, homosexuality was an abomination, a sin against God and Man. Surely, Momma would rant and rave. Surely she would give me the lambasting I deserved. Momma wouldn't let me down.

"And?" Momma said. Her voice was a flat as a pancake.

"I'm *gay*." I yelled as if I were talking to someone hard of hearing.

"Honey, please." Momma waved her hand dismissively. "I watch Ricki Lake. I know all about that stuff." After my heartfelt confession, Momma sent me to the corner store for a six-pack and a box of grits.

With the drama of coming out behind me, I was free to seek out my gay brethren. My initiation into gay culture began in the club, were I shimmied and gyrated the night away. I toured the circuit—Atlanta, DC, New York, LA—and twirled to the beats of the nation's fiercest DJs. As my politics emerged, I joined gay organizations. I sat in hushed rooms, in a circle of other homosexual men, pontificating on internalized oppression, on homophobia in the workplace, and on the odds of another Cher hit. (Could she do it *again*?) I marched in all the parades, chanted in all the rallies, and signed all the necessary petitions. Once I stood up to an employer who refused to hire a man he thought was gay. I reported said employer to the Equal Employment Opportunity Commission and Anti-Defamation League. I was on a roll. I felt as if I had arrived. I was the New Black Homosexual, complete with dreadlocks, too-tight jeans, and rainbow key chain (sparkly bracelets and corset-blazer each sold separately).

For the most part, my new liberal gay world kept me sheltered from the realities of homophobia. Still, there were times when I passed a group of saggy-jeaned black men and felt their eyes screaming *faggot* or, more often than not, heard them say it, their words reverberating with the voice of Ray-Ray Jenkins. My fear was as quick and as involuntary as sneeze. I shriveled. I cowered. I turned around or crossed the street. Inside I acquiesced. I apologized and repented. I imbibed their hatred, adopted their loathing, the stray, rabid dog of it.

Mostly, though, I avoided such confrontations by limiting my traipsing to the boundaries of my gay world. In Atlanta, Massachusetts, and New York, I frequented Mid-Town, South Hampton, and

Chelsea, respectively, areas accepting of homosexuality. Whenever I moved, I scouted out the scene, counting the rainbow flags and the number of winks I received from men in passing cars (strictly a matter of security). For years, I lived in relative safety, sheltered from the homophobia of the larger heterosexual world. This sanctuary ended in Brooklyn.

A combination of indigence, naïveté, and a yearning to be among "my people," motivated me to relocate from the East Village of Manhattan to Crown Heights, Brooklyn. Brooklyn evoked images of sweeping parks, gorgeous brownstones, and beautiful black people as far as the eye can see. Like a black American, idealistic and naive, returning to the Mother Land, the thought of disaffection never crossed my mind. I would be in Brooklyn, among my people who would welcome me with open arms. I did not expect to find myself walking toward Pharaoh, toward the ghost of Ray-Ray and the possibility of a gay bashing, with nothing more to rely on than my stale sixth-grade victory over Big Mike.

"Oh shit," Pharaoh said. He eyeballed me and, to both our shock and surprise, I eyeballed back. Meeting his eyes for that brief moment was as difficult as staring into the face of the sun, but I did it. The rebel inside me screamed, "Say something! Give him the finger. Tell him to fuck off." This time, it was the snap queen who held me back. "Don't be a silly bitch," he warned. "There are three of them." So, having stared my stare, I walked on quivering knees, my heart beating rabbit-fast in my chest, past the lion king and his lynch mob.

I could still hear Pharaoh as I rounded the corner to the Utica subway station.

"I can't believe this shit," Pharaoh said in public-declaration voice. "A gay-ass dread. Goddamn. How the hell did that happen?"

He continued his "I can't believe a gay-ass dread," soliloquy, peppering it with *faggot* and *motherfucker*. His henchmen chimed in with comments about "sissies taking over the block," about "fire burn the batty boy," about "niggas" not knowing "the true meaning of dreads."

I felt them once more, the spitballs, pelting me on the head.

I would like to tell a story of courage and victory, a story where I turned around and met Pharaoh's gaze with my own indignant stare, a story where I stood before him and his two-man congregation—composed, proud, unwavering—and made a poignant speech chronicling the oppression of the homosexual and the black man's hypocritical participation in said bigotry. Unfortunately, there is no such story. Pharaoh's words clenched me in a fist of fear. Somehow I willed my legs to continue their quickened peddle to the Utica Avenue subway station. I managed my way down the stairs, through the turnstile, and into the furthest corner of the emptiest car of the train before I began to weep like a sixth-grade sissy.

What annoys me more than Pharaoh's words is that even now, at twenty-nine years old—having come out to my friends and family, having boasted a rainbow bumper sticker on my car, having marched in gay pride parades and rallies—even now, as I tap these words on my keyboard, composing this proclamation of pride, even now, a part of me feels as if I deserved it. There was a moment, on the train, when I considered changing my style of dress, a moment when I considered wardrobing myself in heterosexual paraphernalia. I would put away my bangles and beads. I would wear baggy jeans and hoodies, trucker hats and triple-X T-shirts. I would retire my exquisitely cut square-toe boots. High-top Nikes would be my new shoe. I would sure up my mannerisms, tighten up the looseness in my arms and wrists. I would replace my jolly gait with a manly, wide-legged swagger. I would keep myself safe by hiding.

On the train, I considered these changes—minor adjustments, I tried to tell myself. Fortunately, before I headed to Sports Authority and put two hundred dollars in Michael Jordan's pocket, my inner queen snapped me to my senses. First of all, I could never face my friends—the fiercest of fashionistas—dressed, as I would have be, like a Lil' Kim back-up dancer. Second, and more important, giving in to such urges would only feed the homophobic monster I have worked tirelessly to destroy. All of my efforts up to this point—from putting down the Gillette razors to picking up a pen and journaling my way to freedom—would have been undone by a black man, a faux pharaoh, and his limited notions of black consciousness.

Needless to say, I passed on the field trip to the Sports Authority, opting instead to sit at my computer and arrange this declaration of independence. Though I did not confront Pharaoh and chance a pummeling at the hands of he and his henchmen, I'd garnered a victory of sorts. I stood in the alley, amid the dust and tumbleweed, my hands hovering over my holsters. I sat in the car, sweating and gritting my teeth, my foot pressing hard on the gas pedal. I did not change my course *or* my homo-pimp gear. I walked past Pharaoh undaunted, with my chin up, my eyes sharp, and my back as stiff as starch. Yes! In my small way, I defeated Pharaoh—this black dread, this African king—and, in doing so, I defeated the Rasta woman who declared me lost. I defeated the turning head and clicking tongues. I defeated Pharaoh and all the ghosts of my bullies past

I would love to say I have developed immunity to homophobia. But I have not. My heart still does a triple lutz when I walk past a group of b-boys, and I still feel remorseful when I meet a black woman's disapproving eyes. On the other hand, I no longer feel a need to apologize for who I am. My run in with Pharaoh and the subsequent visitation by the ghosts of homophobia past helped me to realize that homosexuality and black consciousness are not mutually exclusive. They exist in perfect symbiosis within me, and I will continue to host them—these perfect roommates, these congenital twins—as long as my heart pumps in my chest. Thus, I will grow my locks until they become thick, luscious cords tumbling down my back, until I can no longer walk without tripping over them and yanking a crook in my neck. I will wear my locks *and* I will wear my splendorous bangles. I will strut my sissy strut and sport my fag pimp clothes, while raising a black power fist and reciting the lyrics to "Lift Every Voice and Sing." Those who deem my life a blasphemy, immoral in the eyes of Christ, Muhammad, and Jah Ras Tafari, have two options: they can begin the difficult work of overcoming homophobia—the irrational fear and hatred of gay men—by examining and cross-examining their ethos, by looking beyond their beliefs at the assumptions buttressing their hatred. They can sweep themselves clean of such fallacies, and using their new *tabula rasa* as their map, they can do as I did and venture outside of their boundaries and open themselves to other ways of moving through the world. Yes, they can do the work of becoming free-thinking people, emancipated from ignorance and bigotry, or they can follow in the footsteps of Pharaoh, Ray-Ray, and Big Mike and "Go to fuck, stupid you!"

You Picked a Fine Time to Leave Me, Helen

Mike McGinty

"Oh, noooo!" I wailed, pointing at the dribbling river of grossness streaming down from below the steer's raised tail. "I just combed there, and now look!"

Without a word, the hired hand, Ray, took the circular metal brush from me and swiped the offending brown mess away with one quick motion. I tried in vain to wipe the look of disgust off my face, but my curled lip would not be denied and my nose crinkled like a leg that involuntarily kicks when the rubber hammer hits the knee. As my revulsion surfaced, so did this simple thought: *Maybe becoming an honorary part of the Bradford family wasn't such a good idea after all.*

It was 1975, one year after my dad's job had landed our Boston-bred clan in the black hole of East Tennessee. In the ensuing months, I had never participated in the agricultural or animal husbandry activities so prevalent among the denizens of the area. The surrounding towns of Greenville, Elizabethton, and Jonesboro offered little else though, and I tried to make the best of it, even as I silently renamed them Boringville, Footballton, and HeyY'allboro. I was having a very hard time fitting in. My dad worked a desk job, cooked gourmet meals for us, and filled the house with classical music every weekend. I couldn't relate to the banjo-pickin', the rolling tobacco fields, and the slow-moving tractors all around me. Tyler Bradford—friendly, approachable, and cute—was a bridge. He represented my best chance of fitting into this weird Appalachian culture, where everyone's father but mine worked at the hulking Eastman Kodak plant, the neighbors always wanted to take me squirrel hunting, and you were nothing if you didn't know how to "fake left and go long."

Identity Envy—Wanting to Be Who We Are Not
Published by The Haworth Press, Inc., 2007. All rights reserved.
doi:10.1300/5641_11

I willed the sneer off my face, turned to my best friend, and whispered, "Now there's cow crap all over the brush. We can't use it anymore."

"It doesn't matter, Mike," Tyler said. "Don't worry about it."

Don't worry about it? But there was so much to worry about at a 4-H steer show in Bovineburg. You had to watch where you walked at all times so you didn't step in cow piles. You had to breathe through your mouth when you went near the stalls. You had to pretend that Ray, the toothless, red-faced man with the dirty sausage fingers who spit tobacco juice and talked like the scary guys in *Deliverance,* didn't creep you out. You had to remain vigilant against gigantic flies buzzing in your face, trying to land on you after they had just landed on the cow piles you were trying not to step in, thus leaving microscopic footprints of fresh cow crap—and unimaginable germs—on your clean clothes or, worse yet, on your exposed neck and forearms.

But thank God for Tyler. I can pinpoint the exact moment during our eighth-grade year when our relationship turned the corner from classmates to inseparable buddies. Tyler and I sat next to each other in biology class. Our teacher, Mr. Barnes, put a bonus question on the final exam, one of those easy, everybody-can-get-this-one, gift questions that teachers give when there's only a week of school left. The question read, "You picked a fine time to leave me, _____." I knew the answer was supposed to be easy, but I had no earthly idea. So I took a stab in the dark and wrote "Helen," in honor of my great aunt back in Boston. Auntie Helen's moustache was almost as thick as Mr. Barnes's, so my answer wasn't completely arbitrary.

When we got our papers back a few days later, Tyler glanced over at mine and saw the big, red "X" next to my answer.

"Helen?" he said with a look that didn't begin to mask his certainty that I had lost my mind.

"Yeah. Talk about an unfair question. What in the world did *you* put?" He rattled his paper in front of me. There was no red "X" by his answer.

"LUCILLE?"

"It's a song, dummy."

"It is not." It was the most ridiculous thing I had ever heard.

Tyler rolled his eyes and sighed. "Yes it is. By *Kenny Rogers*? The *country singer*? It's a huge hit."

I felt like a clueless insurance salesman from St. Louis on *The Price Is Right*, who could not come up with an intelligent bid for the washer/dryer set without going over the actual retail price. But what did I know? We listened to Chopin and Ravi Shankar in my house. I was twenty-two before I realized that "Opry" was a redneckified version of the word "opera."

"I can't believe you put 'Helen,'" Tyler teased. "We've got to get you up to speed."

Thus began our friendship. And my education.

Tyler and I did everything together, in school and out. We went to the roller rink on the weekends. We talked on the phone every night. And, slowly, I began to feel like I could actually fit in below the Mason-Dixon line because Tyler and the rest of the Bradfords were different. Oh, they were definitely products of the region, farmers and horse riders and such. But they weren't rednecks. At least they didn't fit my definition of rednecks. They had money and they had class. They lived on a big, working farm in a huge, brand-new house with vaulted ceilings and a swimming pool. Mrs. Bradford played the enormous organ in the living room, filling the tall rafters with strains of "When the Saints Go Marching In" and "The Girl from Ipanema." Mr. Bradford was a savvy businessman with his own highly successful car dealership. There were no rusted-out cars sitting up on cinder blocks in their front yard.

Theirs was a strange, exciting world of privilege mixed with down-home earthiness, of fine crystal and frayed coveralls. Sort of like *The Beverly Hillbillies,* though no one in the house ever referred to a meal as "vittles" or used the phrase "out by the *ce*-ment pond." Coming from a strictly middle-class background, I was enthralled by their affluence. And since the most rural thing anyone in my family ever did was mow the lawn, I found the Bradfords' lifestyle strangely fascinating. I figured if I was destined to live among "cattle folk" I should try to see what all the fuss was about. If people like the Bradfords could embrace a lifestyle of livestock and combines, there must be something to it. Maybe I could relate after all. Maybe I would actually begin to like it. Maybe life in rural America would start to feel more natural and the kids at school wouldn't look at me funny when I told them I didn't own any cowboy boots. I already stuck out for being short and skinny and not saying I was "fixin'" to do anything. If I could talk about bringing in the cows from the back forty or riding horses in the twilight, maybe they wouldn't notice that I threw like a girl and was afraid of bugs.

And maybe one day the pigs on the Bradfords' farm would sprout wings and fly.

As the friendship between Tyler and me grew, the Bradfords brought me deeper into their fold. They took me to horse shows. In fact, the first horse I ever rode was Tyler's mare, Flower. She promptly threw me, but damn if I didn't get right back on again.

I even helped feed the cows from time to time. While his younger brother, Andrew, drove the pickup slowly through the fields (itself a titillating venture: kids allowed to drive), Tyler and I tossed handfuls of hay from the back. The cows would follow behind us, huffing through their dark, wet nostrils. Sometimes when I spent the night we'd sleep in the barn. As the hay from which we fashioned our beds poked and scratched, I'd lie awake for hours and stare at the wooden beams above, imagining all the mice scurrying unseen in the darkness around me. In the morning, Mrs. Bradford cooked pounds and pounds of bacon, heaping it onto our plates. At my house, my parents always cut the bacon in half and portioned out the expensive meat as if each mini-strip were gold leaf. Having as much bacon as I wanted was almost more than I could fathom. So was the way they talked about the beef patties that always accompanied our eggs: "Who are we eating this morning, Mom?"

"I believe this is Harry."

I stopped chewing and wrinkled my brow at Tyler. "We name our steers," he explained. "We breed them, then we show them."

"And then we eat 'em!" laughed Andrew.

"Tyler won first place at the carcass show last year," Mrs. Bradford said proudly.

"Really?"

"Yeah. I got a big, blue ribbon and five hundred dollars. There's another carcass show next month. Wanna come? It's at the Valleydale slaughterhouse."

Carcasses. A slaughterhouse. I couldn't imagine myself in such a place. But I had come this far, I saw no reason to back out now. Besides, if my friend won again, I could share in the excitement. And the glory. "Sure."

The reek of the slaughterhouse was one of the biggest potholes I hit on my road to becoming Farmer Mike. I filed in with the Bradfords and all the other carcass enthusiasts through a thick stench no one seemed to notice but me. I gagged and Andrew laughed. "Don't worry," said Tyler. "It doesn't smell like this inside."

And he was right. What he didn't mention was that I would have to trade the olfactory assault for a visual one. We entered a huge, freezing meat locker, where the line slowed to a crawl as everyone weaved back and forth between the rows of hanging beef to admire the carcasses. Thoughts of *E. coli* crept through my head and I clamped my lips shut. Occasionally someone would reach up and rotate one of the carcasses on its hook to inspect the opposite side and I, with my arms tightly drawn to my sides, would sway back as far as I dared to avoid touching it without bumping into the cow cadaver hanging behind me. Ribs protruded from raw flesh. Leg bones poked out from layers of stretched muscle. Tiny circles of blood mingled with bristly hairs collected beneath each former Bessie, spotting the concrete floor with red circles. The future steak dinners and cheeseburgers and meat loafs both fascinated and repulsed me.

When we came to Tyler's entry, it looked exactly like all the others to my untrained eye, though even I could see the absence of a blue ribbon on it. "I didn't win this time," my friend said.

"Well," sighed his father, "there's always next year."

"Yeah," said Andrew. "Clyde looks like he'll make a good carcass."

I felt immense relief as we walked back through the reek of the slaughterhouse yard, piled into the car, and drove away. At dinner that night, I had two bowls of spaghetti and skipped the meatballs. When the Bradfords invited me to the steer show, I hesitated.

"Are the animals alive or dead?" I asked.

They all laughed. "Alive," Mrs. Bradford assured me.

"It's kind of like a dog show for cows," said Tyler. "You parade your steer in a circle in front of the judges and they mark down your score. You have to make it stand in place while they look at its muscles and its hide and all that stuff."

Again, I felt like I had come down this road so far, I should stick it out. In for a penny, in for a pound, raw or cooked. Besides, in spite of everything I was enjoying my exposure to the cowboy life. I still thought I could integrate showing steers and cleaning out horse stalls with playing my tuba and helping my mom make fancy tortes. And I liked being around Tyler, not just because we were such close friends. I hadn't yet reached the point where I could put words to my feelings, or even recognize them for what they were, but I knew I liked the blush of his cheeks, the dark fuzz above his lip, his musky smell. Whenever he wore a T-shirt and lifted an arm in a simple gesture, I'd try to steal a glance up the sleeve to see the hair in his armpit. I knew I liked that. A lot.

So for weeks before the big 4-H steer show, I'd go over the Bradfords' every weekend and help Tyler practice showing his steer. The main instrument used in steer showing is a long, wooden stick with a nail in the end. The object is to show the steer who's boss by holding the rope around its head tightly with one hand, while gently stroking its belly with the stick, held in the other. Supposedly the stroking keeps the steer calm, which is vital when you're a hundred-pound boy not quite through puberty dealing with a twelve-hundred-pound animal.

"You have to try to get it to put all four legs in a sort of square, or rectangle pattern. So they line up straight. The judges like that," Tyler told me.

"What do you do to move their legs if they're not lined up?"

"This." He stuck the nail gently into the steer, just above the hoof. The thing lifted its leg and set it back down again, making a perfect rectangle with the other three. Tyler resumed stroking the animal's belly with the stick as it stood there, oblivious to the lesson it had just been taught.

"Wow." I chuckled, impressed.

"You wanna try?"

"No, that's okay." I couldn't figure out how, with one hand on the rope and the other holding the stick, I could manage to swat the flies away. In my book, that fundamental task still beat winning a blue ribbon as the most important part of showing steers.

A few weeks later, at the show, I met Ray. "He's an old friend of the family," Mrs. Bradford told me. "He helps us show our steers. He washes them, brushes them down, all that stuff. The boys really love him." I didn't see the attraction, what with the filthy fingernails and the hairy potbelly poking out from under a sweat-stained T-shirt. But again, what did I know?

"We have to do whatever he says," said Tyler. "He's sort of in charge." I was fine with that, as long as he didn't take too much of a liking to me and feel compelled to affectionately ruffle my hair. In my estimation, his hands hadn't been washed since 1964.

Ray gave us orders, and Tyler and Andrew, who each had a steer in the show, demonstrated for me how to carry them out.

"Brush them tails out, boys," Ray said. I understood brushing an animal. Of course, you wanted it to look nice. Even a steer has standards. After we brushed, Ray braided the wiry hairs and stuck a bow on. But when Ray brought out the Aqua Net and told us to "Give her a hose-down," it stupefied me. Ditto when he handed us a can of shoe polish and told us to "smear them hooves right good now, boys. Make 'em shine." Everyone who had entered the show was busy doing the same things to their steers. The whole scene reminded me of the Miss America pageant, only every contestant was from Tennessee and they all had the same talent: standing in a rectangle. Maybe if one of them had played "Malaguena" on the xylophone, I wouldn't have grown so bored. And maybe if Tyler's steer hadn't lifted its tail and made its ugly mess all over the area I had just deigned to brush, I wouldn't have been so exasperated. Or grossed out.

By the time Tyler and Andrew and their respective steers had strutted their stuff on the runway and returned sans tiara, I was over the whole Farmer Mike experience. What had it gotten me, really? I knew how to make a steer stand tall. I could douse it with hair spray and shoe polish to make it look pretty. I had been thrown by a horse and bitten by horseflies. I had slept among rodents in a drafty barn. I was on a first name basis with a toothless backwoodsman who had a second grade education. And I had seen a cow's ribcage—from the inside.

None of it had sparked the discovery of a latent passion. I didn't get butterflies in my stomach at the thought of the East Tennessee Regional Quarter Horse Show out at the fairgrounds. And try as I might, I couldn't care less about how to set a coon trap. It just wasn't me, and I was mentally exhausted from trying so hard to change that basic reality. Some of it was fun, but I was too much of a germophobe and a neatnik to really feel comfortable wiping the sweat foam off a horse's back or operating complicated farm equipment, like a pitchfork. No, Ms. Gabor and I were cut from the same cloth, because farm living was definitely not the life for me, either. I was ready to return to the

Coquille St. Jacques à la Parisienne and Rachmaninoff piano concertos of my own family. We didn't live in a penthouse with a view, but I felt much more relaxed surrounded by the familiar smells and melodies of home, the only place in the entire godforsaken Volunteer State where I felt like I truly belonged. Ironically, the only place I didn't have to try. Realizing that one simple thing suddenly made fitting in anywhere else much less important.

As for Tyler, our enduring friendship was the greatest thing I took from my Grand Experiment. He and I stayed best buddies through high school, and found plenty of other things to bond over—including, to my everlasting delight, the hair under our arms, and in other places.

Wanting

Cheryl Schoonmaker

It started as an itching sensation on my tongue and the roof of my mouth. My throat started to swell. I swallowed my spit a few times, taking inventory of the situation. It was getting hard to swallow. Soon, it would be hard to breathe. That meant my lunch contained a poison deadly to me: peanut oil.

When I arrived at the emergency room, they ushered me in immediately. Five or six doctors flocked around me with needles, breathing apparatuses, and monitoring devices. They shot me full of antihistamines, adrenalin, stomach acid medications, and steroids. The doctors murmured. They were worried. My recovery was taking longer than it should have. My allergy had gotten worse. But finally the wheezing began to fade. I could breathe easily again, physically at least.

Because of the threat of relapse, I was kept overnight for observation. I wanted my pajamas. When I was a kid, I had Wonder Woman pajamas. I wanted to be Wonder Woman with the background music and the spinning and bullets bouncing off my bracelets. I wanted to be impervious. I also, however, wanted to be Princess Leia. She was spunky but more of a victim, and I couldn't decide if I wanted to be rescued or rescuer.

The vigilant attention from the nurses, the open door, fluorescent lights, and beeping monitors led to a fitful, dream-disturbed sleep.

I dreamed I was Snow White but no prince came to my rescue. I hung out with the dwarves, yes, but they weren't much help either. A witch was chasing me. She had a deadly syringe instead of poison fruit, and I half wanted to get caught.

I was waiting for my mom to arrive with my pajamas. I had just done laundry at my parents' house. I found myself in their basement, feeling like some silly version of Lady MacBeth: "Out, Out . . . !" My

Identity Envy—Wanting to Be Who We Are Not
Published by The Haworth Press, Inc., 2007. All rights reserved.
doi:10.1300/5641_12

hands smelled like bleach. I never knew I liked the smell of bleach—
hot tar mixed with sand and ocean's fiery cousin and clean sweat on a
caustic summer day in childhood. I was trying to banish an ink stain
from off-white shorts. I didn't remember when the pen exploded. The
purple-blue splotch seemed to have always been there.

It would not come out. Maybe I was naive to expect immediate results. I poured on more straight bleach, the excess soaking through to
my chewed nails, stinging where I tear at my cuticles. I rubbed at the
stain. I scratched, to no avail. My fingers were on fire, so I tossed the
mess in the wash and sought out cool water.

Before I could reach the top of the stairs, my father started his descent. Without thinking, I shifted into reverse. At the bottom of the
stairs, I turned, walked back to the washing machine. He looked like
he had something to say and the look was unsettling. I wanted to be
close to the soothing, rhythmic sound of the wash.

I was looking at my feet. He asked how long I'd be home this time,
and whether I'd be moving in permanently with "that woman." I
shrugged. I have found it to be the safest response. He kept talking,
but all I could hear was the chugging of water—the circular sloshing,
back and forth. My fingers, my face, my whole body was on fire.
Guilt. Anger. Shame. Not to mention the bleach.

I was not aware of him leaving. I just know that when I finally
looked up, he was no longer there. The wash was still running, but I
couldn't wait. I opened the lid and fished around, retrieving the
heavy, dripping shorts. The area around the blotch was ruined—an incongruous, glaring white. The stain was still there—an uglier color
than before.

I longed for the fresh-from-the-dryer smell of my pajamas. I
wanted to be clean. I wanted to be well. And I wanted to be thought of
as clean and well.

A nurse toting many gadgets entered my hospital room. My favorite was the plastic clamp that went on one of my fingers. There was a
little red light inside and, somehow, the thing measured how saturated
my blood was with oxygen. I scored a ninety-eight percent, which she
said was good. I was proud, but it felt something like getting a ninety-
eight percent on a test in school. I couldn't help grieving over that two
percent.

Like other kids, I suppose, I may have blamed myself for turmoil at
home. Blinking, breathing, I try to remember. Curled up on my child-

hood bed, I screamed, wheezed as he pushed her down, and dragged her back and forth across the upstairs hallway carpet. Afterward, I sat on her bed and rubbed lotion into the rugburn. I became the little glue-girl that held them together. I spent weeks in bed at a time, with bouts of bronchial asthma. Emergency trips to the hospital untied them in the single purpose of keeping me alive. I also got straight A's and won the blue ribbon at every science fair. That was something else they could get behind, united.

In grade school, I developed the unfortunate habit of throwing up at slumber parties. I didn't need any particular reason. Anything would set me off: a dog, a cat, a new carpet, a wood stove, a feather pillow, laughing too hard. I developed new allergies at an astronomical rate—sneezing, itching, wheezing, vomiting on rugs, beds, and friends. If I was sick enough, my mother came to rescue me, brought me home, rocked me in the wooden chair that, to this day, makes a strangely soothing rhythmic, popping noise. I loved being rescued. Did I want to be sick?

My illnesses and academic excellence earned me a lot of attention at school, but I was a scared, silent recipient. I longed to be like one of the cool kids—talkative, brave, self-confident, belting out songs from the *Grease* soundtrack, carefree.

My mother was nervous over me being in the hospital. I should have spent nights in the hospital many times throughout my childhood, but she had always put so much effort into keeping me out. There was the time that I was dehydrated and refused to swallow any liquids or medicines. They told her I had to be hospitalized and she refused. She said she could get me to take the medicine and some water. She never told me what the stakes were. She never threatened me. She simply told me that if I took my medicine I could have anything I wanted. The bronchitis was severe and I could barely speak. I knew what I wanted, though, and whispered to my mother, "a drum." I swallowed the medicine, sipped spoonfuls of water, got a drum, and avoided what she saw to be the trauma of a hospital. I wanted to be a drummer. I wanted to disappear into rhythm.

My mother was more nervous, of course, about me being gay. When she first found out about my girlfriend, she wrote me heart-wrenching letters. We were too afraid to talk to each other about it. She wrote about all the mistakes she made when I was growing up. She gave me pamphlets about how to recover from my sickness and sin. She cried and looked painfully concerned. She prayed. She told me she would get me "help" if I wanted it. I didn't know how to fight that. Maybe it wasn't a matter of fighting. I never meant to hurt her. I did not want to be the source of pain and I wanted to be guilt-free. My parents had a gay-allergy and I did not want to be an allergen.

I remembered the *other* hospital and how I hoped shock therapy would not make me straight. In my granny robe with stubbly legs peeking out, I listened to my roommate talk about her love of knives. I had lost my love of life and that's what landed me in that hospital bed. Tom got theological when manic and preached to all of us. I cried during readings of *Chicken Soup for the Soul* poems. There were too many pastries. I had no energy to put the bottom sheet back on my bed when the elastic gave way. I remembered how the waiting room at my school's counseling center was filled with only women. I started thinking that if shock therapy did make me straight, maybe that wouldn't be a terrible thing. I worried about making my parents worry. I did not want to be the source of worry.

From the very beginning (of me), my mother didn't know what she was getting into. I was allergic to everything and spent most of my infanthood screaming. It took the doctors a while to figure out that things my mother was eating were making me sick when she nursed me. At first, they told her I was a colicky baby and she should just let me cry. She never listened to them. She knew something was wrong. She paced the floor with me at night. When she couldn't think of any more songs to sing, she flipped through a hymnal. I wouldn't even let her sit. I cried if she wasn't walking. I needed the songs. I needed to keep moving. I had no language to tell her that everything hurt. All I could do was scream.

Everything hurt again, and I was looking for a language. The hymns had become part of me, soothed me in my times of distress. I struggled to reconcile my faith with my life. I believed in the Christian basics, yes—the greatest story ever told—but I also loved a woman. Where did that leave me? I wanted to find my place in the story.

I dreamed that good and evil were playing ice hockey with souls instead of a puck. I was defending the goal to hell. I would swing on the top bar and kick the souls away with my skates. None got by me, but I was concerned I was injuring them with my blades. Nevertheless, it was one of the few dreams I've had about hell in which I was not going there, and that seemed like progress.

Groggily, I pushed the buttons on my current hospital bed. Head up, head down. Feet up, feet down. Somewhere along the way, the bed ripped the nurse-call-button-thingy out of the wall, which sent an alarm, and in they stampeded. I apologized, but was secretly amused. I asked for ice cream, graham crackers, a VCR, and movies. I watched *The Good Son*. I wanted to be the good daughter.

Between movies, I played with the faucet in the bathroom. It took me a while to figure out how to turn it on. There were no handles. I thought maybe it was one of those electric sensor ones, but no amount of movement got any reaction from it. Finally, I looked down and discovered the pedals. I pretended I was sustaining notes on a piano. I practiced holding down both pedals with one foot, tilting this way and that to get the right temperature. Faucet maestro, that was me.

The water ran over my hands, long after they were clean. I wanted so desperately to be clean. I thought about my mother, father, and girlfriend sitting by my bedside earlier that night. It was the most time the three of them have ever spent in a room together. My girlfriend was calm and composed, smiling, making small talk. I knew it didn't matter if they liked her. No matter how they felt about her, they separated that from how they felt about my "sinful lifestyle choice."

In high school, I wanted to be a Christian missionary. Or, maybe it started earlier than that. When I was a little girl, I visited our church's pastor and asked him to pray for me. I told him I wanted to be healed from my milk allergies. I had a lot of faith—you know, childlike faith. After he prayed for me, I went straight home, opened the freezer, dished myself out a bowl of ice cream, and ate the whole thing. I didn't get sick. Previously, I had had violent reactions to milk. I promised God then that I would tell people about Him and what He had done for me. So, when I had the opportunity to be a missionary for a month in Venezuela right after high school, I signed up. The opportunity was with a Christian drama team. I headed off to Caracas to be a Christian missionary mime.

Now I wanted it all: a loving God and a loving girlfriend. I wanted to be at peace.

I dreamed that my girlfriend and I were living in a stone tower. Fire had consumed the rest of the building but could not touch the stone.

I wanted to survive intact. I wanted to be stone.

My mother arrived with my pajamas. She had chosen a matched set with little Scottie dogs all over them. They were childlike. They were innocent. I wanted to be innocent.

When I was sick as a child, my mother read me stories. My favorites were the books from the *Chronicles of Narnia* series. I loved Aslan and groped at the back of closets, looking for passageways to Narnia. I wanted to be one of the children from *The Lion, the Witch, and the Wardrobe,* burying my face in the lion's golden mane.

I looked for a hero in high school. I picked a Jewish girl with thick, wavy hair who dressed confidently, spoke boldly, and laughed loudly. She was happy to have a protégé. She lent me clothes, let me tag along after her, and thought I was sweet because I adored her. I felt stronger walking by her side, because of her strength. I wanted to be strong. I started to see Jewish culture as empowering since she was a product of it. I started permanently wearing an Israeli phone token that she had given me around my neck. It was less gruesome than a cross, although I would always love Jesus. I loved mercy, grace. I wanted to be forgiven. I studied the Jewish roots of Christianity and made a Jewish-Christian identity for myself. Two faiths had to be better than one. Or was I fracturing myself further?

I dreamed I was time-traveling in a biplane. I landed in a combination of the Civil War and the Holocaust. Running in the streets, looking for safety, I hid in abandoned houses. Few toilets worked and I was looking for one. I was from the South and that was a crime. A woman, a Nazi, spotted me on the front lawn, but it turned out she was really Jewish, just in Nazi clothing, and she helped me escape. I huddled in hiding with people, forging temporary family bonds. My mom missed me while I was time traveling. My dad said she cried because I didn't call. I had to make it to my plane and fly to Japan where I would prove I was Dutch, not Jewish or Southern. Then I would be able to get home or travel to a time before the war and prevent it from happening and save lives but I didn't know if I had the courage for that and felt guilty. I also had to go to the supermarket and use an ATM and buy a bottle of Sprite. Then everything would be okay.

I started drinking in college. I liked the drunk me. I was unafraid, socially graceful. The pieces of myself flowed together and I was whole. But alcohol turned on me. As I was petitioning it for my freedom, it imprisoned me. I became not as graceful. I became less whole. I walked through a bar once and brushed up against a lit cigarette. It set the arm of my sweater ablaze and I did not even notice until good Samaritans poured their beers on me to extinguish the fire. Drunk, charred, soaking wet, I said to myself, "This is not where I want to be."

I dreamed there was a girl who cried when she looked into a mirror for the first time. I had to swallow a pill to give birth to her again. She froze when I swallowed it. And then a beautiful woman was rowing a boat. The ocean was disappearing and at the same time the waves were too big to swallow.

My parents had to watch me carefully when I learned to crawl. I wanted to be a swimmer before I learned to walk, making my getaway toward pools, lakes, and oceans. When I learned to swim, under the water became my favorite place. I had discovered what Edmond Jabes knew, that "at the bottom of the water, the heart is heard more clearly." I submerged.

At summer camp, my love of swimming was rivaled by my fear of leeches. Despite my fear, I swam.

Home from the hospital, I sneak out onto the early-morning, freshly painted porch. The shine of it suggests it is still wet, but I take the risk (having come from a long line of women who stick their heads in electric ovens). I raise a butt cheek to see if I am adhered to the spot, but I am in the clear. The high-gloss finish glistens in the bare-bulb porch light, and I wonder if such glistening paint would have retarded the growth of mold on the bathroom walls and ceiling. But what could have prevented my sickness and who defines sickness?

Autumn chills and stars linger. The air smells like apples—apples and the fall and the paint still giving off fumes. Fuming, maybe?

Four days have passed since my birthday. My mother attempted to quote a Bible verse in the card she gave me. She meant to write about God's plans to "prosper you and not harm you," but what she ended up writing was, "plans to prosper you *and not you*," which, you can see, is an entirely different thing. My father said to her: "Dear, you butchered Scripture!" I tried to laugh, but was worried about God's plans. I still want to be a swimmer, though. I am determined to keep swimming.

Mishmumken: For Those Who Cannot Choose

Rosebud Ben-Oni

The more alternatives, the more difficult the choice.

—Abbe D'Allanival

Hebrew—like Arabic and Spanish and so many other languages—is gendered. My first Hebrew teacher, Ziva—a middle-aged Israeli woman who did not believe in God and was transplanted to San Antonio, Texas, by a teaching agency—pulled me aside from the other nine-year-old students and told me about the existence of *zahar* (masculine) and *nekivah* (feminine). Up until that point, the class was only learning the letters in block and cursive form. We knew few words, most of them swear words actually in Yiddish and the others being improper conjugations of verbs that we meant as derogatory commands toward another—with the exception of myself.

No one ever spoke to me that way and rare is the sight of children self-conscious around another child, for not only was I the only girl in my Hebrew school class of twelve, I also lived in a different neighborhood and went to a different elementary school where I was the only one of three Jewish students. My friends there did not understand why my parents punished me so: after regular school, I had to attend Hebrew school from four to six in the afternoon and our day of worship was on Friday nights and early Saturday mornings.

At my elementary school, I was an oddity though I dressed like everyone else and wanted to be a point guard in pro basketball, which everyone thought was incredibly hilarious until I started to knock back consecutive three-pointers. I wasn't the shortest kid in the class, but I was the skinniest, and my third-grade homeroom teacher always took the liberty of shouting out my weight to the class when we had

Identity Envy—Wanting to Be Who We Are Not
Published by The Haworth Press, Inc., 2007. All rights reserved.
doi:10.1300/5641_13

our biannual checkups. We would line up in front of a scale and she would shake her head and tell the nurse, "I think her people have to fast every Friday."

Her people. More amusing than her misguided conception of Shabbat—which was actually a weekly celebration *known* for large amounts of food—was the fact that more than once, someone said to me, "You don't look like a Jew," and once this someone was a teacher of mine. I was twelve at the time, and preparing for my Bat Mitzvah after school, although sometimes I hid sheets of the Torah blessings behind *Tuck Everlasting.* At home, my father had me reading through Steinbeck's landmarks. He was religious and critical of religion at the same time so that I grew up in a very secular household.

"How does a Jew look?" I asked my teacher when she made the comment.

"You know . . . Jewish," she said. As luck would have it, she taught Language Arts, which my father thought was more funny than perilous for my education. Indeed, I learned that sometimes people can't say what they mean because it's impolite and sometimes because they lack articulation.

In Hebrew school, the boys were more diplomatic. They passed notes, which somehow fell in front of my desk, that read, "she doesn't look like a Mexican."

One day, Ziva picked one up. After reading it, she dismissed the class for recess, but kept me behind. It was overcast that day and she adjusted the heavy, black frames on her face; they had tinted lenses and partially hid the truth of her eyes. She was in her late forties, had never been married, and wore flowing pieces of cloth that concealed the shape of her body. She almost threw the note in the trash, but then decided to give it to me. I took the slip of paper from her rough hands, but looked over at the wall, which was covered with pictures of Abraham and Sarah on camels and walking barefoot among the dunes of desert. Her sweaty hand patted mine and she said, "I want to tell you something. I think you'll understand what I'm trying to say. I told the class I was from Tel Aviv, but I'm really from a small, dusty town called Afula."

"Why?" I asked her.

She smiled. "Only you would ask why."

She admitted that she had never proud of where she'd grown up, and that I was never to let anyone *dictate*—yes, she used that word in

English—what I was or was to be, for in Hebrew women already had to deal with the gender of language. "You see," she said, "the word of peace, *shalom,* is male, *zahar.* The word for war, *mellchama,* is feminine, *nekivah.* Now does that make sense to you?"

"Who decided that?" I asked.

"Don't complicate things," she warned me. "People will do that for you."

Until I met Amina, I thought I was past such days.

Growing up, I was a tomboy with a boy's body and a girl's face. Now, as I sit here writing this, Amina tells me that I still have these attributes and that if I ever made the decision that she never will, I would be classified as a guy's kind of lesbian since I dream about sleeping with the kind of women they find beautiful. *Hot* women, she says, mocking American English. As she speaks to me, I hear the jealousy and pride in her voice. She knows she has this type of beauty, but in her culture, where they still honor killings, what would her family think of her preference for the ladies? Jerusalem remains divided among the Jews and the Arabs, between the modern and the traditional, but in the darkness of my bedroom, it cannot divide us—for now.

She will be married a month from now.

"Larry Brown went to my temple," I said.

"Who?"

"The head coach of the Olympics. He once coached the Spurs."

"You always bring up basketball when I have something to say," Amina says.

After I promised no more basketball, I add, "You always have something to say."

"I'm trying to tell you that you're very lucky and don't even know it. Americans accept that kind of stuff nowadays. Your parents would get over it. You can be with whoever you want. I don't have that luxury. Some days I don't even want to be with you, if I could *be* you."

That frightens me a little and I say, "I can't believe your advocating for me to see someone else."

"We're not seeing each other. To see someone is to be seen."

"That's not true. People have affairs all the time."

"Trust me," she says, "others know. In this country, the more hidden the girl, the more well-known the womanizer."

"Women choose to have affairs too."

"You can never blame the woman. Arab women have been through enough. You just don't know. Of course I don't want you to see someone else, but it's selfish to only think of myself. You should do it for the sake of all women. You should go back to America and get married to a woman, now that it's legal for your people to do that."

Your people.

I tell her, "I'm not sure if I *am* like that. Fantasies doesn't mean I want to actually marry a woman. I don't know if I ever want to marry. Marriage is . . ." I can't finish.

"You're uncertain about everything," she says, managing a smile.

"Not about you," I say. "I've never once been with a girl, but even a true-blue heterosexual woman would fall for you. It's impossible not to."

She laughs. "You say that and my own culture says I'm too dark."

"You seemed to imply earlier that you were a guy's kind of lesbian, which you mean is attractive."

"That's not what I meant. I was trying to translate it into American terms so you'd understand how I see you and how I see myself. You could have anyone you want," she says quietly.

"No I can't," I say.

Her name isn't Amina; she asked me to change it, but I will not change the details I use to describe her. Here at the university in Jerusalem, Amina is always seen at a long table in one of the cafeterias, sitting between her fiancé and some young European man—usually a Scandinavian of sophisticated alcoholism, strongly made and of few words, who wears shorts in the winter. Her collection of male admirers always outnumbers the women at the table; everyone knows she is already engaged and she knows that everyone knows and that her fiancé knows that she knows that everyone knows. Her fiancé was born in a small Arab village in Galilee and is studying medicine. He is tall and slender and religious, although he doesn't pray five times a day like more devout Muslims. He is also very patient, the kind of man who'd never pick a fight, but would step up to anyone who insulted one of his friends.

I like him and believe he is a good person, but marriage changes people. He seems ready to accept that, but Amina will not want to change or find the middle ground. She says the very act of living is already a compromise for a woman. She's decided that the less that he and she know about each other, the better the illusion of husband and wife.

I met Amina in a summer *ulpan* at the Hebrew University two years ago. An *ulpan* is an intensive Hebrew language course; in six weeks we covered over a semester's worth of material. The class mostly was filled with Jews from all other the world, a few Christians who were studying a Bible course in the coming fall, and an Indian student who was Hindu. We sat wherever and mixed freely among ourselves.

Then there was Amina. She sat on the opposite side of the room with the two other Arab girls in the class, away from everyone else. They would exchange heavy whispers when discussions turned political. They never contributed anything except the smug looks on their faces when Amina answered their teacher, in English, that no one in the class knew enough advanced Hebrew yet to make a decent argument.

The teacher would break the divide in the class other ways. She tried to pair up Amina's friends with other students, but these chosen students would walk over to find the three girls already engaged in the classroom exercise. An understanding that they would always work together materialized between them and their teacher, who would give up on her entire class that summer, as she told me she did every semester.

On the very first day, though, when we were talking about ourselves and our families in slow, flowing Hebrew, I told them my mother's name was Esperanza.

"Ooo," my teacher gushed as the class whispered about what I'd said. "*Yafeh meod*—very pretty. Where is her family from?"

"Originally?"

"Yes."

"*Sefarad.*"

"*Bemet?* Because I didn't know there were Jews in Spain."

"She became a Jew in America."

The class went quiet.

"Oh," she said. "*Oh.*" And went on to the next person.

I wasn't fazed at all by her response—by now I had grown used to the fact that I would never be a Jew's Jew any more than I was an Andulsian like my grandparents—but Amina, who had caught my eye from the moment she walked in late for class, was staring at me while her two friends were looking me over and whispering. Her beauty is hard to ignore, even though she thinks her skin is too dark: she's tall and slender with long, wavy black hair that falls to her waist and big, dark eyes that aren't afraid to look anyone—woman or man—in the eye.

Once her fiancé teased her that women should never look men in the eye, because you know what that means about her character.

She doesn't merely look with those eyes; she somehow manages to bring down those of others. I've seen her do it, and her fiancé was no exception, as a slight blush streaked across his cheek and he reminded her he was only joking.

Once, during a classroom skit, Amina was making fun of the particular behavior of *sherut* drivers—she used the word in Hebrew, but mentioned they had their own in Arabic—who are convinced that a nine-passenger van is designed for twelve people because no American would dare ignore their suggestion—and therefore face their wrath—that they should sit on suitcases piled on the floor of the van.

Someone called out, "If Americans are so weak, then why did we kick ass in Afghanistan?"

But before she could answer, one of the Arab girls, trying to find the word for her uncle's Jewish neighbors in Bethlehem, asked the teacher how to say *settler* in Hebrew. The class went into an uproar until I suddenly heard myself repeating Amina's words that no one knows enough Hebrew yet to make a decent argument, and besides there's no need to get all worked up over a mere word.

"A word is never a mere thing," Amina shouted back, so loudly that the class fell silent. She held her voice steady, as though she were discussing the weather, and looked at her two friends. "None of them live inside this classroom. But we're supposed to, right? We're supposed to take whatever any of them say, but I make a mistake, and that's it for me, right? What about what I give up every day? Did any of them even consider that?"

"Then why are you here?" shouted a voice from the back.

"Why am I here? You think speaking my own language will get me ahead in this country? Do you?" She broke into a coughing fit, then took a deep breath. The clock ticked and someone sneezed, but no one said, *lebrioot*, God Bless You. We waited until the halls begin to fill with students and then our teacher dismissed us.

The *ulpan* was from eight in the morning until four in the afternoon with only a half-hour break around one.

"It's true, isn't it? The long hours of study are punishment for not being *born* a Jew," I heard someone behind me say in English and then felt a hand around my wrist. I turned around as Amina, with her free hand, waved her friends away, but they remained rooted a meter or so from us, silent, with their arms folded.

I remember how the heat of the late afternoon sun was breaking through the windows where one could observe the buildings of Jerusalem stone and the desert beyond. I could never find the Bedouin tents that our teacher promised were there; my eyes would roam west to east and back again, but I was never quite sure what to look for, and for some reason, I felt foolish if I had to ask.

After waiting for an answer and not receiving one, Amina went on in English, "I'm sorry for yelling at you. It's not you, it's them. I didn't want you to compromise the point my friends and I were trying to make. I know you wanted to help us, but I had to say it. I could not go on *not* dealing with them."

I continued looking out the window, searching, and said, "This is a difficult situation for everyone."

"But it is one that will never be my own," she continued. "Listen to me."

"I am." I finally looked at her.

She pursed her lips and regarded me carefully. "Language reflects its culture. You know what you are by speaking your native tongue."

"Not always," I said defensively. "There *are* Jews in the class. Suffering these long hours with us. Jews from all over the world—who didn't grow up speaking Hebrew. Why do you think they are taking *ulpan*? And Radha isn't Jewish. She's Hindu."

"But they *aren't* questionable." She rolled her eyes and nodded to her friends. "The four of us are the only questionables in the class. You know what I'm getting at."

"Questionables?"

"Yes, questionables. For Sanaa and Leila and I, the question is religious, as it is for you. For the three of us, it is: are your families involved in any of the suicide attacks or other suspicious operations? For you, it is: is her mother *really* Jewish?"

"Oh, that. I don't care anymore. I'm not anything."

"What do you mean?"

"You know those ethnicity boxes on college applications and other things?"

"No."

"Well we have them in America."

"So?"

"I leave those little boxes blank."

She smiled. "You can't do that here. There are some things better worth hiding."

"I'm not hiding anything."

"No, that's not what I meant. You do not *choose* to hide. Others *make* you."

I realized she still had her hand around my wrist and she was holding it tighter. "No, not at all, Amina. I just try not to complicate things."

"You know my name," she said.

"That's about it."

"That usually says it."

"That's a misconception."

She took my hand and said quietly, "Yes."

After that, she started sitting next to me in class. Her friends followed, but I noticed they seemed to regard me with a certain amount of pity when I talked to them and I wondered what Amina had told them.

"Oh, nothing. They just think you're too thin, that you're poor," she said quickly.

"What?"

She grinned. "Well you know most Americans are rich, compared to us. The richest are usually too thin, but we can tell otherwise. There's a difference."

"I'm not poor," I said defensively. "I went to graduate school for God's sakes."

"I didn't say uneducated. I said poor."

"I'm not poor."

"I mean comparatively."

"I don't like comparatively," I told her, and there would be a lot of things that I wouldn't like about her—she seemed to want to live her sexuality through me for one—but there are certain people in this world who so lack charisma that, oddly, you never want to be far away from them. The class wasn't enchanted with her; they were infatuated with her fearlessness. When she spoke, everything was in boldfaced or italics.

We soon became inseparable and were seen that way, but not seen the way **we** *really* **are**, she'd say, the way she wanted, even if it just meant picking up my bra strap, which continually fell off my shoulder, without actually touching my skin. But even Amina didn't dare do that, she said, because it meant more than it looked and she worried that it would lead to other, more noticeable displays of what we did while alone—which I never understood, because we are uncomfortable when we are alone. Afraid.

Toward the end of that summer, she invited me over to the apartment she shared with Sanaa and Leila to study for the final. She lived in East Jerusalem, the Arab side. She asked me if I was scared of coming to "a place like this." I knew East Jerusalem better than she thought.

I found her alone, combing her wet hair, dressed in a polo shirt and blue jeans that didn't exactly hang off her.

"Marhaba," she greeted me brightly in Arabic and then asked if I was hungry.

I knew not to ask where the other two girls were and helped her in the kitchen. She seemed taken aback by that, because she knew I couldn't cook, but handed me a pan in which I heated oil and tossed in vegetables she chopped. She added a bundle of thin noodles to boiling water in a heavy pot. The apartment was very organized and smelled of detergent and rose-water before the aroma of cooking took over. The floor, like the rest of the kitchen, was spotless.

"You eat pasta a lot in America, right?" she asked with a straight face.

Here we go again, I thought, and nodded as I reduced the heat on her gas stove. "You know, I never tease you about your European admirers."

"Oh, them," she says. "They are an illusion."

"For what?"

She shrugs.

"Then it is also an illusion that Americans live on burgers and fries. Every day. Or that we take a break with various fried things and mashed potatoes. You know, to shake things up a bit."

"You drink, right?"

I blushed "When I do, one's my limit. I get intoxicated pretty quickly. How do you know that?"

"Oh, I hear things."

"You know, I invited you to go out with us."

"Sure, *they* really want me there." Then she said, "Are you close to your parents?"

I hadn't talked to them in a couple of weeks, so I said, "Are you close to *yours*?"

"No. But your parents, are you close to them?"

"I miss them."

"Would you say that your parents know you?"

"What do you mean?"

She tried to explain and then she said, "What do you miss about them?"

"I don't know," I sighed. "Let's see. Well, right before I left, we went fishing."

"Did you catch anything?"

"Just some small ones we had to throw back in."

"Do you fish a lot with them?"

"I used to. Before college. By then, I was busy with school and work. But when I was in high school, we'd go whenever we could."

"What did you talk about?"

For some reason, I laughed. "Amina, really. Nothing substantial. It's fishing."

"I'm asking you too much."

"No, I just can't give any winning answers."

"It's not like that between you and I," she said quickly, avoiding my eyes as she tried to drain the pasta without a colander by holding it back with a large wooden spoon. Strands of her hair were slipping from the bun on top of her head, and she waved them away and said, "You see, it is difficult for me to answer to my own people. I mean those in the territories. The *real* Palestinians."

"I wasn't aware there were fake Palestinians."

She said, "Well, I can't get too close to them. I'm already too close as it is."

"Wait—which them?"

"I mean the Jews."

"Or close to *your* people. Those in Gaza and the West Bank."

"That's right. It's very difficult when they are . . . But you—you're . . ."

"What?"

"Well, you haven't chosen."

"Chosen what?"

"What you are."

I helped her set the table and said, "I told you, I don't fit into a little box."

She nodded and said, "It's difficult. Some things you can't change about yourself and some things you should and if you can't, you have to hide them. It's difficult enough being a woman." Then she added, "I can't swim. I never learned."

"It's easy. I could show you."

"You would, wouldn't you?" She came up behind me, standing very closely so that I could feel her chest against my back. Some of those stray strands fell across my neck, and I didn't move and neither did she. We looked at the table as if it was the most fascinating thing in the world until she said, her lips almost touching my ear, "You would teach me, even knowing how difficult I'd make it."

Amina makes it clear she is not feminist, because to her it's a Western concept and she doesn't want to become Westernized, yet she admits there are some—okay, many—traditions of her culture that she doesn't like. As a child, she had spoken Arabic with her mother and French with her father, who, when he told his friends that his daughter was smarter than anyone he'd ever known, was met with laughter and affection. He'd stare at them in disbelief: *I'm serious.* He died when she turned eight, on her birthday. She tells me that she loved him more than anything else in the world. Repeatedly, she tells me not to make much of this, the death of her adored father as an explanation for *why* she is the way she is.

I say, "You mean your sexuality."

She shushes me, as if it were a dirty word, even when we are alone.

I never did teach her to swim; she wouldn't go to the beaches in Tel Aviv or Eliat with my friends and me during Shabbat. She was afraid that one of *my people* would give her a hard time or that *someone* would blow up a café and immediately suspect that she had something to do with it, since she was there. Yet she had no problem going with me to any of the cafés in West Jerusalem, the Jewish side.

"If something happens," she says, "I can say I live here." But she doesn't sound like she believes her words. For two years, we have always spoken in English, but never once have we said "I love you" to each other because those aren't the right words for what we feel. I'm not sure those words exist, but if they do, they remain with us, hibernating, like a faded scar that we thought left our faces long ago, but returns as an incandescent red on a cold winter day.

For it is not only attraction and lust and adoration, but pain that links us as well. A pain that I continually deny exists and a pain that she cannot let show because life for a woman is already a compromise.

For two years, she has come over my apartment or I have gone over to hers and we have always shut the door to our bedrooms, even when no one is around. We draw the blinds and turn out the lights and light one candle so we can see each other. We mostly do what she thinks are very stereotypical lesbian acts: we hold each other and nothing more, which worries her because there is already the assumption that women only want to be held and prefer that to sex.

With us, it has never been that. It doesn't seem to matter where she's touching me or I'm kissing her; it is both the same amazing chemistry and pent-up emotion of fear that cannot be destroyed, nor can they destroy each other. Because of that chemistry and that fear, we continue to meet because someone eventually will discover us and that will be it. But so far, no one ever has, and as her marriage date looms closer every minute, we spend the summer days fighting more than anything else, fighting over things that have been decided for her and things for which I cannot decide. In the end, it is always the same: we are too exhausted from our muted shouting and hushed cries to do anything more than be tangled up in each other, and I realize that I do not even think of her as a woman but as the greatest, most compassionate mind I have ever know, whose short fuse and asperity I would endure to be with her until the end of days.

And it hurts most when, after two years, she holds me tighter and says I only believe that because it is a hypothetical.

Last week, I was walking down the al-Wad road in the Muslim Quarter of the Old City, forgetting it was Friday, the day of worship for Muslims. The call to prayer had just ended and al-Wad road was flooded with veiled women and Arab men in *keffiya* headscarves and beards. In front of me, a young boy handed me a religious pamphlet and a very, very old woman without teeth who must be his grandmother asked me in Arabic if I have been to Mecca. I shook my head, and she shouted something about Mecca next year and patted me on the back. It struck that even in my jeans and cardigan and uncovered head I'd been mistaken for an Arab when—and it seems impossible as I write this but in fact it did happen—I saw Amina standing inside an antique shop's doorway, fighting with the owner's wife who claims she's blocking off their customers. She was alone.

Allah forgives! The toothless woman carried on.

With a final decree, the woman pushed Amina out and she tripped down the step, looking small and lost in her black pants and short-sleeves, pushing herself against the side of the wall, waiting for the crowd to pass. Then she saw me and urgently called to me before looking around again and lowering her voice. The crowd unknowingly pushed her up to me. It was very hot, and the crowd seemed desperate to keep moving, when suddenly everyone came to a stop.

Instead of saying hello, she asked, "What's going on? Why aren't we moving?"

As if it were my fault. As if it were *my people* who were harassing the crowd—*our* orders and *our* safety measures.

I raised my head as high as I could and saw that a line of boys with wheelbarrows and hand-trucks are fighting with a storeowner on Aqabat Al-Taqiya. They wouldn't be separated and blocked the crossing as Amina linked my arms with hers and buried her face in my shoulder, saying that she's tired of all this.

Suddenly, she looked up.

"*Mishmumken!*" Amina called out to the line of boys blocking the crossing. Several teenagers in front of us laughed, and called out to the boys, "*Mishmumken!*" But no one pushed—in fact, the delay was celebrated like an intermission at a concert, full of small conversations concerning the hardship of living between such narrow streets and how disrespectful the youth have become since the death of Abu Yassin, and *Allah forgives, Allah forgives!* Abu Ali an alcoholic, Abu Mazen's lead us nowhere, Heba's pregnant again *ilhamdila,* Mahala's studying in Haifa and who knows where she got the money for this and her new car that she hides in a parking lot just outside Lion's Gate where the Gypsies live—did you hear about the death of the child there? *Allah forgives!* They say the revenge killings might soon begin, because the crazy crackhead who murdered the little boy vowed to rid the entire country of their like. . . .

But Mahala needs it to commute, someone argued and another *mishmumken!* from the toothless old woman who came to stand between Amina and myself. The old woman cursed loudly at the line of boys, and grabbed our shoulders when the boys with wheelbarrows and hand-trucks turn around to shout insults concerning such women, as if Amina and the elderly woman and I alone represented the crowd. The storeowner immediately reprimanded them, *show respect!* Amina closed her eyes as the elderly woman let go of our shoulders and moved toward the crowd. Our arms were still linked and I could hear her breathing hard and she whispered, "Let's hope it's nothing, or you'll be in trouble." She let go off my arm and slid her hand down until the tips of our fingers barely touched. *Allah forgives!* The toothless old woman shouted.

"You're wrong," I said and told her what the old woman and her grandson had assumed.

She did not open her eyes, but said, "You'll never really know what it is to be us," to which I snapped, "You're right. I'll never know what it is to be part of *any* us."

She fell silent, and then grabbed my hand and said, "You're right. I'm sorry."

For a moment, I too closed my eyes, just for a moment, suffocating in the heat's sharp sting, the composite sweat, the smell of roasting *shawarma,* the resolute grip of the her hand in mine. Amina whispered to me that she could not breathe, but she sounded calm. A young man in a track suit shouts out if anyone knows whether Abu Sier Sweet's is on this road and I opened my eyes and answered in Arabic, *"la', fi Khan El-Zeit."* The man thanked me and disappeared behind us, determined to go in the opposite direction of the crowd, as someone shouted at the wheelbarrow-boys to get a move on *HALLAS,* but never once did the crowd turn ugly. The wheelbarrow-boys were almost finished in collecting their money as Amina finally opened her eyes and looked down at our hands as if they would turn against her. The old woman continued to complain about the local authorities and the coming feast and *why aren't we moving yet?*

"You'll never have to choose what you are," Amina said. "You don't have to."

"Yes," I said bitterly, "because I have that luxury."

"No, that's not it."

"Yes, I'm wrong again."

"No, it's that . . . *mismumken,*" she said quietly to regain herself. She then assured me that she will breathe just fine in a moment and removed her hand from mine. She didn't know what came over her but she's just fine now, it's a lovely day isn't it, *Yafeh Meod,* she said in Hebrew and a few heads turned her way. She said it again, louder this time, looking up at the sky instead of me, the relief and disappointment wavering in her voice. She closed and opened her eyes, and then changes back to Arabic. *Mishmumken.*

Impossible, she was saying. It meant *impossible.* I did not ask if it is feminine or masculine, because it is the only word that I too pronounced with just the right amount of rising intonation and discontent.

Nanna's Room

Robert Labelle

I grew up on a train. Not only that, the wrong train. I always
thought I should be en route to some proper boys school where Apple
Charlotte and *crème anglaise* are served with tea daily at four. Instead, the lower third of the typical, east-end Montreal triplex I was
forced to call home, with its long, narrow hallway and succession of
cramped, compartment-like rooms, was a train with no destination.
The effect was enhanced on the hour when the real train passed on
tracks only a stone's throw away—a standard unit of measurement in
our neighborhood with its broken panes and maimed stray cats. The
rumblings were especially effective at night, sending tremors through
our metal beds and providing the perfect backdrop to wonderings
about how I got where I was and where my real parents were. I pictured tall, well-dressed figures standing beside me in a crowded station, their frosty hair matching silver fox wraps. They had perplexed
looks on their faces, their aristocratic bearing making them ill-suited
for interpreting destinations and schedules, for sending their child off
on the right track.

Needless to say, I was not a happy passenger. But don't get me
wrong, I did not despise the family I found myself with: my parents,
my brothers and sisters, my adopted Québecois heritage. It's just that
the wished for dollop of *crème anglaise* flowed a little too thickly in
my veins for me to ever fully adapt to life in working-class French
Montreal.

To them I think I was seen as a kind of exotic, slightly dangerous
pet, like an ostrich or spider monkey, kept on more out of curiosity
than emotional attachment. But even they began after a time, to recognize my true cultural heritage. *"Il a l'oreille,"* my mother would
say, looking at my report card with its uncannily high scores in *études
d'anglaises.* Her remark "he has a good ear" wasn't meant to be com-

Identity Envy—Wanting to Be Who We Are Not
Published by The Haworth Press, Inc., 2007. All rights reserved.
doi:10.1300/5641_14

plimentary. It was said with a note of suspicion, tied to that vast world of otherness (English Canada) known as *les autres*. My father called me *"un vrai businessman"* because, at the time, English was the language of the bosses. With his perennial greasy work jeans, his disheveled head of thick brown hair, he seemed more the child than I, as if I'd given up my youth to become dour and administrative. It also absolved him of doling out parental love, which in our family circle was rationed like the warm, sugary squares of *pudding de chomeur*—always devoured faster than they could be replenished.

Confrontations with my brothers and sisters were from the start pretty much of the push and shove variety. One of my earliest and most vivid memories of these involved my baby sister, Guillaine. Attracted by the cries from her crib, I remember reaching through the bars to calm her, to at least attempt the role of loving brother. For my efforts I received not one but two swift bites between index finger and thumb. This instinctual testing of new teeth on this softest of spots produced four little marks, indentations in the truest sense and warnings of future abuse. There were, indeed, many further *bêtises* perpetrated upon me by my family as well as by other children in the neighborhood, but this event became the "primal scene"—not only in my own mind, but as part of my family's supper table liturgy. It was usually my mother who would say, "Remember when she bit you?— *Souviens-tu quand elle t'a mordue?"* playfully accenting the rhyme of the phrase, while Guillaine, wrapped in her arms in an embrace which seemed reluctantly to hold her back, stared me down with the particularly savage look which she used on me throughout our childhood together.

But in spite of this apparent aggression, I later realized that the cries that beckoned me to Guillaine's crib were not meant to trick, nor were they any expression of need or distress. They were pure exercise, exercise meant to expand the lungs in preparation for the loud, territorial hollering necessary for survival in our *quartier.* Up and down the alleyway the children would run in waves like schools of colorful and malicious tropical fish. My own sense of danger at finding myself invariably ten paces behind them was acute: herding animals must stay with the herd or be picked off by predators. So even though I didn't want to take part in their various marauding games of destruction, I tried to stay within their protective periphery. On finding myself left too far behind, I would call out, *"Attendez,"* or try various enticements such as *"J'ai un idée,"* all of which were uniformly ignored.

But if they had stopped to ask me what my idea was, what would I have said? Most likely I would not have been able to put into words my grand schemes of escape. For I did have them. Jumping a slow-moving, screeching freight train at the bottom of the street was the most obvious. I wasn't the first to think of it. Stories about severed limbs found by the tracks were meant to deter, and they did. Merely wandering away was equally steeped in mystery and treachery. The major boundary of our territory was Boulevard Pie IX, named after Pope Pius IX, a name which suited its extraordinary powers and privileges. It seemed as if the actual purpose of the continuous stream of trucks transporting sugar and grain north from port-side warehouses was to create a deadly, moving barrier for the children of the East End. The traffic lights seemed to be timed more for the even flow of traffic than pedestrian crossings. In attempting a run for it one felt like an German refugee during the Cold War, with his or her life and very identity on the verge of being *ecrasé*.

Of course, once achieving a certain age, youth will not be contained. I witnessed these changes in my older brothers and sisters as they made their first expeditions downtown. Marjolaine, about fourteen, seemed sullen after making the trip. The experience didn't live up to expectations, and it seemed as if her afternoon journey was a kind of lost virginity without any of the thrill of love. *"C'etait long en autobus, pis crowdé,"* she said, and referred very little to what her and her friends discovered on their foray to St. Catherine Street and *les gros magasins*.

Oui, les gros magasins. Their emissary, the Eaton's catalogue, came to us with a thump at our door announcing spring, summer, fall, and winter. Eaton's was, at the time, *the* store, the biggest department store in Canada; there was one in every major town and city, and for those who couldn't get to the city or to the store itself, there was the catalogue, from which everything in the world, it seemed, could be ordered. Clothing, furniture, carpeting, musical instruments, kitchenware, and, especially, toys. There was collusion at the time between Eaton's and Santa Claus. Santa, it was assumed, worked for Eaton's, and by early November all the best toys went there. When I got my chance at it, I would circle the things I wanted—not the table-top hockey games favored by my brothers, but other, more unusual

things, things I hoped would somehow appear under the scrawny tree
our father would inevitably drag home from the vacant lot beside the
nearby tavern. There was the Give-a-Show Projector, the Puppet
Theatre, the Complete Viewmaster Set of the Seven Wonders of the
Ancient and Modern World. My choices were always related to escape, which now began to take the form of fantasy. But as I discovered, there was fantasy in parts of the catalogue other than the toy section. Men's Apparel. Women's Apparel. And at the end of these,
coats, sweaters, and finally shirts and blouses were stripped back to
reveal the Underwear Section. Women's girdles and bras were cropped into objectified portions, featuring only the product, and the same
was true of men's briefs, uniformly blazing white within little
squared-off pictures. But the product was filled with something,
something real and breathing, and in the case of the men's underwear,
bulging. In spite of this rule of cropped sections, there was at least one
picture, as I remember, that showed full bodies. It was of a group of
male models all in their underwear, looking, as models always did,
not directly out of the page at the viewer, but upward and to one side,
to some elevated spot of perfection just outside the image, to the place
perhaps where the rest of their clothes had disappeared. I identified
with their longing and I longed for them.

That the Eaton's catalogue was sent to our home at all—for it was
not sent to every home indiscriminately—was not a complete mystery of providence. That was where Nanna's first and perhaps greatest
influence began. For it was to her that the Eaton's catalogue was addressed. Nanna was the name we were told to call the elderly lady oc-
cupying the last bedroom along our long hallway, the last compartment. She was not, as the name implies, a grandmother, but according
to my mother, *"ma tante,"* which would have made her my great aunt,
but as with my own position, I felt doubtful of any real blood link between her and the rest of our family. Nanna, like myself, was a misplaced passenger. She was also my sole ally.

Nanna's age and station gave her special status, and her room soon
became for me and, I assume, for her, a safe haven of political asylum. The decor was French-Canadian Catholic, the kind imbued with
old-lady fervor that had the power to exclude or at least disinterest the
rough-and-tumble interests of my siblings. It was painted a celestial
blue, the same blue as the sky into which the Blessed Virgin as-
cended. Most of the pictures on the walls were, indeed, religious: var-

ious Christs, the most remarkable being one in which Jesus pulls back His robes to reveal the flaming Sacred Heart. In spite of these outward manifestations, I don't think Nanna was especially religious. Only once or twice did I ever see her say the rosary which lay on her night table, and the black Bible sitting beside it had grown a furry coat of dust visible by the warm glow of the little porcelain table lamp. Still, to me she was the pinnacle of Catholic perfection. Even though I can remember her coming with us to Mass only once or twice—before the age when I was finally exempt—I never saw a finger dip itself into the font of Holy Water with such natural ease, and her sign of the cross was performed with the swift movements of true spiritual possession.

But these same fingers could flick through the pages of the Eaton's catalogue with just as much precision and delicacy. Nanna was the one to have the first look at it, and it was only she that made out any orders: sometimes for my mother, sometimes for little Christmas presents for us, but usually for her own "personal" things. Poised on her rocker, or sitting up in bed, she was a combination of frailty and unshakable strength—circling items with her fountain pen and making separate lists of code numbers jotted down with the flourish of a penmanship that was only a little shaky. Indeed, the power of her pen initiated the arrival of boxes delivered by the red and blue Eaton's truck, a rare sight on our street. Sometimes it would be my job to give the delivery man the prepared envelope containing Nanna's check and twenty-fifty-cent tip, and then bring the box down the hall to her door. She would usually lift a hand and wave me away before opening it, but sometimes I was allowed to stay and watch. Unveiled from the tissue paper would invariably be *des robes de nuits* made of a certain kind of flannel that couldn't be found at any of the local stores.

I did ask for, or at least hint at, what I wanted from the catalogue— the puppet show, the slide projector, and she would nod knowingly, as if she were familiar with all these things. My brothers and sisters would also petition her—sometimes through me—around Christmastime for dolls and games. None of us would get what we wanted. Each year, Nanna's present would always be the same: enclosed in the small red Eaton's Christmas box would be a Christmas ball to be hung from the tree, decorations that proliferated year after year. Though I wished she would favor me with a special gift, I was eventually resigned to the idea that she couldn't, that to do so would endanger the bond we had by attracting the attention and jealousy of the others.

Nanna usually strayed from her room only as far as the bathroom and kitchen, where she would occasionally join my mother and her friends for weekly or biweekly afternoon get-togethers. One by one, around four o'clock, a collection of neighborhood women would appear at the back door, and the kettle would be filled to the point that drops of boiling water would spurt dangerously across the floor. The whistling sound would summon Nanna, who would make her slow, regal entrance, her lips covered with deep red, usually creeping up into the wrinkles above her upper lip, creating a moustache of tiny red rivulets. To me these marks weren't ugly or funny but were like the intricate tattoos or markings of remote tribes, marks identifying a chief or shaman. My own role was that of Nanna's page, hovering near her at the table for the duration of the party. This was the closest I came to Apple Charlotte and *crème anglaise*. Instead, there were *biscuits du magasin* produced from one of my mother's hiding places, and usually, though not always, I would be rewarded with my favorite, which had a deep red jelly centre, as red as the exposed Sacred Hearts on Nanna's walls.

My long visits to Nanna's room were usually occupied with the telling of her stories. She would always start by asking me, "What's new?"—in English—wait for my "Not too much," and then launch into a selection from her repertoire of half a dozen or so accounts, switching back and forth from English to French. One of her favorites concerned her meeting with a Sergeant Fabrice Duffault of the Gendarmerie Royale du Canada, which took place at the Marché Centrale, a farmer's market that had disappeared about the time I was born.

"I always choose turnips only after the first frost," she would declare, and I knew what was coming. With every additional point and fact her face would take on a greater distortion. Looks of mock surprise and dismay raised eyebrows, pushed down the corners of her mouth, and caused her eyes to look heavenward or at least toward one of her religious portraits. All this accompanied what often seemed the most mundane of details. "You see, only after the first frost are turnips likely to stay hard throughout the winter," she would say, her eyes widening in alarm. "Down I went, my great, wide basket under my arm, not looking forward to the climb back up the hill." Nanna would then describe her first sighting of Duffault's bright, red jacket amid the market crowds. "I had just picked up what I thought was the largest turnip I'd ever seen—hard as a rock and heavy in my hand; in fact, I really needed two hands to hold it. Well, there in front of me, on the other side of the stall he appeared—taller than anyone else and, in his tight-fitting jacket, as bright as a red flame. It never occurred to me to follow him or to try to meet him, but somehow I couldn't take my eyes off him. Of course, I wasn't the only one that had noticed him; half the marketplace seemed turned in his direction. Distracted as I was, I continued to fill my basket with turnips until it was nearly overflowing. The man at the stall finally stopped me and told me the price. As you may have guessed, I wasn't particularly shy at the time, but pride can equally curtail one's better judgment. Rather than putting half the turnips back, I paid up and struggled away with them, barely able to make my way through the crowd. Well, even if I'd tried, I couldn't have managed a better way to attract the young officer's attention, for he was quick to notice a young girl struggling with a pile of turnips. He made his way toward me and came to my aid. He carried my basket for me all the way back through the streets to Momma's door."

The only reference point I had to this story and the feelings they seemed to impart was what I'd culled from the Eaton's catalogue. Somehow my inner eye linked her sergeant with the models from the underwear page, and those hard, heavy turnips became symbolic of something else, something hidden and thrilling under a layer of glowing white. Perhaps that is why whenever I got the chance to ask her a question, it wouldn't be about specifics from her tale, but about Eaton's. She responded not only by promising to take me shopping there, but to "invite" me to lunch at La Neuvième, the restaurant on the top floor of the store, *"la couronne de Montréal,"* as she called it. Great marble fixtures lit the room, so she said, and there were enormous wall murals as well as a runway for fashion shows. Here, I assumed the models would appear incarnate: perfect men and women gazing off into the distance, while parading back and forth amid the dining shoppers. This would be the place, I imagined, where Sergeant Duffault would be most likely to make a reappearance.

But Nanna and I would only leave the house together once, and it wasn't for a trip downtown. Piscine Publique du Parc Maisonneuve gave neighborhood children some relief to the hot summer alleyways and was, needless to say, a popular attraction to those who could afford the ten-cent entry fee. The city had also prescribed that children under ten years of age be accompanied by an adult, or at least another child over fourteen. My older brother, Jean, was usually given the duty of playing lifeguard for my sister Guillaine as well as myself. And once he got us past the entry to the pool, he would usually disappear into the mix of murky water and screaming young faces.

My inclusion in this arrangement ended the summer of my "condition." Just after my eighth birthday I developed a late case of what is now called nocturnal enuresis. Bed wetting. Although I am aware of its various causes, I prefer to interpret mine as another escape attempt, like skunk spray or octopus ink, meant to befuddle and confuse encroaching predators. The only person trapped, however, would be myself, and I remember the mornings when I would find myself not daring to move out of fear that my state would be discovered by Jean—still in his bed not three feet away from mine. Inevitably my mother's entrance into the room would be signaled by sniffs and snorts and her enlightened warnings to my brother: *"On rit pas!"* thereby letting him know exactly what had happened. To Jean's credit, he never did laugh, nor did he use this potentially lethal weapon against me in the group settings of the alleyway, where it would have caused the most damage. He undoubtedly had *une loyauté à la famille*, which, I confess, I would have lacked if our situations had been reversed.

On the other hand, inside the home, my position evolved with this new element from that of high falutin' oddity to resident monster. My father's usual greeting to me at the after-work supper table, an aggressive *frottage* on the top of my head meant, I think, to remove some of the grease from his work-worn hands, was replaced by suspicious looks. His accompanying line, *"comment va notre anglais?"* a teasing, but somewhat affectionate remark, ceased. As for Jean, his restraint for not completely destroying me was countered by dropping any unnecessary contact. This included poolside guardian. *"J'suis trop occupé,"* he said, a surprisingly lame and diplomatic statement in proxy for what was widely understood: *"Peut être il va faire pi-pi dans la piscine."*

Unfortunately for Guillaine, this verdict affected her poolside excursions as well, and as a particularly warm June turned into a sweltering July, she moped about the house, fixing upon me that well-known stare of hers, looking like a fierce species of young deer. I spent more time sequestered in the blue room with Nanna. Finally one day, in a heroic effort to prove our alliance, Nanna lifted herself from her rocker, picked up her walking cane, and declared *"Allons-y à la piscine!"* What was perhaps most surprising in all this was that my mother permitted this fragile creature out of the safety of her cage. I remember our parade through the kitchen, with Guillaine following Nanna and me, making sure she wasn't left behind. My mother just watched us from her station at the stove, watched as if we were approaching the edge of a cliff, all warnings held back either out of shock or a perverse desire to see what would happen next.

Down the alley we marched, my bathing suit wrapped in a towel and held under one arm, the other grasped by Nanna. Guillaine, following behind, seemed a kind of shepherding force, driving us on or "taking us in," as if we were her bounty-winning captives. Nanna was dressed and made up in a similar way to her *toilette* for tea, with lips and eyebrows a little more fiercely drawn in for the great outdoors. The day was dazzlingly hot, and I thought she would simply melt or dissolve into the shimmering heat waves hanging over the pavement. Somehow, we made it to the pool gate, a walk of about four city blocks. The two little dimes for Guillaine and myself stuck to my hot palm, requiring the girl at the wicket to pick them off. She was probably no more than sixteen, but appeared to me as any other adult public figure. As she demanded our ages, I felt the shudder of official power. *"Neuf,"* I said meekly, hoping to add a year, but not daring to say the requisite ten. Nanna piped in over my shoulder that she would watch from the benches in the shade on this side of the fence.

"C'est parce que c'est trop crowdé aujourd'hui," the girl replied, and added that it was necessary that *la surveillante* be within the confines of the pool itself.

Nanna and I stood there stunned for a moment, not quite comprehending how our regal advance had been so easily blocked by this first, simple encounter with public authority. It never occurred to me to blame Nanna for not being brave enough to accompany me inside the gates. I understood she could no more have entered that wild throng than an aging duchesse from the palace of Versailles could have been expected to pass out *petit fours* at the barricades. Her face took on the same exaggerated expressions it had during the telling of her stories, her eyes widened, her eyebrows arched. The addition of the heat and makeup, however, made the stories from her somber blue bedroom mere rehearsals for this bright, terrible moment. In an almost breathless voice, the rouged space between her upper lip and nose sparkling with tiny beads of water, she pronounced, *"Je ne suis pas sa surveillante, mais sa gardienne."* By this, I knew Nanna meant by the word *gardienne* something akin to one who has taken over in a permanent sense the duties of parenthood. I beamed back proudly at the girl behind the counter. Nanna's pronouncement, however, didn't seem to make the slightest difference, and the girl turned to the next group in the line that had formed behind us.

We took our place on the bench Nanna had intended for herself just outside the Frost fence and stared in at the clamor and pandemonium of the pool. In past years, I'd pretty much hated the rush and violence of it, this tepid, cloudy soup of alleyway children. Only occasionally, finding myself in a neglected corner, could I relax, dunk myself, and feel a moment of departure. But now, sitting in the heat with Nanna, and in spite of the fact that Guillaine seemed ready to explode with frustration, I was able to appreciate something I'd never realized was so close to me. The sea of bodies and faces that merged and threatened on the inside, from this view separated themselves into individuals. I noticed the older boys—grown too large for last year's bathing suits—showing off on the diving board, and felt both a thrill and pang of regret from being able to watch unscathed on the other side of the fence.

After a few minutes of this, Guillaine could no longer be contained, and began to drift away from us. Nanna, with some difficulty, got to her feet, called to her, and we began to retrace our steps back home. Miraculously, Guillaine obeyed, our slow march away from her having prompted her herding instinct, and she brought up the rear. Once again, Nanna promised to take me to Eaton's as soon as the "weather broke." *"On va prendre notre lunch au Neuvieme,"* she said, and though Guillaine looked on uncomprehendingly, I understood. Nanna's words no longer related to actual plans, but rose instead to the realm of unattainable wishes. Our journey to Eaton's had become kind of repetitive prayer, adding itself to the book that also contained those dealing with my long-lost aristocratic parentage.

Not long after, Nanna had to make another trip, this one to Hôpital Notre-Dame. Weeks and months passed with my mother, sisters, brothers, and myself filing onto two bus rides and forced marches through Parc Lafontaine to visit her there. The walls of her semi-private room were a washed-out tone of the same blue color at home, denoting, it seemed, a paling of her life forces. Her usual stories could not or, because of the crowd in the room, would not come out. Instead, she let out only faint murmurings of assent to my mother's questions of how she was feeling, eating, sleeping. Although I sensed that our good-byes would take place here, I felt ill equipped to say anything to her, to communicate anything other than the same silent stares as my brothers and sisters. Here, for once, I was, unwillingly, one of them.

On the last visit Nanna fell asleep before we left. I recall my mother saying, *"Bon, les enfants, on va laisser Nanna dormir."* Silently we headed toward the door, but just before leaving the room I lifted the metal dome from atop an untouched meal tray. Revealed beneath was a bowl of broth, a browned chop, a portion of mashed potatoes decorated with a limp sprig of parsley, and a small cup of day-old vanilla pudding with an obviously rubbery skin. It occurs to me now that this display of tired food, trying valiantly to be a three-course meal, contained a kind of emblematic truth for all of us: domes protecting something meager yet delusively proud. We each exist under our own domes, the same kind used to protect the food in fancy restaurants such as the Neuvieme at Eaton's and, as I well knew, on the dining cars of trains.

Treasure Chest

Darin Beasley

They were boys of a middle-class South that prized its values in history, tradition, and gracious living, and so it was natural their separate bloodlines were steeped in socially acceptable behavior. They were two in number. By the time they met, some of their behavior wasn't suited for refined tastes anymore—but that wasn't a burden; they'd learned to fake their way through almost anything.

Manners, another adult tooth to grow, came easy, as easy as telling tales and living them at the same time. These were the rules of their birthplace and from there they grew.

They outgrew the South. They were its unmentionables, its long johns on a cold night, hitched up to a baying harvest moon. They called all the horses (see dreams) home.

They were cornstalks and Levi's who became city boys easily and remorselessly. Their former small-world skies sent rain to the suburbs and farms.

They weren't coming back. Hell's bells set off ringing. The magnolia trees, without the two boys to whistle at their beauty, were helpless.

The two boys. You would've recognized them anywhere.

Often, they were mistaken for brothers, and more than once new strangers asked if they were intimate.

Theirs was a tale of intimacy.

As in any tale of intimacy, it was one of high adventure.

One boy was given the birth name Warren and the other was christened Darin.

When they came to know one another, it was impossible to separate them. Both were skinny, smoked too many cigarettes, and broke other boys' hearts.

They were unable to say why they were meant to be together and they were never boyfriends.

Identity Envy—Wanting to Be Who We Are Not
Published by The Haworth Press, Inc., 2007. All rights reserved.
doi:10.1300/5641_15

They were boys with proper manners, fond of one another's good graces and perverse highs (the art of sharing, the talents for attraction and appreciation, rides of whorish nights, mouthfuls of tall-tale gossip, and jaunts through naked lust). They were ridiculous and sublime.

They liked to lie down next to one another, on beds during all kinds of weather.

They didn't like to part.

They relied on one another.

They were imperfect. Their personalities were confident and strong, but each boy was stubborn as a mule.

Mules that led all the other mules onto roads of freedom. They inspired admiration.

We miss those mules.

This is a prose poem of sorts; it is not a confession.

I sit here in the dark and think about them. I didn't invent them.

Ryuichi Sakamoto's soundtrack *Merry Christmas, Mr. Lawrence* was a record they both played a lot. Like a soundtrack, what's composed here serves to illustrate a tale, to sing about what two boys shared and how they came to want to be one another and how in the end neither one got their wish. If what you're reading sounds familiar, then join in singing.

This is not a sad tale.

The boys weren't really boys. They were too old to be called boys. They were fine young men (most of the time). It was to your advantage to put on your sunglasses if you saw them coming. The sight of them side by side, in a Jeep, a bar, a bedroom, a club, put a light in your eyes.

Happy trails; blind with love and hungry for affection.

Warren.

And.

Darin.

Who?

I lie in bed at night and wonder where they went. I know where they started.

But the most recent time they were reunited can come first.

They saw each other at their friend Loree's house. Everyone gathered in the kitchen while Loree put the finishing touches on the dinner she'd prepared.

Warren had a gift for Darin.

Warren liked to make himself a Crackerjack box giving you a prize.

It was a belated birthday present and Warren said, "This has been sitting on my desk for two years." The gift was inside a plastic mailer covered in grimy dust and one end was taped shut with a horizontal strip of faded masking tape. Darin pulled the gift out and in his hands he held a limited-edition Jack Pierson book that folded out like a newspaper.

Sing a song to art fags.

Warren and Darin cut some good teeth on art. Art was fucked up and beautiful and they messed around with it themselves, making little books and pictures and plastic tableaux.

Art was fucked up and beautiful like they had been and, in different ways, were now so again. Darin was Warren's Jack Pierson (fondness persists) and Warren was Darin's Matthew Barney (beauty persists too, without similarity between celebrated artist and hot young man making his own, nonfamous world).

Everyone has favorites.

Everyone has a favorite artist. Warren loves Matthew Barney to this day.

Warren loved Darin.

Darin could close his eyes at night and recount Warren by heart.

The stories that happen can go wrong. Instead of hanging back like reluctant boys might, they were brave. They were a sacrilegious pair, foolish and headstrong, one with hazel-colored eyes and the other blue.

It sounds dreamy. It was.

This is the real beginning, way down South.

In Athens, Georgia, a town that belonged nowhere else. Darin loved the deep-hearted, cold winters and the humid, blossoming summers. He fooled around with boys and was faithful to his friends. He called his life in Athens the Rolling Rock puppydog raggedy-ass-clothes way of living. It was a college radio, townie vegetarian, carrot dog, tofu, bleached hair, double scotches, treetop party, dead-end railroad, makeshift cul-de-sac way of living.

Sleepy days followed wild nights and out of nowhere came Warren.

They met in Go!—a clothing store. Within a few nights they were on a date that ended with them sitting on Darin's bed. They kissed. Darin put his hand down the back of Warren's pants. Warren went home. Later he called Darin up and asked him out. Darin said yes but a few days later told Warren he couldn't go.

Darin had problems (a mouth full of bad teeth) and thought if Warren found out just how bad, Warren would get scared and tell him he'd made a huge mistake. So he ran away from Warren.

Warren was better off, but Darin couldn't tell him that.

Warren looked like a fox sometimes. Like you weren't sure if you could trust him or not. He looked like Montgomery Clift. He was handsome and his widow's peak never lied because his eyes said look at me. He loved being noticed.

Darin didn't care how Warren looked. He had an inkling he loved Warren's guts.

Though neither planned it, they lived in Seattle around the same time, both of them eventually working for a hip retail chain. Seattle was a gloomy old thing.

Darin high-tailed it to San Francisco, a place that would prove to be tenderness, horror, and all the good things one needs.

Boys and men and the city everywhere and beyond all of it the Pacific Ocean.

One Saturday afternoon when the telephone rang, Darin was in the flat. Warren was on the other end. The sun was shining outside. "I'm coming there," Warren said. "Can I live with you?"

I'm living here, Darin thought. You can come.

Some moments put the glue in the glue gun and squirt it out in the right spot. They shared that spot. It was a voyage into pleasure, the discovery of a kindred spirit.

Checking out guys, bottles of wine, hair dye, cigarettes, dot dot dot.

Eating together like every day was a day for thanks.

They could have been hit by the proverbial bus—they cared about everything.

Coffee in the morning together was a historical event: clouds parted, tree limbs bloomed, and gods looked down transfixed over the serious A.M. rituals of French Roast and Parliaments, boom box Bjork, and Pet Shop Boys.

Together, nonstop.

A spring night's entertainment beginning at a gallery. Chummy friends are inside. Plastic cups full of wine. And leather men. The bathroom door is a fuzzy green blanket. Macaroni noodle paintings hang on the walls, Dolly Parton's up there and it all takes place in a gallery named Kiki. Darin writes a couple of stories inside himself. Surrounded by art he writes *we're living it* and steps out for some fresh air.

Warren walks back up the street with a new pack of cigarettes and *the sun is setting around him*. It is a prelude.

When the show's finished they truck over to a bar, Este Noche, where all the Latino boys you can want strut around in tight jeans. They don't pay Warren or Darin any mind. Warren and Darin just drink some good, shitty beer and head home early. This is what you do when you live in italics: *stay happy and don't ask too much of anything*.

They felt lucky to have one another.

You're the one. No, you're the one.

You are the man.

I love the shit out of you.

Shit stuck to them and didn't stink.

Boys came and went for Warren. For the longest time, Darin didn't feel jealous. Darin was happy being himself and trying to figure out which parts of himself were like Warren. This felt reciprocal because one thing was certain. Although Warren was successful with boys, something was missing inside him. It wasn't Darin, but Warren wanted to be around him. He didn't trust anyone like he trusted Darin.

Meanwhile, boys kept flocking to him. Most of the time Warren let them go. They'd fall in love with him and he'd have already had his fill. Warren couldn't help it.

Darin wanted to go as high as possible too, so he gave in and loved Warren more.

For a short time, Warren went away. He flew home to help take care of his father who was ill. The plan was once he'd helped out as much as he could he'd return to California and he did.

As soon as Darin and their friend Megan picked Warren up at the airport, the three of them knew something was wrong. Warren didn't look like himself. He walked like a zombie. His eyes were yellow. A couple of days later he came out of the bathroom and said his pee was thick.

After seeing a doctor, he came back to the flat where they lived and went to sleep—but not before leaving Darin a letter on his bed. The heart of the letter said, *I'm sorry but I need to go home.*

Warren was fast asleep with hepatitis C that he managed to pick up from a plate of oysters at *Dollywood* (Tennessee sure knew how to travel).

Darin cried like a fucking baby and didn't have an ounce of shame over crying. The tears poured out of him. The day shut down all over them.

They knew they weren't anything alike but they pretended they were. When the time came, they said good-bye like it was easy.

Fly the friendly skies, cowboy; go west.

They had.

Darin stayed. His teeth were made beautiful and he fell in love with a boy named Tom. Back home in Georgia, Warren fell for a guy who drove a forklift.

They tried their hands at love (those are other stories).

Warren moved to Oregon. Darin moved to Oregon.

Good-bye, sweet California. Hello, personal danger.

Rock shows, June rain showers, pints of Northwest beer, and a Victorian house.

Some things that happened between Warren and Darin were frisky.

It wasn't the first time. It was harmless, like teenage boys.

Darin did it though, he fell in love (see Warren) and Warren did not.

Darin got a little more stupid with each passing day. The more stupid he got, the more neglectful Warren grew. They wanted out.

But—and this was the big but to come into their lives—impossibilities sometimes get their chances.

Darin and Warren were jackasses. They didn't have to initiate anything; another boy came along and saved them that grief. The boy's name was Michael. He liked Warren and Darin liked Michael. In this case, three wasn't such a magic number.

Who the fuck were they trying to kid?

They remember the sound of each other's voices.

If they were the last two people alive and the world was surrounded in darkness, they would call out and find each other. But this is a little too kind even if it's the truth.

Say they're reunited. They'd lick their wounds and then they'd get serious and write down their tale. Most of which would have to be left out. Identity takes up too much space when you let it take over (and two identities take up even more).

They'd write down their tale and when it was finished, they'd say, looks like it's done and nice work. Their heads would spin and they'd have to lie down, not beside each other but not too far away.

This is the tale they will leave behind.

Maybe someone in a new world will find it.

It goes like this:

X and Y were not like friends, brothers, or lovers.

They were modern-day pirates—each of them a rummy, sweaty combination of good and bad, grounded around one principle: see what you can get away with.

They didn't have grand schemes.

They swam in high seas of desire.

California was everything. Guys who laughed like flowers and guys who pretended to be ferocious and guys who looked disgusted with everyone except anyone who looked exactly like themselves. And then (sweet) the guys in the middle, unknown rock star-material boys who loved art fags with understated style, not in a hurry to get anywhere, except in bed together.

Shirts flew off in flashes. Pants gathered around the ankles lickety split. Canons fired!

And the pirate ship continued to sail around the world. Somebody came into the moving picture with a parrot on his shoulder. The parrot said, "Ahoy, ahoy, chips ahoy." Cookies. For everyone.

X and Y. They made it a habit to be good and bad. It seemed the only way to keep a balance between their separate natures. The god and bad in one pirate complimented the good and bad in the other.

Darin was pirate X. His unbearable lightness of Y was a pirate named Warren. And likewise so that in the end, they made each other walk the plank.

All that finery and such a great swell of water.

When they swam up for air they were alone and when they broke through to the shining surface they were free, except for one little thing.

Their hands were tied.

A Serene Invisibility:
Turning Myself into a Christian Girl

Perry Brass

From the time I was about seven to the time I was eleven, I had two secret wishes that were very much based on the facts of my growing up Jewish in the Deep South in the 1950s. Being a child who was fairly sissified and from a working-class family left me without any handle I could find to hold a place for myself in the world. My only space then was an inner one of longings and fantasies, and the splendor of whatever I could create to try to make some kind of place for myself. I needed to invent this place, and even re-invent myself to be in it. Like a lot of other queer boys, I was dreamy and withdrawn. And I had these two adults around me called parents, who themselves not being a complete part of the Southern landscape around them, could be alternately understanding or violently disapproving.

First, it would be good to give you some kind of background: at the time that I was growing up, Southern Jews still lived in fairly closed communities that seemed like ghettos within a white, basically An-glo-Saxon, culture. The ghettos were based on generations of real anti-Semitism and genuine fears of it, mutual feelings of distrust between Jews and the Christian world, and also a need to preserve the community, even though as "Southerners," most Jews frowned on "flaunting" their Jewishness. It was considered a private, personal thing that for the most part you did in your own home and with your family, friends, or "tribe."

Savannah, Georgia, had had Jewish residents since colonial times, but within the community there was a pronounced hierarchy reflecting Southern society itself. Jews who'd been down South longer and were more "Southern" in their speech and manners, who could "pass" easier through the social and professional gates of society, occupied the top rungs of social standing, money, and status. Jews who

Identity Envy—Wanting to Be Who We Are Not
Published by The Haworth Press, Inc., 2007. All rights reserved.
doi:10.1300/5641_16

had come down South between the World Wars, who were seen as being pushy, immigrant, and too "obviously" Jewish, occupied lower ones. My mother's immediate family were recent immigrants from Poland and very "Jewish," despite some success among her cousins in the dry goods business. My father's family were shopkeepers from Lithuania, considered the "aristocracy" of Eastern Jewry; therefore, they felt themselves to be above my mother's Polish roots. But in truth, although well read and with the Southern courtly manners he had picked up as a child, Daddy, who had served well in the infantry in World War II, was still only trained as a meat cutter and always remained stiffly outside the polished status of Southern Jewish professional men.

When I was eight my father bought a small grocery store with a filling station attached "way out in the country," where we were the only Jews within about thirty miles. Our most immediate neighbors lived on a long dirt road off the highway that stopped in the woods. They were poor white country folks, barely up from being sharecroppers, some of them without indoor plumbing. Farther away, past the woods and some pastures, were several black shanty settlements whose inhabitants timorously ventured in groups into our store. In the store I was known simply as "Boy," a name which seemed so unlike what I felt inside. Inside, I wasn't "Boy" at all: "Boy" seemed alien to me, threatening, more like a taunt, like calling someone "Whitey" who was really black. But my father wanted to call me "Boy," because he wanted me to be a part of his own idealized boyhood, as a very loved, often headstrong, only child.

My father lived in a dream world himself, in a rugged pulp magazine 1950s man's world, filled with war stories and that kind of buddyhood that came out of the war. Out in the country, away from a Jewish community, he could engage in his own unapproved passion for guns and hunting, highly unusual among Jewish men who were usually tied to wives and work. He immediately set aside part of a large dark storeroom in the back of the business, next to fifty-pound bags of chicken feed and sacks of flour, for his rifles, shotguns, pistols, and reloading equipment. When he was not out front cutting meat or even pumping gas, he would be in the back while my mother had to watch what was going on out front.

This rural male pursuit of guns and killing animals terrified me; I became nauseated around it. My father would spend hours with his country friends talking, smoking Camels, drinking black coffee, and talking about hunting. They'd go into the backroom while he refilled empty ammunition shells with gunpowder, topping them with bullets he'd cast himself from lead. Some of his friends had boys close to my age who went out already with their fathers into the woods. They could not believe that I didn't like to kill song birds with BB guns, or shoot rabbits and squirrels with a kid-sized shotgun. Away from their fathers, they'd ask, "Ain't you a boy? Come on, show us. We don't believe you're a real boy!"

I was petrified. Suppose what I had under my clothes did not prove that I was a real boy, because nothing about me seemed to be what real boys actually were? Boys never cried. They liked to kill things. They avoided anything that was pretty, out of the ordinary for boys, and to me exciting. They liked the scary dark, a time to play tricks; and nature was only something to be destroyed, not wondered at.

If boys were like that, girls on the other hand seemed to be totally self-contained. They had a serenity, a secret security boys could not touch. They did not need the approval of other boys, the way boys did. Girls were born girls, but boys had to prove themselves to be boys. The greatest proof was that you were unafraid of death in the form of dead animals in the woods, or war, like the Big War my father had so proudly fought in.

Being a girl would be wonderful, a sanctuary from all my fears, I decided in my most secret heart. I'd seen enough television and movies to know that girls could cry and even fall into an attention-getting faint if things called for it. They could wear glamorous clothes and wonderful makeup. Who could forget Ann Miller in billboard-sized Cinemascope in *Kiss Me Kate,* with her banner of purple eye shadow and glossy red lipstick streaming across the big screen? Or all those English beauties in *Forever Amber* in acres of seventeenth-century silk dresses, wigs, and jewelry, while the men wore mostly drab black and handsome Cornel Wilde got wounded in a duel? I didn't want to be wounded in a duel; I'd rather hold Cornel Wilde in my arms, wearing one of those great dresses.

It would be better, I decided impulsively, to be a girl, and a Christian one at that. Christians could have things that Jews couldn't: wonderful Christmas gifts and decorations; brightly colored Easter clothes and Easter baskets, which I wanted desperately to decorate. The thought of fantastic baskets holding crinkly plastic grass, colored eggs, and little bunnies that were not bloodied and killed, but were adorable and acrylic, made me cry inside with longing. Being a Jew was so difficult; it felt like the negation of any brightness. I felt like a spy taking envious notes in a Christian world. The only thing worse, more alien and distrusted, would be to be a Communist, whatever that meant, because I'd heard my parents talk a lot about Communists then.

"Communists," Mother informed me, exhaling from one of her Chesterfields, "lie all the time. They're always trying to set traps for you: you can't tell from the outside what they really are, but inside they live in secrets, disgusting horrible secrets." She looked directly at me. "If you ever hear about someone who's a Communist, let me know at once."

I had no idea what to do. I wanted to be a girl and a Christian; suppose I was a Communist? Suppose wanting to be a girl and a Christian was the same thing as actually being a Communist, since they lived in secrets, disgusting horrible secrets? I was sure my mother could see all the way through me as she puffed on her Chesterfield, resentfully watching the store. She scared me with her talk about the Communists. She seemed so certain of what she knew and probably knew already about me. She and my father argued a lot about me, and I began to understand that maybe they were engaged in a secret war of their own.

Whatever it was, it turned my father into a great escapist. Besides his guns, hunting, and fishing, he loved to read, mostly adventure sagas from the period, like *Kon Tiki* and *The World Atlas of True War Stories*. He liked to bring books to me and gave me one of his childhood favorites, a deliciously unexpurgated volume of *The Arabian Nights*. I was in heaven. Here men wore silk harem pants and jewelry, traveled through space on the backs of jinnis, and felt a wonderful surrender to magic that I barely knew existed. I devoured all the tales, reading them over and over again, wanting to re-create them somehow. I started playing with dolls. At first they were things I made myself, cutting them out of paper or out of comic books, like Katy Keen or Prince Valiant. They did not have to be Arabian, only "fantastic."

My mother became furious and horrified. It was bad enough that her husband never acted like a real Jew, not having a real profession with security, the hunting and the fishing, but now her son was playing with dolls! She lashed out at me, humiliating me in front of the country people in the store, saying, "My son's a sissy; he plays with dolls! Where'd he ever come from?"

I asked that myself: where did I come from? But no one could tell me.

But my father, realizing he was perhaps not the most regular of Jewish men, decided that instead of playing with dolls, his son could play with puppets: boys could do that. For "Boy," puppets were better than dolls, although Mother could never see a difference between them. To her, they still put me outside of the real boy race. But Daddy stood his ground. And since he had a gun workshop of his own, he insisted it was only fair that Boy should have a place to make his puppets. "You're only spoiling him," Mother argued. "He'll end up like you. Never realistic. Only good for things that never make any money."

She was sure that Daddy's hunting and fishing kept him away from his work in the store, just as puppets would keep me from ever being a real boy. But my father cleared a place in the back of the garage and built a puppet stage for me. The stage was like opening up a miniature world of my own, made from a wooden fruit box that Daddy had painted and fitted with a drawstring curtain. With his help, I started to make hand puppets out of papier-mâché. Now I could be anything I wanted to, as long as I was a puppet as well. I could be a glamorous girl with eye shadow, a Christian king, a powerful queen. I'd already known that it was okay for girls to do this, but not for boys. Boys could only be boys, but girls could be anything they wanted. They could wear pants or dresses, could cry and be strong, could be quiet and left alone and nobody cared. Nobody ever tried to start fights with them. After all, they were only girls.

I would stay for hours alone in the garage with my puppets and their stage. I made six of them, using directions from a book Daddy got out of the library for me called *Puppets and Puppetry.* I don't remember who wrote it, but I do remember that the author considered puppets to be living and with feelings, too, almost as soon as the idea to create them was born. The heads were first modeled out of clay, the way Adam was, and then a shell of papier-mâché was placed over that; the papier-mâché dried and the clay was carefully scooped out. The heads were painted, and wool yarn was used as hair. I could dress my girl puppets, do their hair, faces, and makeup. The boys seemed kind of drab, but they had crowns of course, since they were kings or at least knights. I made one puppet with a glittering Arabian Nights turban, and wanted to make puppets who looked like Shakespearean characters in magnificent costumes, but they were too difficult.

This was the happiest, most serene and joyous part of my childhood. It was the thing that joined me, at least on the outside, to my father, but inside I was a secret girl who made puppets, not a boy, since the boys around me did nothing like this. They still sneered at me and called me names when I ventured out to play down the dirt road. I knew nothing about Christianity, but I was a Christian because being a Jew seemed too drab, too fearful of the "graven images" that I was now absolutely crazy about. I was in an Eden of my own, where like Adam, I got to name the beings around me, the ones that I'd made.

But the one thing I could not name was myself.

Who was I really? Where did I come from? And was I authentically a boy, even if I took my pants down? I would not find out for a long time, but strangely enough, the only thing that made me want to be a boy, a real *actual* boy, was, when, at age eleven, after my father had died of cancer, Mother's family decided that in order to become a boy, I should join, of all things, the Boy Scouts.

Boy Scouting was an alternative to Little League baseball and football; but it was a boy-thing in a kind of secret, old-fashioned, and nerdy way. Now with other kids my own age I learned that being a boy was more than hunting and fishing and never crying. It was more than never being scared. It was a kind of bonding and yearning for a closeness we could not name that had nothing to do with being Jewish or Christian. Suddenly being a boy could contain all the secret codes and messages of Scouting; earning merit badges about Indian lore and cooking outdoors; and learning in Scout camp that there were other boys like me, who had secret lives of their own, though none of them ever told me that inside he was a girl.

Plantation Fantasies
or,
One Hillbilly's Journey to the Tidewater and Back

(for Cindy Burack)

Jeff Mann

The Old White, they used to call it, when Robert E. Lee and other Southern aristocrats, fleeing the Tidewater summer heat, used to visit the mountain resort. Torn down in 1922, rebuilt in the late 1920s, it is now called the Greenbrier, still a luxurious resort for those who can afford it. For most of my life, I have wanted to spend the night there, but considering the cost of the rooms—$228 per night is the cheapest rate I can find on their Web page—I doubt that I will ever fulfill that particular dream.

Those mountains once were Virginia; since 1863, they have been part of West Virginia. In particular, Greenbrier County, which is just east of Summers, the county where I spent my adolescence. I remember the first time I entered the Greenbrier, when I was a shapeless pre-teen visiting relatives there. My mother's sister, Aunt Jane, had married well, a Chrysler executive whose company treated him to occasional visits to the resort. I walked into the lobby, admired its high ceilings, its expensive furniture and wallpaper, its air of gentility, and proclaimed, "Ah, the elegance I was born for!"

At that point in my life, I had yet to realize that I was gay, but on some level I certainly knew I was different. During my first ten years, in my mother's hometown of Covington, Virginia, my peculiarities were not all that remarkable. I played with the other neighborhood children, attended grade schools, tinkered with my rock collection

Identity Envy—Wanting to Be Who We Are Not
Published by The Haworth Press, Inc., 2007. All rights reserved.
doi:10.1300/5641_17

and my chemistry set, watched *Batman,* and passionately collected comic books. My only salient oddity was an interest in the occult.

After age ten, however, when my family moved from Covington into the mountains of West Virginia, my father's original stomping grounds, and, after a few years, when I entered junior high in Hinton, it became clear to everyone that I did not fit in. Along with the continuing enthusiasm for witchcraft and magic, which horrified the local devout Christians, I was not interested in sports, I was not interested in band (which all the popular kids joined), and I was a straight-A student in a region only beginning to value education. This led to a bit of name-calling: the word "queer" was lobbed at me well before my sex drive began to take shape and long before I realized that the admiration I felt for some boys and many men was sexual.

I responded to such hostility with one haughty conviction: my intellect made me superior to my persecutors, made me an aristocrat amid peasants. It was this self-defensive belief, I suppose, that led me, a descendant of Appalachians and all my life a denizen of small towns in the Highland South, to identify with European royalty and the antebellum aristocracy of the Tidewater South. Thus my sense of entitlement, of coming home to luxury and expensive grandeur, when I entered the lobby of the Greenbrier.

Though none of my ancestors or my immediate family had possessed anything even approaching the finances appropriate to an upper class, I quickly learned the phrase "genteel poverty" and soon set about emphasizing my genteel differences. If I could not have the money (and no future career that caught my adolescent interest would provide more than a decent wage), I could possess the other attributes of nobility: a wide-ranging education, fine manners, a well-developed aesthetic sense, an enthusiasm for things cosmopolitan.

These "high-falutin'" interests of mine my parents more than approved of. Though both came from modest backgrounds, neither were typical Appalachians of that time period, the 1960s. They possessed many of the traits I yearned for, and they encouraged my intellectual development. My father, the grandson of mountain farmers, was the first on the Mann side of the family to earn several degrees. He taught English and French in high schools and colleges and then later became a lawyer. As soon as I learned to read, he pointed me in the direction of serious literature and music. He bought me comicbook versions of classic novels and an entire set of encyclopedias, read me stories from King Arthur's exploits and from Greek mythology, taught me bits of French, and played me records of Puccini, Beethoven, and Brahms.

My mother, daughter of a nurse and a machinist, had dropped out of Longwood College to get married but continued to read novels of depth and share my father's passion for classical music. In one major respect, however, she differed from Daddy. He had traveled a good bit as a soldier in the Second World War and had had more than enough of the outside world. He was content never to leave the mountains again. She, on the other hand, though immured most of her life in two uneventful little towns—Covington, then Hinton—yearned for international travel and passed that yearning on to me. Luckily, her sister Jane lived far from Appalachia, in interesting cities like Chicago, then Detroit, then San Diego, so that gave my mother an excuse to escape the monotony of the mountains, to take her children—my younger sister Amy and me—into the outside world and expose us to classes and cultures not our own.

Along with my parents' relatively genteel tastes, then, another factor that encouraged my longing for elegance was my Aunt Jane and her well-off lifestyle. Her husband, Uncle Garm, the Chrysler executive, had scads of money (at least compared to my father, who as a schoolteacher made little and as a novice lawyer made not much more). In Chicago, they lived in Deerfield, one of the more affluent suburbs. In Detroit, they lived in Bloomfield Hills, with the other well-off. In California, they lived in La Mesa, a wealthy suburb of San Diego. What a treat it was to visit them, to get on the train in Hinton, to see the mountains diminish, the flat lands and the cities begin, and, at journey's end, to be whisked from the rail station to their home. Always a living room reserved for special occasions, with furniture too expensive for children to touch. Always exotic foods: lobster and cheese broiled on English muffins, shrimp cocktails, crab enchiladas, avocado salad, and the adults' fancy cocktails from which I occasionally got a tiny sip. In Detroit, a huge boat on which to explore the Great Lakes, big enough to spend the night on, rising to chipped beef on toast in the mornings. In La Mesa, a pool surrounded by rustling palm trees and birds-of-paradise.

These were my first tastes of the life of the rich and the wide world beyond Appalachia. After glamorous and novelty-filled weeks with Aunt Jane and Uncle Garm, it was always a letdown to return to

Hinton—the shift from colorful otherworldly adventure to black-and-white home that so many have noted in *The Wizard of Oz*. My father rarely went with us on these visits, having, as I've said, lost any interest in travel, and he always seemed to resent my aunt. It was clear to me even then that he regarded her values as trivial, materialistic, and shallow. It's only now, from the perspective of a forty-five-year-old, that I realize that he must have feared that she might kindle hungers in me equally shallow, desires that his means and my region would never be able to satisfy.

A few other elements of my youth were to sharpen this hunger for wealth, privilege, and my fascination with aristocracy, whether in the form of American mansions or European royalty. Those stories my father read me as a child—how clearly I can remember lying with him on the chaise lounge on my grandmother's back porch, the Howard Pyle edition of King Arthur's exploits held between us, the wonderful illustrations of Merlin, Lancelot, and Vivian. Here, and in Edith Hamilton's *Mythology,* another early favorite, were castles, kings, warriors, fortresses, magic, and heroism. This is the sort of fare that both fertilizes the imagination of a bright child and also, for many of us, makes quotidian reality forever inadequate. When I finally got to junior high and had access to the library, the first two books I checked out were big photo collections of European castles and cathedrals, grand edifices very, very far away from Hinton, West Virginia.

The third book was *Dracula. Dark Shadows,* the Gothic soap opera that ran from 1966 to 1971, would also prove to be a huge influence. Already fascinated with the occult, I took to its stories of witches, vampires, ghosts, and werewolves with avid interest. And there it was, an American castle, Collinwood, the huge family estate on which most of the storylines centered. Baronial fireplaces, ancestral portraits, grand staircases, looming turrets, romantic terraces and gazebos…and American royalty, the wealthy members of the Collins family, who lounged about in formal clothes and sipped sherry (or brandy, when they needed resuscitation after the latest supernatural shock). How I hankered for the vampire Barnabas's characteristic Inverness cape, onyx ring, and silver-wolf's-head-handled cane (all souvenirs I have since, as an adult, acquired). Such props might not only add dash to my appearance—and as a pudgy, insecure, bespectacled bookworm, I needed all the dash I could get—they might also invite adventure into my life or distinguish me from my inferiors. They might reveal to the world my inner aristocratic nature, so far quite efficiently buried within a doughy, asexual body and quiet mountain towns.

❋

Needless to say, this interest in things grand and aristocratic made me look down on my own culture, that of Appalachia, with contempt. What had I in common with hicks and farmers, railroad workers and miners? I recall one particular expression of this contempt. One autumn night when I was about fifteen, I went out to dinner with the playwright Maryat Lee and her partner at the Oak Supper Club near Pipestem, West Virginia. Maryat, a family friend, occasionally invited me off on jaunts without my parents in tow, perhaps sensing my potential as a writer, or, more likely, as a budding queer. What a sense of arrival: a fancy restaurant with candles and silver, a menu on which brown beans and cornbread did not appear. I ordered duck, my first. The fact that it turned out to be all dark meat, and dry at that, didn't matter. It was the sort of entrée I imagined might be enjoyed at Collinwood, or some Tidewater plantation. When a family of locals sat at a nearby table and began talking, I quietly mocked their accents as indicators of ignorance. Maryat smiled, but gently told me not to make fun of them, admitting that she liked this region's dialect. I smiled back, rolled my eyes at the table of "hillbillies," and began contemplating the cheesecake menu.

When I tell this story now to my Appalachian Studies classes, I use it as an example of cultural hegemony: how mass media prod us into assimilating into mainstream culture and encourage us to deride and reject our regional or ethnic legacies. Where did a high-school kid who had spent almost his entire life in the Highland South get the idea that mountain accents revealed stupidity? What Appalachians on television or film are depicted as anything other than provincial laughing stocks? There are exceptions, but they are few. For both "queers" and "hillbillies," mass media often spread the seeds of self-hatred.

But these were realizations I was far from achieving that evening in the Oak Supper Club. I did not belong in my native mountains, I felt sure. I belonged elsewhere, in a faraway world of privilege from which only an accident of birth had exiled me. Somewhere, a turreted house or massive plantation awaited me, with, perhaps, a passel of servants. After all, the Ferrells, the Irish side of my father's family, were descended from royalty, a fact my grandmother was fond of pointing out, a fact I clung to in order to make sense of my pervading and inescapable sense of displacement.

Soon after, when I turned sixteen and, through the help of lesbian friends, realized I was gay, that sense of displacement grew, and my attitude toward Appalachia grew more fraught. Now I had another reason to seek the outside world: not only might there be some aristocratic life awaiting me, there were, I knew from my furtive reading of gay novels borrowed from my lesbian friends, places Out There where gay people could live openly and safely. I knew that, in my hometown, to live as an open queer would invite pariah status, verbal abuse, and violence.

My rapidly developing sexual tastes added a sharp complication, however. I found myself attracted to the country boys I'd grown up around, the same "peasants" I feared and looked down upon, the intolerant straights from whom I did my best to hide my desires. This was thoroughly confusing: how could a would-be aristocrat yearn for rough mountain men? Shouldn't I be turned on by men like those I wanted to become, gentlemen in suits, men with the visible attributes of the upper class? Hopelessly ambivalent, I wanted both to flee the culturally backward country for big cities and gay ghettos and to stay in Appalachia and sleep with its men.

This lust for the locals, by necessity, I never acted upon, and I knew that as long as I remained in Hinton my desires were irrelevant, condemned to suspended animation. Nothing could change till I finally made it to college, where I could cultivate my gentility in the rarefied halls of Higher Learning. In high school, I already had a reputation as a bookworm that was inescapable. (I was declared "Biggest Bookworm" and "Most Polite" in my senior yearbook.) Hanging around discernible lesbians didn't help my reputation any: I "associated with known ducks" and was thus tarred with the same brush. After my lesbian friends graduated a year ahead of me, I kept to myself, concentrated on my studies, and survived as best I could during that slow and painful time between the realization of my sexual identity in early 1976 and my escape to West Virginia University in August 1977. I was meticulously nondescript, except for the rebellion of shaggy hair. Striding around blue-collar Hinton looking like Barnabas Collins or an elegant Southern gentleman or any other upper-class ideal would only have encouraged catcalling and jeers.

Once I made it to Morgantown and WVU, where few folks knew me, where I had no reputation and could be someone new, I took that opportunity to transform myself. And it is here that my lust for Appalachian men took an interesting twist. Despite my aristocratic pretensions, I had to face facts: men in suits did not appeal to me. Scruffy mountain men did. An erotic syllogism: country boys are sexy, I want to be sexy, so looking like a country boy will make me sexy. Plus, blending in would be a way to stay safe. I used mimicry, not unlike the Viceroy butterfly, whose coloration imitates the foul-tasting Monarch so as to dissuade the hungry interest of birds. I took up the very signifiers of masculinity that I admired in local men: jeans, work boots, flannel shirt, beard. Queer novels I discovered in Morgantown's bookstores mentioned the leather community; my fantasies about tying and gagging handsome men were thus given a context that helped them make sense, and so I bought my first leather jacket. As I strode around Morgantown's bars with my lesbian buddy Bill, two self-conscious butches in search of a good time, my fascination with a far-away and long-ago aristocracy faded a bit, and when I decided to major in forestry as well as English and began hanging around with other booted, bearded country boys, my yearning for a world of sherry-sipping, fashionable, courtly, plantation-owning gentlemen began to wane.

Other factors have eroded that early passion for Tidewater elegance, those antebellum dreams. When I moved to Washington, DC, to teach in the fall of 1985, I did not take to the city at all, and, in fact, realized how much of a small-town Southerner and hillbilly I really was. Yes, my mother's careful training had given me sufficient manners to get along at fancy parties in fancy queer townhouses—in fact, for a West Virginia boy who'd never had money, I felt fairly secure in such settings—and yes, there I was, at last surrounded by what I had come to call "piss-elegant" furnishings, the same wood paneling and the very crystal decanters displayed at Collinwood. But the sense of arrival I'd felt as I first entered the lobby of the Greenbrier as a preteen, that was not there. Instead, I missed the mountains, I missed the down-home cooking, the slower pace, my family. The few folks with Southern or mountain accents whom I met in DC I immediately took a liking to: they sounded like home.

At the end of that semester, I returned to West Virginia. I had had enough of city noise, Beltway traffic, and too many people. Somehow the yearning for a plantation house, a Newport mansion, or a crenellated Irish castle had transformed into a desire for an isolated plot of land in the mountains, with a vegetable garden and a big farmhouse.

Teaching Appalachian Studies and Appalachian Literature at Virginia Tech has completed my fondness for my native region and further dwindled my Tidewater-plantation aspirations. How fond I am, how protective I am, of local kids in my classes, kids from West Virginia or Southwest Virginia, bright well-mannered kids who tell me shocking stories of being mocked—by other students, even by some of their professors—for their accents, their backgrounds, whatever makes them discernibly Appalachian. As I have learned about the history of Southern Appalachia—the exploitation of the natural resources by outside interests, the consequent environmental destruction, the courageous battles of coal miners to form a union, the economic declines and out-migrations—I have been moved and saddened and angered, and my allegiance to my region has immeasurably deepened. Encountering the fiction of Harriette Arnow, Lee Smith, James Still, and Denise Giardina, or the poetry of Louise McNeill, Irene McKinney, and Maggie Anderson, I have come to feel more and more respect for the struggles of the mountain working class, and I have learned to take pride in being the descendant of country farmers.

In my identification with Appalachia I have achieved, I suppose, an awareness of class issues and class conflicts, a recognition effectively obscured for most of my life by my haughty craving for aristocratic privilege, my "identity envy." And recently, race issues have also tarnished my Tidewater fantasies.

To the shock and disapproval of many, I respect the Confederate flag. I have a small magnetized one on my refrigerator and a large one draped over my guest room door. That flag means to me, as it does to many Southerners, "Heritage, not Hate," to use a T-shirt slogan. However, this is an opinion I keep pretty much to myself so as not to offend the many people for whom the Stars and Bars are a symbol of racism. My in-laws are black, as are several of my favorite col-

leagues. A double minority myself—Appalachian and gay—I immediately gravitate to minorities. And in the company of several African-American colleagues, I have been given gentle reminders of their
perspectives on the antebellum elegance I've admired.

Brilliant, deliciously acerbic Grant, joking, as we entered a faculty
reception held in the grand mansion in which the president of Virginia Tech lives: "Well, my kind are traditionally asked to enter edifices of this sort through the back door." My snort, mingling contempt
and camaraderie: "Hahh! Well, you can be damn sure if they asked
you to enter there, I'd be right by your side."

Lucinda, the chair of my department, one of the most exceptional
human beings I've ever known, who, during my first year as an
openly queer assistant professor worried about achieving tenure in
conservative Virginia, passionately defended me from a homophobe
who sent around a vicious e-mail note to alumni about my Web site
and the gay-themed publications listed there...Lucinda, as we entered a fancy restaurant in New Orleans with other colleagues attending a national creative writing conference, "Hmmm, so this part used
to be the slave quarters, according to the waitress. Well, Larry," ad-
dressing her husband, "I guess this is where you and I would have
ended up."

My aristocratic pretensions and cravings are far from dead, I freely
admit. Much of my travel revolves around visiting the remnants of
empire in one form or another, the monuments left by an opulent past.
In Richmond, I have toured the White House of the Confederacy, then
driven down to the James River to quietly drool during tours of
Berkeley Plantation and Shirley Plantation. Like any Southerner with
an historic sense, I have toured Mount Vernon and Monticello. In
Charleston and Savannah, amid azaleas and Spanish moss, I have
swelled with envy over the great white-columned homes there. Near
New Orleans, I have sipped a mint julep on the back porch of Oak Alley Plantation and wished I could own it (with, preferably, a stable of
beefy, hairy, perpetually shirtless, black-goateed young men to keep
the property up for me while I write and read).

My jaunts in search of aristocratic relics have, over the years,
ranged farther and farther from home. One Spring Break I dragged

my partner John to Newport, Rhode Island, to see Seaview Terrace, the great mansion that served as Collinwood in the original *Dark Shadows*. When I make it to Europe, I have to push my way into Prague Castle, Neuschwanstein, Edinburgh Castle, and the Hofburg with all the other slavering tourists. Obviously, I still have a fondness for royalty. The lives of the Windsors interest me to some extent, and the thought of a United Kingdom without a queen or king disturbs me. The fate of the Russian Romanovs is so painful to me that for years I have carefully avoided learning the details of their deaths, and visiting their tomb in St. Petersburg, I was wet-eyed. I have eagerly read biographies of gay royalty like Edward the Second of England and Ludwig II of Bavaria, and I have visited their tombs to pay my respects. If I ever make it back to Vienna, I will not only snap up assorted pastries but also revisit the Hapsburgs' imperial burial vault.

When I finally got to Ireland in 1994 and visited Longford, home of the once-royal Ferrell clan whose blood has, diluted, descended to me, I discovered that the ancestral castle I would gladly have claimed as my rightful inheritance had long ago been razed. In its place was a parking lot. Once I realized that there was no royal edifice left to lust for, what seized my sympathies in Ireland was the many ways in which it is like Appalachia: small towns and rural dwellers; crumbling, abandoned homes and other signs of out-migration; high unemployment and poverty in a scenic landscape. I stroked the green leaves of huge potato plants, admired the colorful cottages with their plumes of peat smoke, listened to old ladies planning another round of gooseberry-jam-canning, sat in pubs sipping stout with sexy Celtic country boys and watching televised soccer, and felt pretty much at home, with farmers and livestock herders, with people who have never known money and who make do, as we do in Appalachia, as best we can.

I am now, and probably always will be, a hive of hopeless contradictions. The refined and cosmopolitan traits that as an adolescent I dreamed of acquiring I have to a great extent achieved. In my home, there are crystal decanters like those in Collinwood, sherry and brandy snifters, a rack of good wines. My cookbooks range from Ireland to Germany to Greece—in fact, most of the countries of Europe.

My travel-photo albums are numerous: I have been to just about every European country that interests me, though Iceland, Norway, Spain, Italy, Poland, and Romania are still on the Yet-To-Be-Ravished list. With a little practice, I am competent in French and German, and I can speak a little bit—a very little bit—of Greek, Hungarian, Czech, and Dutch. I know a great deal about certain aspects of literature and mythology, a smattering of history and philosophy, and a good chunk of botany. I listen occasionally to Puccini, Beethoven, and Brahms, as my father still does. Right now I am enjoying Ovid's *The Metamorphoses*. Next summer, I hope to return to Greece and show my partner John the delights of Mykonos and Santorini. Unlike many of my fellow mountaineers, especially those caught in the economic crisis of the coalfields, I am obviously not poor, though I am certainly not well-off. English professors rarely are.

However, beside the Inverness coat I bought in Edinburgh, the coat almost identical to my aristocratic role model's, *Dark Shadow's* vampire Barnabas, there hang the coats I wear more often: the scruffy brown duster John's sexy straight ex-roommate left me, the new biker jacket John bought me for my birthday in a San Francisco cycle shop, or the worn black-leather jacket with a patch on the chest depicting the Celtic god Cernunnos. Kept in the same guest room are my boots: lumberjack boots, cowboy boots, harness-strap boots. In them conveniently converge two worlds, often mutually exclusive, that live side by side in me: the world of the Appalachian countryside, the world of gay leather bars.

On the dresser, beside the elegant onyx ring I sometimes sport, *à la* Barnabas, are the black-leather cock rings I often wear as wristbands. In the front hall are my collection of baseball caps—"redneck caps," I call them, since many, many mountain men wear them, and I have finally come to terms with my innate streak of native redneck. For baseball caps, mine are, I must admit, a mite unusual. One is from Lost River, a gay guesthouse in West Virginia, one celebrates Joni Mitchell's CD *Both Sides Now,* one commemorates *Dark Shadows'* thirtieth anniversary, one displays a black-and-blue leather flag, and one bears the logo of Mr. S, a leather store in San Francisco, where I have bought quite a few restraints over the years.

Odd how a regional identity I so wanted to escape as a younger man I have almost entirely come to terms with in my middle age. These days I drive an extended-cab 4x4 Toyota Tacoma pickup truck

I bought off my father, and I am so delighted with the way my "Macho Mountainman Mobile" climbs steep dirt roads and maneuvers in the snow that I have sworn never to live without four-wheel-drive again. The country music I so loathed in my adolescence is, other than my continuing passion for folk-rock stars like Joni Mitchell and Carly Simon, my primary musical enthusiasm. There is little I love more than driving the back roads of West Virginia and Southwest Virginia in my truck, watching the woodlands and meadows shift colors with the seasons, and listening to Kathy Mattea, Mary Chapin Carpenter, Toby Keith, or Brooks and Dunn in my CD player.

Then there is my favorite country-music star, Tim McGraw, with whom I am so infatuated that his handsome goateed image appears on my fridge, on my bedroom wall, and even in a bookcase nook in my office. Listening to his new CD *Live Like You Were Dying* on my way to Charleston, West Virginia, or Washington, DC, to give poetry readings has been a real delight this autumn of 2004, and my partner John and I will be attending McGraw's Charleston concert in a few weeks. With any luck, John's rational grasp will prevent me from rushing the stage like a lust-addled thirteen-year-old girl.

All this is surface detail, obviously—clothes, truck, CD collection. But these details accurately reflect a deep change in attitude. Yesterday I gave a talk on Appalachian poetry and fiction and played my mountain dulcimer for an Elderhostel group at Mountain Lake, Virginia. Last night I read poems at a rally against the massive environmental destruction caused by mountaintop removal mining, an invention of Satan if there ever was one. In a few days I will be speaking on a panel focused on language diversity and will discuss how Appalachians are often mistreated due to the ways in which their pronunciation and usage are perceived as ignorant. Later this autumn, at a symposium on mountain music, I will be reading a series of poems I composed about the dulcimer, and next spring I will be moderating a panel of West Virginia poets as part of the Appalachian Studies Conference. My career as a writer and a scholar is, obviously, pervaded thoroughly by my Appalachian identity.

Despite the homophobia and religious fundamentalism of this region, pestilences common in Southern Appalachia but certainly not exclusive to it, I intend to stay here, albeit in the sheltered environment of a university town, where I can be openly queer without having to engage in street brawls every day. Someone needs to stay—not to flee to New York City, DC, or San Francisco—to stay here and continue the fight. I intend to, and to fight on two fronts: for Appalachians and for LGBT people. I have, after all, inherited from my hardscrabble ancestors an innate orneriness and a taste for battle. Despite my cherished sword and dagger collection, despite my hot temper, I know that, in the twenty-first century, the pen (or, rather, the laptop) is a handier weapon than a honed blade and more likely to be free of uncomfortable legal consequences. I intend to use this keyboard with pugnacious regularity—as claymore, mace, dirk, or battle-axe—to attack conservative stupidity, as well as using it—as lyre, dulcimer, banjo, or guitar—to praise mountain and queer cultures and to tell the truth about my life as an Appalachian gay man. Beneath my earlier yearning for a Tidewater plantation and a life of privilege I have found an inescapable fondness for underdogs, for the persecuted and the marginalized.

Today I am taking John to lunch at the Greenbrier. The main dining room and the Sunday brunch are far too expensive to be worth it, but luckily there is a small, reasonably priced restaurant in the basement of the hotel, surrounded by shops selling garish golf clothes and jewelry. After a rainy stroll around the autumnal grounds under John's huge umbrella, we settle into a table and examine the menus. It takes me only a few minutes to realize that all the other diners are palpably well-off and Not From Around Here, and all the water-servers and waitresses are locals who speak like I do. Yes, their accents are deeper than mine, more prominent. Education often smoothes the edges of dialect, and it has mine, though my accent deepens considerably when I am angry, drunk, amorous, or around others of my region. Nevertheless, I feel that immediate kinship that common language can create.

This afternoon I respond to the restaurant staff the way I usually do when courteous people are waiting on me. I have enough empathic imagination to guess how hard their jobs are—much harder than mine—and I do my best to return their friendliness and to be appreciative of their efforts (though I will be the first to admit that unfriendly service brings out in me the supercilious aristocrat faster than anything, except, perhaps, waiting in line). The fact that they sound like fellow mountain folks only makes me friendlier. I have lived long enough to realize that the differences between their education and mine, their salaries and mine, are nothing I could take credit for, but are, rather, caused by chance, luck, fate, or accident.

As John and I sip our sweet iced tea and wait for our meals, I watch the overworked staff dash back and forth while I sit comfortably in my chair. I think about class differences and regional identities, the luxury of free time that allows my reading, writing, and contemplation. I think about the gentry I once wanted to be and will never become. Being waited on makes me feel uncomfortable and apologetic, I realize, as it did when I was a child at my grandmother's, where the women would cook for hours, and after dinner the men would retire to the living room to watch TV while the women cleaned up. As much as I like dining in the fancy atmosphere of the Greenbrier, I would not have made a very good Southern aristocrat. In fact, considering my penchant for underdogs, I would probably have done a lot better as a member of the Underground Railroad than as a plantation owner.

Social injustice, class differences, and unequal distributions of wealth have created so much of the beauty I love: the castles of Europe, the plantation houses along the Mississippi and the James, the mansions of Newport. Always driven more by aesthetics than ethics, I cherish that beauty despite its origin, as I am today relishing the opulent surroundings of the Greenbrier. It is a world I love to visit.

But I know in which world I belong, if I belong anywhere. What I want to share with John one day is not a plantation but a cabin or a farmhouse with a big porch, in the countryside or in some liberal small town. A wood-burning fireplace would be nice, and an orchard, and a small garden, and a wood-lot for chopping kindling and splitting chestnut oak—though, admittedly, I am so immersed in reading and writing that those elements might work better in fantasy than in fact.

Our chicken-salad croissants arrive, and our spinach/English walnut/mandarin orange salads, and as I thank the waitress and hear my home in her inflections, as I not-so-elegantly dig into my food, I remember a phrase I often use with my best friend Cindy.

My People. It started at one of the big gay marches in Washington, DC, when I was much younger. A kid used to the homogeneity of small towns, I studied with dubious fascination what I regarded as a cavalcade of shockingly colorful queers—some of them, to my inexperienced eyes, extreme and ridiculous freaks. I rolled my eyes with scorn—as I did years before at the Oak Supper Club, when I mocked those Summers County accents. I sighed resignedly, then said to Cindy, "These are . . . my people?"

My sense of irony is as sharp as many a gay man's, but there is little irony left in that phrase now. When I think of the drag queens, the radical fairies, the transgendered, when I think of the coal-miners, the truck-drivers, the railroad workers who live along Cabin Creek, down in Logan or up in the Potomac Highlands, I am certainly aware of our differences, but now, in the face of a world hostile to both hillbillies and queers, I am more interested in our outsider commonalities. I know them for who they are, and I know who I am. Today in the Greenbrier, amid aristocratic elegance I was not born for, as I smile at my lover and order my pecan pie, I am grateful at last to know my own people.

Tania, Sometimes

Will McNamara

April 21, 1974

"She's a Class A con artist, that one," my father said. In disgust, he threw the *Sunday Register* onto the floor, as if it had tainted his fingers. He reclined in his black Naugahyde chair, the orangey tip of a cigarette dangling from his mouth. I was stretched out on the floor in front of his stocking feet, pretending to look at the comics, but listening to them. "I'll bet she planned it all along."

"Oh, Bob," my mother said from her matching La-Z-Boy, across from him. "She's a rich girl, a co-ed. You think she wanted to be locked in a closet for fifty-seven days? I'm sure she had better options."

"Ha," he snorted. "Don't be so gullible. We're not talking about Des Moines, Iowa, here. No, sir. That's San Francisco, California. Land of fruits and nuts. I'll betcha she was caught fornicating with the Black Panthers and her father used all that *Citizen Kane* money to hush it up with this cockamamie kidnapping story."

Who's Citizen Kane, I thought, and made a mental note to ask about it later. I eavesdropped for a bit longer, but they continued to repeat things I'd heard them say before. I already knew what they thought about her.

For weeks, one of the main topics of conversation in our house and in the news was Patty Hearst. It had all started several weeks before, in early February, with her abduction. It was a Sunday night when *Mutual of Omaha's Wild Kingdom* was interrupted for a Special News Report. At first I thought it was going to be more boring stuff about Watergate and President Nixon with his bulldog wrinkly face, and I almost left the room. But then they started talking about a kidnapping and a newspaper heiress and California, and I was immediately hooked.

Identity Envy—Wanting to Be Who We Are Not
Published by The Haworth Press, Inc., 2007. All rights reserved.
doi:10.1300/5641_18

My parents probably didn't even know that I was aware of what was going on, because I was only nine years old at the time. But I did know about it, and just as the nation was obsessed with the case I had my own, more personal, obsession.

Every chance I got I listened to the radio, watched television, and scoured through newspapers and magazines for any new details about Patty. I am sure I knew much more about what happened than my parents did. I knew how she was taken from her apartment that night in her bathrobe, and put into the trunk of a car. I knew how she was kept in a closet for weeks and weeks while this group called the Symbionese Liberation Army—the SLA—brainwashed her. I heard the tape where she sent a message to her parents. "Mom, Dad, I'm okay." she said. "Just give them what they want."

That morning, when my parents weren't looking, I took the newspaper that my father had discarded and hid it under the comics page. As they continued talking, I left the downstairs family room and hurried up to my bedroom. From under my bed, I pulled out the shoebox where I kept my collection of clippings. I quickly scanned the latest front-page article. There were new details of the bank robbery and the woman who was killed. There was information about a new tape that had been released. The article said that Patty now called herself Tania and had announced that she would stay with her abductors and work to "free the planet from oppression." I didn't know what oppression meant, so I retrieved the dictionary from my desk. Oppression: a sense of being weighed down in body or mind.

I closely examined the grainy black-and-white photograph of Patty/Tania at the bank robbery. She stood between two rows of short thin poles that were roped together, like the kind they had at Sierra 3 Movie Theatre to block off the concession stand. She was wearing a stocking cap, but I couldn't tell what color it was. She held up a shotgun with both hands. I carefully cut out the headline and article, storing them in the shoebox. I then cut out the picture, but instead of the shoebox I hid it in my desk drawer, so I could get to it more easily.

Later that afternoon I rummaged through the front coat closet in the downstairs hallway and found a poofy red-knit stocking cap that my mother sometimes wore. I also found a brown suede coat that looked to be about right. I bundled up these items into a tight ball and ran upstairs to hide them.

That evening, as my parents became engrossed in the latest episode of *Barnaby Jones,* I said I had homework to do and excused myself for the evening. Once upstairs, I retrieved the cap and coat and locked myself in the bathroom. With the newspaper picture taped to the mirror, I quickly got into costume. I had to play with the cap for a while to make it look like the one she was wearing. But finally I had created what I thought was a fairly accurate likeness. I stood back and looked at myself. With an imaginary shotgun in my hand, I mimicked the way she stood behind the bank ropes. "I am Tania," I said quietly but fiercely into the mirror. I looked at myself from various angles. "Call me Tania." I stayed in the bathroom for a good hour, deep in fantasy, and then took off my costume and went to bed.

Several days later after school was out, the McAllister twins from across the street walked home with me and I asked them inside to play. Although they weren't identical, it was often difficult to tell them apart, so they wore different colors to distinguish themselves. That day Pam was in pink and Paula wore purple. The twins were aspiring little actresses and very active in the West Des Moines Community Playhouse. I enjoyed their company because with their theatrical tendencies it was easy to persuade them to act out my fantasies. Often we would run around my backyard with hooded sweatshirts tied over our shoulders to represent capes. They would be Wonder Woman and Batgirl. I played Robin, and we would spend hours running through the yard in passionate efforts to find Batman.

That afternoon we were upstairs in my bedroom. My mother was downstairs preparing dinner. "Let's do something different today," I said. "Let's play hostage." They were generally agreeable and we began to assign roles. After some negotiating, I convinced Pam and Paula that it would be more of an acting stretch for them if they pretended to be the kidnappers and I played the victim. I produced our props from under my bed, some long pieces of gnarly rope that I had taken from my father's tool chest in the garage, and my teenage sister's red bandana. The twins did not question why I had these props so readily available. I instructed them to blindfold me and tie my wrists and ankles tightly with the rope. I then crouched down in a fetal position in my closet. The area was appropriately tight and congested. My tennis racket and sneakers pressed against the small of my back.

Along with being the star of this production, my secondary role was director, and accordingly I gave the twins precise instructions for

what I wanted them to do and say. I pulled the closet door shut and became enveloped in darkness. The sticky, slightly ripened smell from
the inside of my closet filled my nostrils.

"PIG!" the twins shouted in unison, as I had instructed them, and
pounded on the door.

"You aren't ever going to get out of that closet!" Bang! Bang!

"No one is coming to get you, EVER!"

There was sudden silence, but I remained enthralled, deep in fantasy. I immersed myself in the imagined torment of Patty. I writhed
around in my closet and moaned theatrically. The blackness of the
closet was a hole into which I kept falling, deeper and deeper.

I heard the closet door open abruptly. Light seeped through the
cloth wrapped around my eyes. Suddenly the bandana was ripped off
and my mother stood above me, with the twins behind her. She
looked alarmed and confused. Pam and Paula immediately started
crying. "He made us tie him up! He made us say those things!"

My mother turned back to toward me. I saw in her eyes something
I'd never seen before, or at least not in that particular way. It was fear.
Fear of me, for me.

"Girls, I think you better run on home now," she said.

January 25, 2002

I am trapped on the Pacific Coast Highway. It is taking me almost
two hours to get home from work. I am held hostage by what seems
like an endless army of militant BMWs and Porsches. The only thing
that keeps me from going completely psychotic and doing major
damage to the car in front me is the thought of the double martini that
I will fix immediately upon walking through my door. I finally make
it home, get out of my suit, fix my drink, and get comfortable in front
of the TV. Two hundred channels to graze through. What's on? A
blizzard in Minnesota. Who cares? Vicki Lawrence in her Mama
drag. Skip. Ron Popeil spraying black paint on some pathetic man's
balding head. Give me a break.

Then there's Larry King's frog face staring out at me. His suspend-
ers and glasses are almost comical given the state I'm in. Usually I
can't tolerate him for very long, with his insipid questions and grating
habit of interrupting his guests. But I always check to see who he
might have on. His roster of guests often satisfies my appetite for

mindless pop culture. Where else can you find a full hour reserved for
Raquel Welch or Rock Hudson's ex-lover?

"Tonight, exclusive!" Larry brays. "Patty Hearst discusses her kidnapping by the Symbionese Liberation Army in 1974. New charges
brought in a notorious murder could put her back on the witness
stand."

Hmm, this will be interesting, I think. The last time I saw her was
in that John Waters film, *Serial Mom,* where she was bludgeoned by
Kathleen Turner for wearing white shoes after Labor Day.

She looks good, sophisticated. A Westport mother of two. It's great
that she's doing so well now, after all that trauma. When was it? Mid-
1970s? God, almost thirty years ago. Patty's on the show to discuss
the recent arrest of one of her female captors, who had been on the run
from the police for thirty years. Apparently this captor had been living quietly as a suburban mom in St. Paul. Her neighbors had no clue
of her terrorist past. Larry doesn't fail to waste precious minutes of
the hour with his inane questions. "So what was prison like?" he asks.
"Well, I wouldn't recommend it," Patty deadpans. Classic. You can
tell by the smirk on her face that she thinks he's a moron.

Suddenly a memory flashes in my mind. It emerges clearly and
without warning. I see my nine-year-old self, tied up in my bedroom
closet. A blindfold comes off my eyes and the light flashes in. My
mother is staring down at me, horrified, like she doesn't know who I
am. I flush with embarrassment, even though I am an adult man sitting alone, years and miles away from that incident. I had forgotten all
about that. What was I thinking? Who tied me up? Oh, yeah, those
McAllister twins from across the street. I organized it all, instructed
them on how to do it. Told them what to say. God, I was a weird kid. I
laugh at the thought of it, it seems like another lifetime. Yet, it also
makes me feel unsettled.

I certainly had my share of childhood obsessions. Most were fairly
reasonable, at least for a sexually curious, prepubescent gay boy.
There was Peter Tork of the Monkees. Everyone else (well, girls that
is) fawned over Davy Jones, but I went right for Peter. His sweet,
slightly dazed smile and the dishwater blonde hair. Then came Donny
Osmond and Fonzie. I gave a great deal of thought to what it would be
like to be married to both of them.

Of course there was Farrah Fawcett-Majors. She dominated my
thoughts all through 1977, her posters covering every inch of my bed-

room wall. I even sent a letter inviting her and Lee to stay with us if they ever came through Iowa. My parents encouraged this interest, as they thought it was perfectly normal for an eleven-year old boy to have little fantasies about the beautiful blonde Angel. What they didn't know was that I didn't want to kiss Farrah, I wanted to be Farrah.

But what was the deal with Patty Hearst? What was the appeal with her? There must have been something there, as I was completely fixated on her for months. As I get slowly more intoxicated, I sit on my sofa and ponder this. Larry King's interview has ended, and I am still churning over childhood memories from thirty years ago. Could it be that as a child I tapped into a psychological association with the whole closet thing? Patty was trapped in a closet, gay people come out of the closet. No, that's probably martini logic. Even now, that explanation is just too poetic to be accurate. Maybe I romanticized her kidnapping. The danger and excitement of having people—let alone an entire nation—searching for you. To a child who felt overlooked and unappreciated, in a warped way having all that national attention must have been rather attractive. That explanation is getting closer, but it doesn't seem quite right either.

Then I suddenly know the reason. It's Tania, of course. Along with the image of being willingly tied up in my bedroom closet, I flash on my bathroom monologues. I see myself standing before the mirror, imaginary gun raised toward the ceiling. The truth of the matter is that I coveted Patty's alter ego Tania. Whether it was created as a result of brainwashing is beside the point. Patty was an innocent, a good girl. Tania was a revolutionary who robbed banks, held machine guns, and told motherfuckers to get down on the ground.

Patty wasn't to blame, Tania was. Tania did those things, not Patty. And yet they were both part of the same person, weren't they? Which one was real? Which one was manufactured? My thoughts are getting tangled up, deluded by the alcohol. But, yep, that's it. That explains my childhood obsession with her. It must be. Granted, I wouldn't have been able to come to this realization without years of psychotherapy. Obsessing over Patty Hearst was the least of my troubles.

But I suppose even as a kid back in Des Moines, I sensed that the duality of myself would be one of the subterraneous foundations of my psyche. The inner life of thoughts and desires that no one ever sees, but they are always there. The good kid who people see and think they know. The expectations that must be met. It was certainly the part I played. My identity was clearly based on how other people saw me, and as long as I furnished that image upon their demand then I would know who I was.

But what about that person underneath, what about him? The one who has the ongoing inner dialogue of thoughts that he can never share. The one who wanted to be something that other people didn't want him to be. The one who is living a life that is so different from the way he thought it would be. Is that person the real self, and is the one who everyone sees just a fabricated shell? In my own duality, which one is the alter ego?

It's late . . . I've got to go to bed, I think. I stumble upstairs, brush my teeth, get into my pajamas. My head will throb in the morning, no doubt. Taking one last glance into the mirror, I laugh a bit. No one's around, so why not?

"Goodnight, Tania," I say. "Sleep well."

Child Star

Max Pierce

Few child actors sustain a career beyond puberty. It is a difficult time physically and emotionally, and Hollywood has never suffered from a shortage of fresh juvenile talent eager to seize the spotlight. The luckiest ones fall into obscurity, trading camera angles for meaningful careers. Others become notorious casualties.

By age twelve, for the talented Laura Pierce, as both a television star and having several memorable films under her tiny belt, the only way to go seemed down. Personal tragedy kept her mostly off-screen from age thirteen until seventeen, but she rebounded with a vengeance, propelling forward to new acclaim and a cinema endurance that a select few from the golden age (Roddy McDowell, Natalie Wood), and even fewer of her contemporaries (only Jodie Foster comes to mind) have achieved.

Coming to prominence as the death rattle of the studio system became a final gasp, the Dallas-born moppet, at the ripe old age of five, was the last contract player signed by the once-mighty MGM. With the ink barely dry, the studio loaned her to Twentieth Century-Fox while deciding what to do. She made an auspicious debut on TV's *Batman* as the young sister of Boy Wonder Robin during the show's last season. Returning to MGM, where the famous "little red schoolhouse" was reopened amid much fanfare, she appeared in her first feature film, *Happiness*. In late 1969 she played a ghost in the television "Movie of the Week" *Daughter of the Mind,* starring old-timers Ray Milland and Gene Tierney.

After hearing rumblings of a clever family sitcom being produced at Paramount, MGM-TV, whose successes had been limited to *The Man from U.N.C.L.E, Flipper,* and *Dr. Kildare* jumped feet first in the water. Utilizing their old back lot sets from the Andy Hardy movies and *Meet Me in St. Louis,* they filmed their sitcom concept on a mod-

Identity Envy—Wanting to Be Who We Are Not
Published by The Haworth Press, Inc., 2007. All rights reserved.
doi:10.1300/5641_19

est budget. The show was *Riverview Mansion,* and ostensibly focused on a trio of mischievous siblings who lay claim to an abandoned estate as their clubhouse. Running on ABC Friday nights at eight o'clock from the fall of 1969 through the spring of 1975, *Riverview Mansion* joined an evening of classic favorites such as *The Brady Bunch, The Partridge Family,* and *The Odd Couple.*

Buoyed by the audience's response to its younger talent, MGM dropped most of the adults in the second season and dusted off their Our Gang franchise, adding a new Spanky, Alfalfa, and Darla (but avoiding a latter-day Buckwheat) to join Pierce, her seldom-seen older brother (Eric Shea), and younger sister (Kristy McNichol—in reality one month older than Pierce). The show stayed in the Top 20 its entire run.

Off the set, MGM was undergoing a dramatic change; after decades of boasting "More Stars Than There Are in the Heavens," declining fortunes and revolving management led to a 1969 sale to billionaire Kirk Kerkorian, and Pierce was there as the historic studio sold off its costumes and props in April of 1970. "I didn't understand it," she recalled later, "but I knew something terrible was happening, yet was powerless to stop it." Despite a photo of the eleven-year-old Pierce smiling with Kerkorian at the grand opening of the original MGM Hotel and Casino in Las Vegas, and another posed shot of the mogul presenting her with a brand new car upon her eighteenth birthday; today she holds no affection for him.

Riverview Mansion sustained the studio during these lean years, a fact not lost on its star's parents, who negotiated her earnings higher each season and banked the money away. As the series' popularity grew, so did its budget and fanciful nature, and the gang's clubhouse would witness elaborate musical numbers, ghosts, and numerous preteen crushes.

Although a veteran of several films, Pierce famously lost the role in *Paper Moon* that brought Tatum O'Neal an Oscar, and of Regan, the possessed child in *The Exorcist.* Her best big-screen success, without a doubt, was the disaster epic *The Poseidon Adventure,* where the character of Robin—in Paul Gallico's novel a boy who drowns—received a sex change and survival on film.

By mid-1975, with *Mansion* on the chopping block (both *The Brady Bunch* and *The Partridge Family* had been axed one year before), it was rumored Pierce would transition full-time to the big screen. Although considered for the role of Iris in *Taxi Driver*, her mother's refusal to allow her daughter to play a prostitute provided Jodie Foster a leap to stardom. A year later, Pierce took over for Foster in the family-friendly *Freaky Friday*.

Tragedy struck in June 1975, when Pierce's mother was found dead of a drug overdose. With her father unable to care for her, she moved in with relatives in rural Texas. Finding it difficult to shake fame in a small town, she returned to Los Angeles and attended private boarding school, with plans to enroll in UCLA after graduation. In 1979, *People* magazine caught up with her working part-time as a salesperson in a Bullock's department store near the college campus, contentedly retired from movies.

But fate had other ideas. Shortly thereafter, she returned to MGM, cast in the comical and chilling remake of the campy Joan Crawford film *I Saw What You Did*. Released in May 1980 and riding the wave of teen horror films, the movie became a sleeper hit of the summer. This success led to an audition with Steven Spielberg, and Pierce landed the role of Marian Ravenswood in *Raiders of the Lost Ark*. At age nineteen, she found herself receiving an Oscar as Best Supporting Actress for her efforts. Although her on-screen chemistry with Harrison Ford was dynamic (and both denied rumors of an affair), she was not cast in the subsequent prequel, wryly observing, "Steven had met Kate [Capshaw] and I was good friends with Amy [Irving, Spielberg's ex-wife]."

Neither her career nor love life suffered, for also in 1981 she starred in the romantic comedy *Love Among the Millionaires,* earning her place among Hollywood's top comedians. Although her screen appearances became more infrequent in the last decade, Laura Pierce nonetheless remains a popular and influential player in Hollywood. Having invested wisely, she pursues projects of personal interest versus commercial vehicles, including her fondness for remakes of films from the Golden Era. She also honed her writing talents, often as an uncredited (but well compensated) script doctor. Her honest, yet tongue-in-cheek look at her childhood career in 1987's *The First Hundred Years* became a bestseller.

As for *Riverview Mansion,* the original program has rarely left television since 1975, becoming an early staple for cable's Nickelodeon, then resurrected on TV Land. With reluctance, Pierce gave in to appearing in a reunion show in 1988 that topped the ratings, but later stated she found this "return" "emotionally cleansing." While many of her former co-stars rue their legacy to the former show and have had public scrapes with the law, Pierce holds fond memories for the past, but "doesn't like to go there," declining any interviews about her days as a child star.

Unlike her old nemesis Tatum O'Neal, Laura Pierce has escaped a scandal-plagued adulthood. Of her now thirty-something years in the spotlight, she laughs, perhaps a bit too sarcastically, "I wouldn't have changed either the good or the bad, and continue to look for the good. After all, this is Hollywood."

Actress—Selected filmography (2000s) (1990s) (1980s) (1970s) (1960s)

- E! The True Hollywood Story "The Curse of Riverview Mansion" (2000) . . . Herself (archival footage)
- Something's Got to Give (1998)·. . . Ellen Arden
- Ghost (1990) . . . Molly Jensen
- Holiday (1989) . . . Slim Wilson
- Return to Riverview (1988) . . . Laura
- The Time of Their Lives (1987) . . . Melody Allen
- Spitfire (1986) . . . Lola Burns
- Desperately Seeking Susan (1985) . . . Roberta Glass
- Thursdays 'Til 8 (1984) . . . Cynthia
- Risky Business (1983) . . . Lana
- Personal Property (1982) . . . Crystal Weatherby
- Victor/Victoria (1982) . . . Norma Cassady
- Love Among the Millionaires (1981). . . Pepper
- Raiders of the Lost Ark (1981) . . . Marian Ravenswood
- I Saw What You Did (1980) . . . Libby Mannering
- Freaky Friday (1976) . . . Annabel Andrews
- The Poseidon Adventure (1973) . . . Robyn Shelby
- Shipwreck! (1972 (TV) . . . Dana
- The Jungle Adventure (1972) . . . Sara Browning
- The Pet Motel (1971) (TV) . . . Alice
- Happiness (1969) . . . Charity Hope
- Riverview Mansion (1969) TV Series . . . Laura Pierce (1969-1975)
- Daughter of the Mind (1969) (TV) . . . Mary Constable
- "Batman" (1966/II) TV Series . . . Jennifer Grayson (1968)

The End. Roll credits. Made in Hollywood, USA, by Metro-Goldwyn-Mayer. A Division of Loew's Incorporated.

Nice bio, huh? I write a lot about movies, television, and stars, and this particular actress's life is a subject quite close to home. Although almost a modern fairy-tale, like any classic movie it features moments of pathos, yet a dash of music to keep things light and the requisite happy ending. The theme is Triumph over Adversity.

What's that? You can't quite place the actress or her hit show? And those movies—you think many of them starred other people?

Well, that's how I'd like it to have been, complete with selected filmography. Movies and television were my rock growing up; giving me places to aspire, to visit, rainbows to follow. I credit them with shaping my life, in fact, saving my life. Max Pierce may not have attended MGM's little red schoolhouse, but I learned to talk, walk, and survive from film, that portal to other worlds, alternately as an instructional tool and life preserver. Read further and you'll find what happened in my "first hundred" years, and how various ingredients I collected became the elements of fantasy that dominated my thoughts—a fantasy that showed me an escape hatch existed from narrow-minded towns too small to have sidewalks, and led me to strolling the Walk of Fame in Hollywood, where I live today. My successes are tinged with sadness, for the two who never doubted my ability to accomplish any goal did not live to share my joys.

Only children are terrifically spoiled: for my fourth birthday in 1966, I received a Texas-sized color console television. Like others, my parents used the TV as a babysitter. I spent countless hours watching that big rounded screen and became hooked on the images. I can even recall the shows I watched: *Batman, Peyton Place, Ozzie and Harriet,* even a bad TV remake of *Laura,* starring Jackie Kennedy's sister Lee Radziwill, Farley Granger, and Arlene Francis.

We were an odd family, never serving as role models like the Nelsons, not as eccentric as the Addams, more suited for a soap opera. Daddy was fifty-nine when I was born and had two grown children from his first marriage. He had worked for Al Capone; "repossessing

cars" was the official job description, but long after he'd left Chicago
for Dallas, he slept with a revolver in his nightstand drawer and a
small pistol under his pillow. His second marriage, the one *before* my
mother, was to Helen, a small-town Catholic girl nineteen years his
junior. Helen and Daddy liked to drink—a lot—and their relationship
could be characterized as, uh, volatile. Here's a glimpse: one night after too much Scotch, Helen attacked my father with a butcher knife,
and he responded by knocking her through a plate glass window.
Helen's adventures didn't end with her divorce from Daddy; she
turned up dead, and her boyfriend—believed to be responsible—disappeared thereafter, dispensed with by my father—or so his admirers
claimed. I never received clear answers to the myriad of questions
these stories inspired. Our family, true to its deep Southern roots, remains excellent at not discussing history and experts at reinventing
facts.

Daddy owned a collection of hamburger stands, also called beer
joints, although Mama politely referred to them as restaurants, and
my earliest memories are invested in sitting in warm kitchens, swip-
ing cheese slices out of a walk-in refrigerator, or skipping behind
enormous metal cases that smelled of barley. I played pinball or chose
songs off a Rock-Ola jukebox. (Another of Daddy's ventures was a
vending machine company that supplied his cafes and other busi-
nesses with cigarettes, pin ball, and records.) If I was hungry, I either
went to the kitchen and had the cook (almost always black and treated
like a member of our family) whip up something, or plopped down at
a table and the waitress (always a white older woman) would take my
order: the child star alone in the complicated world of adults. And the
stories: besides people being knocked through windows or threatened
by knives, extramarital affairs and the settling of scores were related
as casually as if we were talking about the weather. These tales filled
my days and nights and, combined with television, fired my imagination.

After a cyclone like Helen, with her penchant for dramatic exits, no
wonder Daddy was attracted to my mother—another simple country
girl twenty-five years younger than him. In my father, I imagine
Mama saw a worldliness and adventure far removed from her roots in
the soil of South Dallas County. Before Daddy, my mother's link to
glamour had been via my Uncle Pick, who lived next door to actress
Linda Darnell's family. Mama brought her own baggage, never re-

covering from divorcing her high school sweetheart and the loss of her two brothers to war. Mama also hid, but not too well, a prescription drug addiction. And although he tried, Daddy couldn't stop her from popping pills.

As for me, child of these two different people, I was a combination of their best and worst traits, and it's easy to see how my yearning for drama was inherent. I began reading at age two, and thus was considered a child genius. It wouldn't do for me to be average, and the pressure was on from an early age to achieve greatness and avoid mistakes, but that's where the definition of "great" is conflicted. As long as I "made him proud," Daddy had no long-term strategy for me. Mama's plan had me becoming either a doctor or lawyer (or ideally both) and my professional success would rescue her from her multiple depressions. She even forecasted her own involvement with my career: as receptionist in my law (and/or medical) office, a side effect of her love of *Perry Mason*. It was working for a doctor that she first became hooked on pills, so by having a doctor for a son I reckon she thought she'd get a substantial discount on her drugs.

Mama didn't exactly live in the real world. She admonished me to never fight, never argue, and always turn the other cheek. Her Golden Rule pacifism got me called names, shoved, and looked upon as the stereotypical sissy "brain" with four eyes, buck teeth, and a Little Lord Fauntleroy wardrobe.

So that big color television, broadcasting the three major networks, PBS, an independent station that ran old movies, and, if the rabbit ears were pointed right, an occasional UHF channel, began shaping my dreams and shined a welcome light into our rambling, totally electric, ranch-style house. A house located on the outskirts of a dead town thirty miles northwest of Dallas. We were in the country for a reason: city living was deemed unacceptable for my father's seesawing health. Not one to retire and obey doctor's orders, Daddy escaped to Dallas every day, while Mama and I grew bored in the sticks. Mama's goal was clear: get back to Dallas, where there were grand movie theaters, all-night pharmacies, and people didn't wear overalls and twang every other word. Daddy was expected to die at any moment, and I would grow up, get that law/medical degree, and buy Mama a big 1920s house on Dallas's elegant Swiss Avenue. But I had other ideas.

My fascination with Los Angeles started about age four, believe it or not, when our next-door neighbor Andrea Duane took a bus trip to California, a concept akin to an all-expense-paid trip to Mars. Then between age five and six, the twin tragedies of Bobby Kennedy's assassination and the Manson Murders piqued my interest in this mysterious city Where Things Happened.

Back in Dallas, Daddy paid his monthly visit to Mr. Hatley's Pharmacy, and he'd buy me the current issue of *Famous Monsters of Filmland* as a treat. *FM* was edited by one Forrest J. Ackerman, also known as the Ackermonster, who lived in a "lair" called the Acker-mansion in Horrorwood, Karloffornia. I got the joke. I devoured these journalistic retellings of spooky movies, with great photos and what I'd term "campy" humor. This only increased my desire to go west. By the time I watched the *I Love Lucy* episodes set in Hollywood, I knew my destiny lie not in Dallas as a doctor or lawyer, but in Hollywood—lunching at The Brown Derby, dancing at Mocambo, and working at Metro-Goldwyn-Mayer.

My parents listened patiently to my request to move—I wanted us all to go immediately—but they did nothing to either encourage or dissuade me, assuming that anything I set my mind to do, I would. But taking me to see Disney on Parade as it traveled through the Fort Worth Coliseum only made me pine for the real Disneyland more and I pitched numerous scenes of kiddie hysteria. Stubborn as a mule, my mind was made up: I would live in Hollywood. The trick was how to get there. This goal conflicted entirely with Mama's own dreams for our future, and had she lived, my life would be quite different. In fact, I expect I'd be dead and buried in the family plot in Keller, a victim of repressed desires, unfulfilled dreams, and easy access to Seconal. But I refused to be a victim.

In the third grade, a wonderful thing happened. Our teacher read us Laura Ingalls Wilder's Little House books—most of them, skipping *The Long Winter* and *Little Town on the Prairie* due to time constraints. After hearing *On the Banks of Plum Creek* read aloud, I decided, at age eight, I would be a writer and create my own series of books. Being an unimaginative little plagiarist, I came up with titles such as *Little House in California* and *On the Banks of Hunters Pond* and created cover art for both epics not dissimilar to Mrs. Wilder's. About this same time, the kids on our street passed around Nancy Drew and The Hardy Boys to compare. I stuck with Nancy Drew, who accomplished every goal with wits and a chic wardrobe. Girls just seemed to have an easier life: being able to read, being quiet, and using their intelligence to get something, while not playing sports any more strenuous than jump rope. So rather than making myself the main character, I borrowed "Laura" from my new favorite writer, but she and I were essentially the same.

I skipped over to what I planned as the third book in the series and scribbled out three chapters. The plot revolved around Laura and a brother/sister team who discover a haunted house. Loving television, I segued from the idea of a book to an episodic comedy called *Riverview Mansion*. The name came from a location in Nancy Drew's *The Hidden Staircase* and I pulled plots from my favorite TV shows like *Dark Shadows,* a gothic soap opera. For the next few months, I walked around the extensive woods that surrounded our house with my four dogs, acting out scenes from the show.

I liked being in this new world where spooky and magical things happened, where problems were minor and wrapped up in twenty-five minutes. If the going got tough, a song and a tap dance cured all. This was the opposite of home, where the soap opera continued. Daddy was in and out of the hospital, each trip predicted to be his last—although my grandmother foretold "He will outlive us all." Which Daddy did. Grandma's death, another link to the past broken, hastened my mother's decline; pills became a way of life rather than an occasional escape.

Being the smartest kid in class and perhaps a little too aware of the adult problems around me meant I adopted a too-serious demeanor, bursting into tears at any slight. As a boy who preferred Barbies over baseball and Nancy Drew over the Hardy Boys, my life invited challenge, but I couldn't rely on the adults to make things easier. Having a mother addicted to painkillers and an absent father due to illness added to my isolation. I didn't want my real-life friends to see what kind of haunted house I lived in and I stopped inviting people over. I amassed a sizable collection of board games that I played alone.

But with my pack of imaginary friends, culled from reruns of *The Little Rascals,* I was happy and no one cared what my parents were like. Maybe on some level I connected with child actors who grew up too soon. Imagination ran wild and I loved every minute of it. Each night, when my parents retired to their respective ends of the house, I went into the living room, arranged the furniture like a situation comedy set, and put on records. No longer was I stranded in Keller, Texas, population 820, but I was on a hit television series, living the high life in Hollywood. Daddy slept; and as long as the stereo wasn't too loud, he left me alone. Mama was always conked out in the den.

This parallel universe became infinitely more pleasurable to be in: where children ruled, parents were nonexistent, and everyone had a grand Technicolor time. Aside from the Technicolor and grand time, it was pretty much similar to my real life. I spent hours in front of the stereo playing soundtracks to Disney films and a grab bag of oldies (The Platters, The Andrews Sisters, and Tom Jones), and acting out episode after episode of *Riverview Mansion*. Laura developed her first crush at age eleven, on my neighbor John Drake, an eighth grader who never knew either of us existed. My fictional television series was a ratings hit, and this led my characters on to feature film appearances and more. When Tatum O'Neal took home that Oscar in 1974, I cried and cried, feeling cheated and that time was running out. In a way it was.

The life I shared with my parents began reaching a climax of disastrous proportions shortly after my twelfth birthday. Reality started sticking its ugly head in more and more, upsetting the delicate balance. Mama, zonked out on Miltown, crashed her car in front of the school bus, and I heard the jeers of my classmates as the police carted us home. Two months later the same car got stuck in a swollen creek and Mama almost drowned. One by one, my beloved dogs disappeared, their fates unknown.

On top of this, former child actor George "Spanky" McFarland, of the *Our Gang* comedies I cherished, lived in our town, and his daughter was one grade ahead of me. Naturally, or by force, she participated in the eighth grade play. The school was abuzz that the reclusive Spanky was attending his daughter's theatrical debut. Nervous at seeing a real movie star in the flesh, yet being aware that the Spanky I loved from circa 1937 had grown up, I was not ready for the sight of an overweight, middle-aged man with a permanent scowl on his face, as far removed from youth and innocence as one could be. My smile at him garnered a frown in return, a scarier sight than anything in *Famous Monsters of Filmland*.

I can trace my obsession with MGM to the summer of 1974. KERA, Dallas's PBS station, broadcast a series of MGM's silent films, with Greta Garbo, Lon Chaney (who I'd read about in *Famous*

Monsters), and Joan Crawford. These films captivated me; they had a look about them, a sheen that was indeed magic. Added to this was the fact that most of the *Our Gang* shorts I loved were preceded by a roaring Leo.

Within the next year, my mother's addiction took her life, an act that none of us had calculated, and Max Pierce was thrust into a new reality-based series, one far removed from a musical soundstage. This storyline featured my father's declining health and ultimate death, which triggered a custody battle for me—or more importantly my trust fund. In the chaos, my records (the soundtrack to numerous *Riverview Mansion* episodes), my last remaining dog, the toys, the fifty or so precious issues of *Famous Monsters,* those childhood drafts of *On the Banks of Hunters Pond,* indeed all the tangible elements of my life, including photos from age six to twelve, were lost, sold off or scrapped like the trappings of MGM. By divine intervention, the Laura Ingalls Wilder books and most of the Nancy Drew Mysteries were spared, and I carried them with me in a battered peach suitcase as I moved from one relative to another, no longer a precocious moppet to be petted and pampered, but a teenager growing up too fast. My travels took me to different towns, different churches, different schools, included sexual abuse, betrayal, and what seemed to be perpetual abandonment, but never once did I stop my search for that Yellow Brick Road that led to Hollywood. Lying in yet another new bed, the old characters from the living room visited me in mental reruns and grew up with me as I went through high school. For a while, the fictional Laura gave up acting and married either a student council member, high school jock, or the richest boy in school, depending on who I had a crush on that week, and as I settled into one high school, she did too, with our mutual career goal to be a high school Spanish teacher.

As soon as I could get away from my remaining family, I abandoned my mother's plans for medical/law school and became a theater major, learning to sing somewhat on key, tapping out a weak time step, and joyously reconnecting with the part of me that yearned to be on stage. I curtailed my drawl by parroting movie dialog. In the process, I found that being a professional actor took a lot of commitment—something I struggled with. After a time, I realized I desired a steady income over the quest for fame and landed a job in retail, moving up the management ladder rung by rung. It would be this career choice that took me west.

Although acting was behind me, I never stopped writing, keeping diaries, creating parodies of *Dynasty* and *Falcon Crest* based on my own life when not writing clever copy to sell satin pajamas or Calvin Klein's Jeans. My primary hobby became watching and reading about old movies. I thank God for the VCR.

Life has a way of working itself out, even in the darkest hours. I left Texas and moved to Hollywood. The Brown Derby had closed and there was no Mocambo to mambo at. I donated to Goodwill my child's suitcase, the one that had taken me through my transition from poor little rich boy to adult. Although they weren't there to cheer the realization of my dream, I knew my parents approved.

Eager to absorb everything about Los Angeles I had missed, I immersed myself in the city's legends and became an advocate for historic preservation. As a volunteer, I've given walking tours of Paramount, Fox, and the old MGM studio, where, in another dimension, *Riverview Mansion* was filmed and my fictional friends worked and played.

I began writing more and more: journalistic pieces on classic Hollywood, the city that captures my interest still, and was astonished to see them published. Still determined to create a book series, I now modeled my fiction after Armistead Maupin instead of Laura Ingalls Wilder. If you're familiar with her *Little House* series and Los Angeles neighborhoods, you may get goose bumps, as I did, to realize for a while I lived *By the Shores of Silver Lake*.

I even met the Ackermonster, almost choking up when I shook his hand and thanked him for *Famous Monsters* and for inspiring me, not only as a writer but also as a movie fan. This meeting happened not in his lair, but at a corner coffee shop where, before his health declined, Mr. Ackerman and I ate breakfast twice or so a week, although at separate tables. My childhood experience with the grouchy Spanky McFarland prevents me from talking to icons who might prove disappointing, and Mr. Ackerman was perennially surrounded by a young crowd of sycophantic ne'er do wells, content to let him pick up the check.

Despite what you may have inferred, the actress Laura Pierce is no longer a prevalent or dominating part of my life, although when a good film role comes along I can easily see her in it. No, I have never harbored any desire to change my sex and "become" her. I haven't even done drag on Halloween. I'm much more appealing and comfortable as a leather daddy than as the new Jean Harlow, if I do say so myself. Laura is more like the sister I always wanted, a mirror image when I was young, but now complementary, the feminine to my masculine, the salt to my pepper. Neither of us enjoy reflecting on the past—I don't like "going there" either—and while Laura's biography was a breeze to write, Max's True Life portion was a difficult execution that brought agony and another round of tears. I will always miss my parents.

But one statement transcends the line between reel and the real: Hollywood remains a place where dreams come true. And I continue to look for the good.

Acting American

Robert Boulanger

Les Grèves was a vacation colony run by the good Franciscan Fathers, forty miles northeast of Montreal. Every summer, three hundred boys spent weeks or months there. My older brother Michel and I stayed the entire summer. All the boys slept in a large two-floor dormitory—a big, airy barn of a building with rows of beds on several floors. Michel and I had our beds on the second floor, about thirty beds apart.

It was 1949 and I was eight years old. On one of these hot, humid summer nights in Quebec, by the Ouareau River, I woke up crying from a nightmare. Afraid to stay in my bed, I got up, walked over to Michel's bed, and gave his shoulder a tentative shake.

"What's the matter?" Michel said, his voice deep from slumber. "Why are you crying?"

"Because I can't become a priest. I'm not like the others. I'm different."

"Go back to bed, and stop bawling," Michel groaned.

I had realized at that very young age that I was different. For three summers at Les Grèves, I would fall in love with one of the Brothers or lay workers. It was always very platonic, yet extremely intense and consuming—full of guilt and mixed emotions, with hours of late-night fantasies.

That summer Albert was the one I fell for. Albert was mysterious. He was quiet and kept to himself, and I could sense he was hiding something, some deep pain inside. He was the organist and singer at the small little white-steepled church run for the boys by the Franciscan Fathers. I sat at the top of the stairs that led to the organ balcony, looking up at him playing and singing Gounod's *Ave Maria* and I would cry my eyes out. Once in a while he would look down at me

Identity Envy—Wanting to Be Who We Are Not
Published by The Haworth Press, Inc., 2007. All rights reserved.
doi:10.1300/5641_20

and smile warmly and I would feel this tingle all through my body. The tingle of being alive.

Over fifty years later, I can still remember the beautiful fabric of his pants—thin lines of beige and red and green forming a plaid against an earth-tone background. Albert had taste. He was not your usual French-Canadian of the 1950s. He had lived in the USA—"O Zetas Zunis." He was everything I ever wanted to be.

My father Raymond worked for Alcan, the Canadian equivalent of Alcoa, and everyone called him Ray. My grandfather was François, a machinist for the newspaper *Le Canada,* but everyone called him Frank. I was next in line to have an anglicized surname. I was never Robert, pronounced "Robaire." I was Bobby, pronounced "Bahbay."

In the 1950s in Canada, being French-Canadian wasn't easy. Colonized by the British and brainwashed by our beloved Catholic religion, we believed we were all "born for a little bread," born poor and meant to mind our place. My father knew that for his son—a French-Canadian—to get ahead, he would have to learn English. I did my first through third grade in French. I took fourth grade twice—once in French and once in English. When I started, I knew very little English but I was an excellent mimic.

The very first English phrase I learned in Mrs. McEvoy's fourth grade class at Saint Domenics was "Blessed Is the Fruit of Thy Womb Jesus." I had no idea what the words meant. "Di Um Jesus Di Um Jesus," over and over and over. I had not yet perfected the "th" sound—the most difficult Anglophone sound for a French-Canadian to achieve. When I was older, I would always say "Excuse me" in English if I bumped into someone. I soon realized that I did not want to be who or where I was. I didn't want to be the good little choirboy praying before he goes to sleep, dreaming of one day becoming a priest. I wanted to be the bad boy, torn between God and Albert, dreaming of those pants, and pretending to be American.

It was easy for me to pretend I was someone else. I certainly didn't want to be who I was.

Thankfully, I had an insightful mother. Knowing my talents as mimicker and pretender, she sent me to a private dramatic school for children and grown ups—the school of Madame Jean-Louis Audet, the teacher of all the best French actors in Quebec of the 1940s and 1950s. My mother must have sensed that this would give me purpose as well as being a way to retain my French heritage while attending an Anglophone school.

At twelve I was "Bobby" on Madame Audet's weekly CBC radio soap for children. Things took off from there. I had my own television series for teenagers on the French CBC when I was fourteen. And at fourteen, I was sexually active with much older men. There seemed to be willing men everywhere I looked. And I was looking. Looking for acceptance, attention, love. I was a very talented young actor but unaware of it. I certainly wasn't disciplined. My sexual drive, my other self, was what motivated me. In many ways, it dictated how I lived and how my future would be played out.

As I grew older and discovered new places to meet men, I soon realized that if I saw a handsome man and then heard him speaking French, I would completely lose interest. I wanted English-speaking men. And I knew where to find them. My favorite men? Americans. By the time I was seventeen, I had slept with an English-speaking man in every hotel in Montreal and had fallen in love with some of them, if only for one night. I can remember walking home one morning from downtown Montreal to my neighborhood miles away, walking so I could remain in the moment, smelling the man from the night before on me, tasting him still, not wanting to be contaminated by others on the bus or trolley, reliving the bliss I had experienced the prior night, a bliss made more sweet because I knew I would probably never see him again. I was walking home, singing and humming. "Once, I had a Secret Love . . ."

I acquired a certain flair for identifying Americans in a bar. By their socks, shoes, buttoned-down shirts, or even just a plain white T-shirt and, oh yes, the graduation ring. This was a dead give away. If the man sporting the graduation ring wasn't an American, he was at least someone who went to school there, spoke English, and could play the part.

But my religion pulled at me—a cycle of confessions, communion, and the promise and conviction that I would never have sex with a man again. But I always did. With Americans, though, it was different. It just wasn't a sin for me to have sex in English with an American. If we were having sex and speaking English, then I wasn't in Quebec and I wasn't really me and I wasn't committing any sin. I was someone else—an American or English boy. I didn't have to feel guilty about anything.

After a few more years of successes on live radio, live television, and the stage in both French and English, I ran away from everything I knew. I could not breathe the air of Quebec anymore. My sexual self, that bad American boy, convinced my other self, the good Catholic French-Canadian boy, that I should set out for London, England, to audition for the Royal Academy of Dramatic Art (RADA). I convinced everyone else, too. In retrospect, it was quite a crazy dream for a young French-Canadian. Other French-Canadian actors who left Quebec to better themselves headed off to Mother France and the Academie Française. I couldn't conceive of going to France. As much as I convinced my parents and myself that I was going to London to become a great actor, I was going there for sexual freedom. I found nothing about French men attractive, so how could I go to France? They all seemed sissified, feminine. When I would hear dirty phrases in French, I wasn't excited. I was just disgusted. On the other hand, hearing a man, any man, say "suck that cock" in English made me weak at the knees.

Of course, it's easy now to see why I found French and French-Canadian men so unattractive. It had nothing to do with them. They were too much like me—the language they spoke, their suspect masculinity. I had been raised to believe that being French was being second-class. It was the English-Canadians who were the important ones. As long as I stayed in Quebec and stayed French, I would never amount to anything. I would never be free. And being a Canadian, I was a British subject. In England, I could easily find a job and get health care. In America I would have to fend for myself. I wasn't ready for that. And besides, everyone knew that all the great actors were British.

I booked a trip on the HMS Caledonia, a small British cargo ship that sailed from Montreal, up the Saint Lawrence River, across the Atlantic, and ended up in the port of the city of Ipswich, just sixty miles from London. It took fourteen days and cost me fourteen dollars. And I had sex with some of the crew while crossing, of course. After all, they were English.

I arrived in London in early December 1958. I was seventeen and yearning to discover more about myself. In my teenage shortsightedness, though, I only thought about discovering more of my sexual self. My talent for acting and the idea that I would become a great actor in English vanished as soon as I set foot on British soil. I never made it to RADA—not to audition, not even a walk in front of the building on Bayswater Road. It was all a sham, though I don't think I knew that consciously at the time. Like a good Catholic boy from Quebec, I convinced myself that I wasn't good enough, that the instructors at RADA would laugh me off the stage. My salvation, I decided, lay in finding a handsome Englishman or American to fall in love with. Instead of acting on stage, I went in search of Americans in the coffee houses and private gay bars of Soho's Wardor Street.

With the connections I had made at an English-language theatre company in Montreal, I easily found a temporary job and lodging. After only a few months, however, I became homesick and got tired of sleeping around. My evenings seemed an endless cycle of one-night stands with older men, few of whom seemed interested in anything besides the sexual thrill of bedding of a teenage boy with a French-Canadian accent. I was as exotic to them as they were to me and it left me feeling empty. I had come to London to accomplish something and what did I have to show for it? My mother sent long, tear-stained letters pleading with me to come home. When she offered to pay for a ticket on the SS America, the fastest ship of its time, I finally caved in. I would return home a failure, but at least I would be home.

It was springtime in Quebec when I arrived, the best time to return because it is the beginning of nature's cycle. Everything was awakening from winter's grip, and despite my feelings of regret and guilt and failure, it seemed I really could start over again. Like my escape to London, this too was an illusion. My first task was to get back into the theatre scene. But in the very short time I was gone, something had happened. There were no parts and few auditions. I didn't understand. I'd been a popular actor on radio and television. How could they have forgotten me so quickly? Despite the smell of spring in the air, I had to face the facts—I could not find an acting job, I was once again living with my parents, my freedom was gone, and all I could do in my deep depression was reminisce about my failure and dream about what could have been.

I tried to pull myself out of my depression, with no success, until one Saturday morning an idea came to me. I didn't bother to get more information or find out if it was possible. On that Saturday morning, I announced to my parents that I would join the American Air Force. My father laughed at me.

"They will never take you," he said. "You're just not man enough."

He kept on saying this, but I didn't listen. I was determined and nothing could stop me once I had convinced myself. Where this idea came from, I don't really know. I wasn't even sure I would be allowed to join, being a Canadian. I only knew that I didn't want to be where I was and who I was. I had to get away again and reinvent myself. I had to finish something I started. I wouldn't be happy until I did.

On Monday, I contacted the American Consulate in Montreal. They told me that first I had to enlist and be accepted. Then I could apply for immigration to the United States at the Consulate. Upon my honorable discharge, I would be given a green card because the American Air Force would be my sponsor and would vouch for my upkeep. It seemed so easy. Once again I had a goal to take me away from Quebec, but this time, I could become an American. I could prove to my father that I was man enough. I would prove to everyone that I wasn't going to be "Bobby" from Quebec. I was going to be "Bob" of the American Air Force.

The nearest United States Air Force Recruiting Center was in Plattsburgh, New York, about sixty miles south of Montreal. I took the Greyhound bus early the next day, arriving in Plattsburgh around noon. On the second floor of the tiny City Hall, I found the Recruiting Center—the Navy, Army, Marines, and Air Force all sharing the same space. I expected it to be full of people, but there was just one recruiting officer there on that Tuesday in August of 1959. The rest had all gone to lunch. By the time the Air Force recruiter returned, I had already enlisted in the Army. It was an easy decision. The Army recruiter gave me a lot of reasons why the Army was better, but two factors sealed my fate—the Army only had a three-year enlistment as opposed to the Air Force's four years and, since I had not graduated from high school, the Air Force would probably not have me. The Army wasn't so particular.

Flushed with excitement, I was anxious to return to Montreal that day and confront my father with my United States Army enlistment papers. Finally I had found a way to start and finish what I had begun. I would have to. I had no choice but to finish or get thrown out of the Army and the United States. I couldn't afford another failure. So there I was in late September 1959, eighteen years old, sitting in my seat on a Greyhound Scenicruiser, on my way to Fort Dix, New Jersey, to become a genuine GI. Little *moi* from 5302 Rue Fabre on the

Plateau Mont Royal in Montreal, Quebec, Canada, would soon be wearing the uniform of an American soldier.

Basic training was a shock. It was soon clear how little I knew about America and Americans and how ill prepared I was for what lie ahead of me. When I heard someone was from Arkansas or Kentucky, I wasn't sure if the names were states or cities. The first time I was required to recite the Pledge of Allegiance, I had no idea what I was saying and why. I just mouthed words along with all the other men. And I was completely horrified by the crudeness and vulgarity I encountered in the barracks. When, in casual conversation, I heard one man refer to another as "motherfucker," I couldn't believe my ears. I had never heard that word before and took it literally. In a panic, I ran out of the room, found a quiet spot, and started to cry.

Oh yes, I was different . . . definitely not like the other soldiers in my company. And they saw that immediately. My accent was thick and the other men thought of me as French because most of them had no idea there was such a thing as a French-Canadian. All the soldiers had their family name printed on their fatigues, but because Boulanger was somewhat difficult for Americans to pronounce, I heard all possible pronunciations. So I was nicknamed "Alphabet" or "Lucky Pierre," but the name that stuck was "Frenchy." They would say, "Frenchy's not queer . . . he's French." They had the same impression of French men as I did, and fortunately this saved me from being ostracized or beaten up. The other men actually seemed to like me.

At the end of basic training I was given Army M.O.S. # 130: Tank Crewman. Tank crewman? *Mon Dieu,* I didn't even know how to drive a car. I had to report to Fort Knox, Kentucky, for two more months of advanced training and there I learned to shoot a .45 pistol, even though I had never even played with a toy one as a child; how to drive a Jeep; and finally, how to drive an M48: a fifty-ton tank. If only my father could see me now—I *was* man enough. But it was also becoming clear that I was not and never would be American. I was French-Canadian to the core, and as my training progressed, I got very, very homesick.

The worst time was after six o'clock in the evening. During the day there was always work to do or class to attend. Every minute was planned out, and there wasn't time to think about anything except the task at hand. But in the evening, we were on our own and I soon grew lonely. I craved the things I knew from home—the language, the food, the smells, but mostly the music. I knew I could not quit this time. I had to finish what I started. So I used music to get me through the loneliness and the pain of being so far way from everything I knew.

To keep myself company on guard duty, I would sing French songs. At the base library, I checked out the same three records over and over again. They had no French songs, but they had a few albums of classical music that I knew very well—*Madame Butterfly,* Sibelius's *Finlandia,* and Glazanov's *The Seasons. Finlandia* always reminded me of Quebec. I could see the hills and rivers and sky of my home whenever I heard that piece. *Madame Butterfly*'s allure was less apparent to me then, but now I think it was the passion of the doomed love affair that comforted me, reminding me that I too had a secret passion I must hide. Exposing my true feelings would lead to disaster. And *The Seasons?* That was easy to understand. One of the sections of the Glazanov piece, "Autumn," was the "Petite Adagio," which was the theme music for the most popular and long-running soap operas in Quebec, *A Man and His Sin.*

When at last my two months of advanced training at Fort Knox were complete, I was given new orders. I hoped to be stationed in Europe, but instead was ordered to report to the U.S. Army 40th Armor Division at Camp Beavers, a very small U.S. Army camp nicknamed "Dogpatch," which was nestled in the hills a few miles north of the 38th Parallel in South Korea. I would have to report to Oakland, California, to be shipped out, but first I was given two weeks' leave to go home to Montreal.

Nothing else mattered. I was excited and proud. I would go home having successfully completed four months of intense training and I wanted to show off—first to my father and brother Michel who had made fun of my decision and were certain I would fail, but also to all of Montreal as I walked around town in my U.S. Army uniform with a newfound swagger. Before I left Fort Knox, I bought a summer dress uniform, the exact uniform I had seen so many American actors wear in so many American movies. It was beautiful, so fresh and crisp and the color of sand on a sun-drenched California beach.

It was 1960 and I was nineteen years old. On one of these hot, humid summer nights in Montreal, Quebec, I woke up—not from a child's nightmare, but from my wildest dream come true. I was dressed in my U.S. Army uniform, about to enter my favorite gay bar in downtown Montreal. As I walked in, everyone was looking at me. I stopped for a moment just inside. I could see men's heads turn, feel their interest and energy pull me forward. I could hear the chatter. No one here would guess that I was a French-Canadian. Surely I must be an American soldier in town on leave. But I *was* French-Canadian. I was still little "Bahbay" from the Plateau Mont Royal on the inside, but ever the actor, I kept that hidden. I was still not like the others. I was "different." This time, though, it was nothing to cry about. Instead, I nodded to a handsome man seated at the bar, smiled, and strode confidently toward him.

Escape from the Appalachians

Frederic B. Tate

As a child I simply did not fit in. I grew up in the 1950s in the heart of the Appalachian Mountains, where the tips of North Carolina, Tennessee, and Virginia all blended into one. Like the other children, I ran barefoot in the summer, swam in the cool mountain lakes, and caught fireflies in jars at night. Each autumn I was amazed by the beauty of the colored leaves extending as far as the eye could see. When the soft snow fell in the winter, I would hike with my friends to the top of the mountains far above the timberline and watch the white flakes cover the dormant mountain laurels.

Any similarities with the other kids stopped there. I was gay, precocious, and found religion ludicrous, none of which were acceptable traits in the South during the 1950s—especially for a child. However what alienated me the most was that I loved to climb up in trees where I remained reading for hours. I would put my book down the back of my pants and, with my hands unencumbered, climb until I found a good branch at a reasonable height. In a neighborhood filled with kids and me having an older brother, it was one of the few places where I could get some time to myself and see my world from a different perspective.

For some reason this behavior, which I saw as perfectly logical, caused my poor parents more concern than my inability to play sports and my refusal to participate in a meaningful way with anything that was even remotely religious. My parents were less worried about my mortal soul than what the neighbors might say. Occasionally, my mother would bring out a peanut butter sandwich or some freshly baked cookies and hand them up to me. She always admonished me not to fall, and with look of grave concern, headed back to the kitchen to which most women of the 1950s were slaves.

Identity Envy—Wanting to Be Who We Are Not
Published by The Haworth Press, Inc., 2007. All rights reserved.
doi:10.1300/5641_21

My father was perpetually inventing activities that would turn me into a boy who better fit his definition of masculinity. He started with baseball. This lasted for a month until I was knocked unconscious by a ball. Next was Boy Scouts. During the day we worked on merit badges and at night we drank, smoked, and had circle-jerks. None of these activities had the desired results. I have to give my idiot of a father credit for at least being persistent.

Being gay or agnostic may not be so rare, but what was unusual is the fact that I came out of the womb that way. Even before I had heard the word "gay" or "homosexual" I was well aware of my attraction toward other boys. Being a smart kid, however, I learned that one needed to be very cautious about expressing these feelings. I also understood that I would have to travel far away from the mountains to ever be free.

I attended a sterile, austere Presbyterian church because my parents made me go. The windows in the sanctuary were clear because stained glass would have been too ostentatious, which would have pissed God off. I remember sitting in a Sunday school class as the teacher read the story of Jonah in the belly of a big fish. Even at the young age of five, I knew you could not breathe or write poetry in a whale's stomach and I dismissed the story, and the entire Bible, as a bunch of poorly written parables. Interestingly, I never had any guilt about this. I have had gay friends who were damaged by the fact that they could not reconcile being gay with their conservative, religious upbringing. Luckily, and I am not even sure why, I was spared all this. Is it possible to come into a life with some type of prior knowledge?

I spent a good portion of my childhood up in the trees. I was safe from the religious fanatics and my feelings for other boys while communing with the squirrels and birds. They were a lot less judgmental. Mostly I read books about Ireland. I went through every book on Ireland in both the school and community libraries. I read anything related to the island: geography, history, mythology, and Viking invasions. The myths were my favorite. If I found pictures of Ireland in *National Geographic* or *Life* magazine, I cut them out and taped them to my bedroom wall beside the large map of the Emerald Isle. My fascination, which at times bordered on obsession, had no clear genesis. My parents simply chalked it up to being one of my many strange behaviors, like enjoying books. My attraction to Ireland was like my attraction to boys: it was just always there, a part of me from the beginning. I accepted these facts without a lot of questioning.

My paternal ancestors were Irish, but I have been unable to trace my DNA across the Atlantic. My last name, Tate, was also spelled Tait and Tayte, and this tended to muddy the genealogical waters. It is just as well; I am sure most of my Irish ancestors were horse thieves and heavy drinkers. Maybe this interest in things Celtic was because the island was literally in my genes. Or maybe as a young child I heard someone talking about Ireland and it triggered an interest. Another hypothesis, probably the most plausible of all, is that the hold Ireland had over me could have been the result of a desire to escape to an isolated, far-off place that, in my mind at least, was safer. As a child, the tall oak in my front yard was the best I could do and I was thankful for that.

It is interesting; I have always had dreams of Ireland. These dreams were different, more real and vivid, than my other dreams. I would wake and feel as if I had actually been standing on the craggy, Irish coastline. The smell of the salt air would linger for a few minutes. Even when I was a small child I just somehow knew that the place I visited in my sleep was Ireland. It seemed somehow familiar.

About ten years ago some friends suggested that I attempt past-life hypnotic regression. I did not fully believe in it but had always been curious about this process and the possibility of reincarnation. Let's say I did not disbelieve in the possibility of living many lives. My friends were much more convinced than I was, that some of the dreams I had were related to a past life.

The hypnotic trance came easily and quickly. During the regression I saw a young woman with red hair. She was in Ireland and the date was around AD 990. She had joined a nunnery, more for survival than for religious reasons. One of her duties was to leave food for the lepers by a crossing in the road. On her walk back to the nunnery she would stop by one of the forbidden stone circles where Druid and other pagan religions had practiced their rituals for centuries. She felt much more at home there than she ever did in the church. The therapist counted to ten and I was again fully conscious, feeling relaxed and rested.

Maybe it was a memory of a past life, or simply a fantasy from deep within my subconscious. I did conduct some research after the experience and confirmed that there were in fact lazarettos in Ireland at that time in history. They were run by the nuns and monks.

Anyway, the parallels between the memory and my current reality were apparent. Like the red-haired woman, I am much more pagan than anything. In the 1980s, I did volunteer work at an AIDS hospice, feeding those dying of the disease. Society's treatment of people with AIDS at that time was no different from how the lepers were treated hundreds of years ago. The therapist told me that if one believed in reincarnation, there were lessons to be learned from previous lives. He felt that my lesson was to help and serve others, but without totally sacrificing myself like the Irish nun had.

On the drive home I gave it some serious thought. I decided to leave the hospice. I was ambivalent about this decision, and it was a painful good-bye for me. I stood crying in the garden behind the hospice. I thought of all the time I had spent there in the past five years, helping the men who lived and died there. I had done good and important work, but it was time to move on. Quickly drying my eyes, I went out and bought a piano. The next day I opened the yellow pages in the phone book and found a piano teacher. I decided to put the time, money, and energy that I had put into AIDS work back into myself by learning to play the piano. I had always wanted to play but my father had rigid ideas about what a boy did. Reading was bad enough, but piano lessons were not going to happen. He would never have been convinced to add "musically inclined" to my already long list of shortcomings.

Hospice work taught me several important lessons. One was that life is short, and another was that having regrets is hell. I sat on many beds, holding hands and listening to the regrets of those who were dying. It may be unrealistic to expect to die without some regrets, but I want to have as few as possible when I die. If I had been diagnosed with some terminal disease at that point in my life I would have had two regrets: never having learned to play the piano and not traveling to Ireland.

I have had several years of piano now and I dearly love my teacher. She is eighty years old and her twisted, arthritic fingers can still play a run of notes flawlessly. She is infinitely patient. I am not very talented, but my goal of playing simple classical pieces for myself is realistic.

So that left one potential regret to eliminate—not seeing Ireland. I went in May. I drove from my home in Williamsburg to DC, and flew into Shannon. My heart raced as we descended over the island. The sun was coming up and I could see the ocean and the green fields below. It is no wonder they call Ireland "the Emerald Isle." It is hard to describe the various shades of green. I picked up my rental car, cashed a few traveler's checks for Euro, and off I went. I quickly adjusted to driving on the left side of the road.

Though Belfast and Dublin contain much of interest, I had no desire to see Irish cities, to shop for Waterford crystal, or to kiss the Blarney stone covered with the slobber of thousands of Jersey tourists. For me, I knew the rewards were to be found in hiking the most isolated countryside. I wanted to meet the people in the fields and in uncrowned village pubs, take in the geography and atmosphere, and walk among the prehistoric stone circles. I was searching for a sense of being enfolded by the mythology of the county. I had a desire to wander and avoid the prepackaged experience—sort of a nontourist tourist, if you will.

I headed down to the Beara Peninsula in the southwest corner of the island. My dreams had directed me to this specific location. The landscape was filled with rocky earth that spilled into the ocean. Every turn of the road opened up to a new, breathtaking panorama. Its mountainous and almost stark landscape is in sharp contrast to the Ring of Kerry that most tourists love so much. I visited Neolithic burial chambers, ruins of ancient castles, friaries, and churches, stone circles, and a Bronze Age fort. More than once I would come over a hill into some ancient ruin that was not even listed in the guidebooks. There are few things more humbling than standing in the center of a ring of stones built 2,500 years before the time of Christ.

I hiked to one collection of ancient stone huts above Smerwick Harbor. These huts were made entirely of stacked stone, built without the advantage of mortar. Each had a small entrance that I had to crawl into. A small opening in the roof would have allowed for smoke to escape. These ancient dwellings survived the Vikings and Normans, Atlantic gales, and were later used by Christian monks who lived in solitude. When a thunderstorm hit, I quickly escaped into one. I sat for about an hour in the house that was 1,300 years old and still completely waterproof, as I tried to imagine what life was like for its original inhabitants who hunted deer and caught fish, cultivated some plants, dressed in leather and fur, worshiped a fertility goddess as well as the sun and moon, and for whom the average life expectancy was about twenty-two years. Maybe even the red-headed nun had spent some time in this stone hut?

The people were wonderful. They have easy smiles, tend to mix fact with legend, and though it may be a bit of a cliché, they do have an air of melancholy about them. It was embarrassing to see so many American tourists who had a need to talk about their Irish ancestors. The Irish are gentle and affectionate people. But they must get sick of tourists and the trend to turn the entire fucking country into one lace-curtained B & B. I kept my need to be Irish to myself.

If you asked me if the trip was a spiritual experience, I would say yes. But in a very subtle way. There were some gentle feelings of déjà vu and often a sense of familiarity. More than once I came around a bend in the road and knew what would be on the other side. I had a calm feeling and one of "being home." But there were no dramatically mystical or earth-shattering spiritual experiences. It simply felt good and comfortable. It felt right.

In the evening, when the shadows have sacrificed themselves to the dark, I sit at my piano playing the first movement of Beethoven's *Sonata Quasi Una Fantasia*. Is it played brilliantly or without error? No. But nobody would deny that the piece is played with great passion. I feel happy and safe—like I did as a child sitting in the trees, reading. The feelings of alienation that I had when I was young are gone. Either I do feel I belong or I no longer care if I do not. I look around my simple home and feel at peace. The Irish have a saying in Gaelic: *nil aon tintean mar do tintean fein*. The best translation would be "there is no place like home." I fell in love with the green jewel called Ireland. I guess I had been in love with her long before I visited. I met wonderful people, and more important, I even encountered myself.

Living Mythically

Keguro Macharia

> Speak to me. Why do you never speak. Speak.
> What are you thinking of? What thinking? What?
> I never know what you are thinking. Think.
> . . .
> Twit twit twit
> Jug jug jug jug jug jug
>
> T.S. Eliot, *The Wasteland*

On Mythology

I have never been able to tell a linear narrative. I guess that is one reason why myths have always appealed to me. Myths create. Myths destroy. Myths do not need to explain. Myths are explanations. Myths make me and I make them. Myths are dialectical. Welcome to the myths of me.

1. Myths of Origin

I once heard it whispered that in my tribe, the Agikuyu of Kenya, there were ways to change one's sex. These whispers said that if one were to go around the sacred Mugumo tree backward seven times, one's sex would change. In my prepubescent state, already tired of years of being called sissy and "girl," I was convinced that all my problems would be solved if only I could go around this magical tree seven times. Only, I did not know what this tree looked like.

In my naiveté, and influenced by a commercial culture that proclaimed "bigger is better," I searched for the biggest tree in my school compound and proceeded to go around it a number of times. As with all myths, though, there were a couple of problems that had not been

Identity Envy—Wanting to Be Who We Are Not
Published by The Haworth Press, Inc., 2007. All rights reserved.
doi:10.1300/5641_22

addressed. For example, what would happen if I were to lose count? If I were to get dizzy and stop? If the playtime I had allotted for this act were to be shortened? If I were to be caught by my friends?

I don't know how many times I went around that tree, but I doubt it matters. My sex did not change, the name-calling continued, and I had to learn to create new myths for myself.

But, as with all myths, are they ever really enough?

2. Myths of Discovery

I have read several times of men who claim that they were aware of their sexuality when they were quite young. All I remember is watching Doris's chest at the swimming pool in a haze of adolescent lust. I also remember Paul grabbing at my crotch when I refused to give in to him, and the shock with which I looked at him, perhaps afraid to admit to myself that I had a penis. The uncomfortable feeling I would get when Tito would gently stroke my thigh (in retrospect, I wonder about him). It's hard to know what to call yourself and your desire when there is no name for it in your language, at least no name that you seek to claim for your own.

It was in the two-paragraph passages in cheap fiction that I discovered myself as the body longing to be penetrated. The body longing to be felt and to feel. It was in the cheap and dirty pages of despised magazines that I found names for myself: "fag," "sissy," "homo." The Kiswahili "shoga." But what I discovered was that I was none of these. So, I set out to discover myself.

January 19, 1997

Once again, bitten by the bug of insomnia, I sit at my word processor and proceed to record thoughts. I have been coming to terms with my sexual identity and have discovered quite a few things about myself, how I feel toward the gay movement, and how I choose to define being gay for myself. So far I think I have gone through three distinct stages: one, an intensely physical stage; two, an intensely emotional phase; and three, my current phase, a highly intellectual phase.

I suppose it would only be natural for me to have gone through a physical stage first. From a heterosexist point of view, it is not that one is attracted to people of the same sex that makes one a homosexual; rather, it is that one chooses to validate this attraction by having sex that defines one as a homosexual. Coming from a "purely" heterosexist society, I felt compelled to validate my sexuality, affirm that I was homosexual, the only way that made sense: having sex. Of course, from a homosexual point of view, I was only doing what comes naturally. The often hedonistic and uninhibited view toward sex that many in the gay community carry seems to affirm over and over again that one is defined as a homosexual because one chooses to have homosexual sex. In my case, it didn't last long, for which I am grateful.

My intensely emotional phase, which I am still not completely over, demanded that I seek someone like me with whom to have a relationship. It was characterized by an intense need to have someone of my own whom I could flaunt in the faces of my straight and gay friends as an affirmation that my sexuality was not a passing phase. In American society (at least the little that I have observed of it), having a person by one's side affirms one's sexuality, individuality, and sense of self-worth. My first foray into this realm of emotional wonder was to develop feelings for a friend of mine, a person I had never met, but had spoken to on numerous occasions. In retrospect, I wonder if my feelings were prompted by the "need" that was instilled in me through living in a society "defined" by relationships, or if this was simply another way for me to validate my sexuality: "I have a boyfriend so I must be gay . . . I am attracted to a male, so I must be gay!" The search for this one special person that society dictates one must have, or else there is something wrong with one, has been a source of conflict for me. My notions of relationships are strongly colored by contemporary romance fiction. I believe in that "One" special person. I believe in falling in love; I believe that intimacy is special; I believe that love lasts through time. I often describe myself as a hopeless romantic, yet, at the same time, there is something of the pragmatist in me. I am quick to disabuse myself of the notion of "a perfect lover," while, at the same time, I am not willing to "settle" for whatever may come along.

My current phase is my intellectual phase. I am interested in finding out about gay history. I want to find out who the famous homosexuals and lesbians in history were; I want to find out how they lived their lives; I want to find out how society has traditionally looked at homosexuality and how society looks at homosexuality today. I want to find out how the gay mind works. I want to know what gay people say and think about themselves. I refuse to be an ignorant homosexual. If there is a fight to be fought, and I believe that there is, I want to know what I am fighting for, who fought the fight before me, and how I can fight the same fight.

My sexuality is not based on my emotional or physical attachments, contrary to what many may think about the gay lifestyle. I live a whole gay life, one filled with hidden nuances, space to explore my whole character, exciting discoveries about the world, in short, a whole world exists for me. I love it! I hate it! I live it!

I'm still searching.

3. Myths of the Closet

There are so many myths about the closet that I am not sure where to begin. Perhaps the most pernicious ones?

> "Come out and the world will recognize you!"
> "Come out and refuse to hide!"
> "Your silence will not protect you!"
> "There is safety in visibility!"

I have learned to be skeptical. What is being out? How does one ensure that one is consistently out? What does it mean to be out to some people and not to others? If visibility is life, then why are so many queer people being bashed?

My coming out experience can be summed up in two phone messages from my mother: "I am extremely disappointed in you," and "You either stop this or this is the end between me and you."

I discovered that being out does not mean that people see you. It means that they take what they have seen of "your kind" and impute it on your body. In subsequent conversations, my mother was to clarify that I was a "sick person," a "drug addict," "probably infested with AIDS," "irresponsible," "immature," "hedonistic." All this. And all I wanted was to be visible.

My best friend's parents know about my sexuality. I guess that means that I am visible. When I go over to her house for dinner and her relatives are there, we always get sly looks cast at us. Little phrases fall like raindrops saying, "how wonderful," "two people coming together . . ." I guess that means I am not visible to them.

So I decide to wear my rainbow pin to school. So I have a massive ring with an upside down triangle on my left hand. So I carry around my rainbow flag in school. The only people who notice or care are the queer people. They know what it means. It matters to them. Not to anyone else.

So I ask: visible to whom? And does it matter?

4. The Myth of the Dance

Everyone knows that gay men can dance. But does everyone know how and why gay men dance?

I learned to dance standing in front of a mirror. Not able to go out in my neighborhood in which there were no gay clubs, I learned to dance by watching MTV videos and imagining myself some great star. I learned to dance when I went out and discovered that I had to sell myself.

Entering a gay club for the first time is an experience. It cannot be qualified or modified by adjectives or adverbs; it just is. I saw men. Beautiful men. I saw dancing. Beautiful dancing. I saw dancers. Beautiful dancers. No one would dance with me.

I saw dance moves that MTV had not prepared me for. I saw moves that BET did not feature. I saw body contortions and contractions that made my heart sing. I was way out of my league. I saw tight tees on perfect bodies. I saw grace and motion and movement and magic and I wanted to be part of it.

So I created my own dance moves. Drawing from what I saw around me, drawing from what I liked around me, like a *bricoleur* engaged in a most intricate piece of *bricolage,* I put together my costume. The eye makeup that would make my eyes look different, at least to me; the tiny T-shirt that would expose my love handles and protruding tummy; the loose jeans that would fall off my hips as I moved; the dance moves put together as an exhibit; and I stood in the spotlight.

And I whirled around on the dance floor, claiming it as mine. And I felt my blood sing. And my skin came alive. And my body came alive. And I was alive. And on the dance floor, I forgot I was not the most beautiful. I forgot I was not the most appealing. I forgot that I was not the best dancer. I forgot the name-calling. I forgot the people around me. In a blaze of lights and beats I lost myself.

Then, the music would end. The harsh white lights would come on. I would feel the cold, clammy shirt on my back. The love handles would be evaluated. My body would pass under the eyes of the meat inspectors. My now dried and salted face would not pass muster. The emptiness I had tried to forget would, once again, assail me. And I would walk back to school, as I walked to the club, alone.

But when I danced . . . I counted.

5. The Myth of Family

A useful little word "family." Depending on who is using it. I learned it in the queer community as a euphemism. Was it to show the solidarity of the movement? Or was it because we were too scared to say "gay," "lesbian," "queer," "homo," "fag," "dyke"? And why was it always said in an undertone? Why do I still say it in an undertone? Is it because I'm frightened that if I look too closely at it I will discover that it is a myth, a fiction, a lie?

In these "families" there are arbitrary rules that apply. Black men and women call themselves "Same-Gender-Loving," "ADODI," "Family." This is because they say that they are not "Gay" or "Lesbian" because these are white names.

We have our "size queens," our "snow queens," our "dinge queens," our "rice queens," and queens of all shapes and sizes. All that royalty is a bit too rich for my blood.

There are the "acceptable" family members: "Men who act like Men." And the "unacceptable" family members: "Men who act like Women." There are the "acceptable" bodies: pumped, buffed, and beautiful, and the "unacceptable" bodies: weak, loose, and slack.

In this vision of family, there is a language in which one may speak. A sanctioned language. A language punctuated by "girl-friend," marked by desire and availability. In this family of "brothers loving brothers" (a form of incest?), I have discovered that I cannot exist. So.

I have created my own family. In my family we hug and kiss. In my family we share what we have with each other. In my family we cry when we hurt. In my family we don't need to upstage each other. In my family we are not defined by our sexualities. In my family we are not ashamed to say we are family in public. In my family we do not set arbitrary rules for admission.

6. The Myth of Conversation

Queer men are so funny; they are the best conversationalists around. While I can spin a good yarn or two, I have discovered that I often do not like the color of the thread.

There are acceptable topics for conversation: music, fashion, some kinds of politics, and *always* sex, sex, and more sex. Frequency, positions, number of partners, number of positions with one partner, age, size (most definitely size), period of session, aids to the act, favorite porn star, favorite porn movie, favorite porn scene, multiple partners, anonymous, penetrative, non-penetrative, the best lube, no lube . . .

And in this little world of topics my mind has learned to shut off. I yawn repeatedly. I've heard it all before. Who is sleeping with whom, who is cheating on whom, why he is cheating on him, why we all should not like women, the merits of topping over bottoming and vice-versa.

And in this little world of topics my mind has learned to shut off.

Creating My Own Myths

> My realities
> are
> Shattered bones
> and
> Silicone Implants

I have learned to create my own realities. To create myths that do not destroy me. I have learned to use words that empower me. I have learned to choose not to sleep with lies. And I see a world of possibilities.

But first, I have a few myths to face.

In The Beginning

In the beginning there was me, my parents, my siblings, my tribe. In the beginning there was laughter and pain. In the beginning family meant people who cared no matter what. I have learned that families change. And I have to create my own beginning.

Coming out to my mother was the hardest decision that I have ever made. Of course, it was to be a decision that I was to make in college. Because college was where I was to discover my sexuality. That she would have problems accepting my sexuality was something I knew would happen. However, since my father's death we had developed a strong relationship that I thought would hold up under the pressure. It did not.

We did not talk for two months after I came out. When I received her first phone message I went out with my friends. I warned them to

take care of me. I went wild on the dance floor. It was cleansing, healing, cathartic; I could face her. And I learned that coming out trans-
Atlantically does not work. As far as my mother is concerned, I have
been corrupted by America. As far as she is concerned, homosexuality has always been and will always be a Western concept.

So, we have learned to talk around it. We have learned to ignore
that I am not heterosexual. And nightly she prays that I will find a nice
Christian girl to marry. I long ago stopped praying.

Be Fruitful and Multiply

I have learned to distrust sex. I would go so far as to say that I am
inimical to the idea of sex. My first forays into the realms of the queer
world were tinged by pornography and sex shops that smelled of cigarette, sweat, desire, and cheap sex. That I was part of it I do not regret. I regret that the only reason I ventured into the worlds of the sex
shops was because I did not know that there were any alternatives. I
regret that I never learned to value my body, my whole body. I regret
that I came into a culture where my penis and my color mediated my
path. I regret that my foreignness still mediates my way.

I tried to learn how to stop feeling dirty after furtive fumblings in
darkened sex booths. I tried to learn not to want to scrub away the
feelings of violation. I learned to try not to hate the anonymity. I never
learned.

Instead, I learned to be distrustful of the eyes that would look at
me. I learned to despise the men who would try to hug me without
first asking my name. And I learned how to build walls of ice that
would not thaw. And I healed within my walls of ice.

And I learned to feel my body again. And I learned that I was beautiful. And I was able to fall in love.

Falling in Love

I remember how he would kiss my back slowly, tenderly, all the
while whispering, "Your skin is so soft." I remember waking up next
to him, feeling his warm body next to mine. I remember wanting to
leave my mark on him: the little love bites on his lush flesh that
marked him out as mine. I remember sitting in a fast-food restaurant
and running my toes up and down his calves as he tried to pretend that
nothing was going on.

And I remember telling him I loved him. And I remember him telling me that he loved me. And I remember that he made me feel beautiful. And I remember that when he said that I was beautiful I became beautiful. And I remember breaking up because I had given too much of myself and I was afraid that there would be nothing left if I did not hold back. And I remember him crying over the phone and how I wanted to hate myself for what I did to him.

I called him up again recently. It is almost a year to the day that we started going out (on my birthday no less), and I still care for him in a way that I cannot define. We have grown up some since we broke up. We can now tell each other that we love each other. Falling in love taught me to say, "I love you." More than that, it taught me how to love myself.

Negotiating Minefields

So here I am in college studying English. And I read books in my areas of interest: queer theory and gender theory. And I get excited about the transformative power inherent in destabilizing gender, and I think about how the world would change if only everyone else would read the same books. And then I am told by my colleagues that I "read jargon," that it "doesn't make sense," that it "takes away from the text." And I fight to explain that for me this is not theory; this is an act of survival.

I call myself "queer" now. I hate labels because they constrict and constrain and choke if you allow them to. I like the label "queer" though. It's not "gay," and it's not "Same-Gender-Loving." It's not black or white, male or female. It defines where I feel I am right now. And where would that be?

I am caught in between cultures and histories that would, if I let them, rip me into shreds. My postcolonial body struggles in the wake of neocolonialism not to be either the colonizer or the colonized. And yet, I am writing this essay in English, I am attending college in a Western university, and I ask myself if I am simply a white man in blackface.

The West has people with desires like mine who do not have to crawl around in the shadows, afraid that their shadows will betray them.

The Luyha tribe have a legend about a man whom they call Lwanda Magere. Lwanda Magere was the mightiest warrior in the land. He was invincible. Enemy spears and arrows bounced off his body and as long as he was alive his tribe was in control. Unable to destroy him, his enemies decided to send a spy into his house in the form of a young wife, who was offered as a peace offering. She discovered that his body was merely a form, and that he truly lived in his shadow. Armed with this information, she went back to her tribe and informed them. During the next war, his enemies attacked his shadow. He died.

I am afraid that my shadow will betray me.

To live queer in a culture that is not my own, but where I am at least acknowledged as such, or to live queer in a culture where queer does not even exist. And does it really matter?

> And
> do I care
> about the dreams
> I lose
> in choosing not
> to sleep with
> lies

Who Am I?

Margaret Cleaver

As a librarian at the Santa Monica Public Library I found myself
dreading the beginning of the school year when the "Who Am I" project was being assigned. The middle school students in Santa Monica
are annually assigned this research project, entailing a visit to the
public library. There they are required to look up newspaper head-
lines for the date of their birth, research the meaning of their names in
name dictionaries, and make a list of historical events that happened
on their birthday.

For weeks, my colleagues and I were terrorized by several hundred
squiggly, squirmy thirteen-year-olds who, after ganging up on the
newspaper reading machines and making the reels race back and
forth, made for the multivolume sets of historical events encyclopedias like they were heading into a football game. The fact that Valium
became a prerequisite for surviving the duration of the assignment
did not prevent me, however, from sporadically wondering about the
meaning of it all. If I were doing this assignment what would I think
about the idea that "Who I Am" consisted of a handful of events
which happened to take place in the world at large at the time of my
birth and the derivation of a name conjured up for me by my parents.

While for most of the students a certain amount of fun is involved,
notably getting to play with the newspaper microfilm machines, for
others the assignment proves more challenging. The name research is
an especially tricky proposition for those whose ancestry is other than
European, as most name dictionaries do not include names that are
not Eurocentric. But what interests me most about this endeavor is
that, according to this assignment, a person's identity is somehow assumed to have a connection to events tangential to, or maybe even un-
related to, his or her life. Conversely, could someone's identity be de-

Identity Envy—Wanting to Be Who We Are Not
Published by The Haworth Press, Inc., 2007. All rights reserved.
doi:10.1300/5641_23

veloped in a vacuum, untouched by events taking place in the world, particularly during one's formative years?

I can't remember when I might have first thought about "Who I Am," but I know that as far back as I can remember the others around me seemed to be telling me who they thought I was supposed to be. Any ruminating I might have done at that age, which could be construed as leading up to forming a concept of self, was more likely to have been in the direction of "identity by adversity." It was not about who I thought I was, but rather, about who I wasn't. A description of my middle school–aged "self" as viewed by others probably read like this: black, female, heterosexual (or assumed to be so at the age of puberty), small for her age, and called by a first and middle name (which happen to be the given names of each of my grandmothers). A description of my "self" at the same age, according to me, might have read like this: Native-American, male, heterosexual (heterosexual male as a masque for my budding homosexuality—not that I knew anything about these actual words), the same size as everyone else, and called by any one of a variety of names I had made up for myself.

Looking back on my thirteen-year-old invented self, I find that I can still tap into the fluidity with which I was able to assume an identity that I knew to be different from how others perceived me. How did I know this and how did I arrive at the turning point—that place in time where the desire to become someone else would become a conscious need? I can see myself at a crossroads, the prescribed path with all of the scenery filled in criss-crossing an empty path, which was waiting for me to populate it with images of my own creation. Had I been able to read the newspaper at the time of my birth, I would have been informed of the perils associated with being born a girl of African ancestry in the United States of 1943, a mere introduction to the real story lived by my family and the social, racial group to which they belonged. The road that I was trying not to follow would have been surrounded by the same negative imagery that plagued anyone growing up black in the United States at that time. Had I been reading the newspaper at age eleven, I would have found out that *Brown v. Board of Education,* a historic Supreme Court decision, happened because someone made a case that it was impossible for black kids to develop positive self-images in a social environment in which they were consistently negatively cast, discriminated against, and in which they were consequently segregated.

These events on the national front could have had another, indirect, impact on me. My family's response to the negative social position of blacks was to make the kids appear to be nonblack. Not being able to change the color of our skin, we were brought up to look and to act in every other aspect like the kids in families on the white TV shows, in the white magazines, and so on. The message communicated to me was that in my natural form, I was not right. In order to become "okay" or acceptable, I had to act like I was someone else. Puberty brought on a new fascination with girls—especially older, developed girls, or more appropriately, women. With the new fascination came waves of wanting to be close, very close, intimately close, to other young women. Without saying anything, somehow I knew that these feelings were most definitely not "okay."

Coming of age had brought me to this metaphoric crossroads, and it's probably no surprise that I responded to the need to escape by making furtive slips down the pathway of my new identity. Books provided a lot of the raw material. Books being my main source of entertainment, I gathered up the images that could be me in a different context. My brown skin could just as easily be Native American as it could African American. Not yet being fully developed as a woman meant that I could easily look like a boy. Loving the idea of a lifestyle which included horseback riding—something rudely missing from my inner-city neighborhood—I of course had to be someone who rode a horse. And I had to have new names. A school mate who claimed to be related to the Native-American ballerina Maria Tallchief (and who also had an older sister on whom I had a secret crush) provided the inspiration for one of my names, "Little Tallchief."

"Little Tallchief" remained unknown to most folks I came in contact with; the small amount of evidence I ever gave of his existence included claiming to be "Indian" at the odd moment when there might have been an opportunity to make a statement about my ancestry, wearing pants whenever I could get away with it (not to school, of course—it was still the 1950s), and insisting on keeping my hair in unfashionable braids while the other girls were all getting cute bobs.

My new identity was doubly useful in that it was not only more "me," it was also more socially advantageous. Notwithstanding how Native Americans were discriminated against—to the same degree as blacks in many parts of the United States—there existed a certain romanticization of Native Americans in literature, and especially in children's literature, that made it seem better in my youthful mind's eye to be Native American. I was not the only black kid of my era claiming falsely to be Native American.

By being a boy, I not only got to wear pants and ride a horse astride, I could also have girl friends—the real, romantic kind. Loving women remained a secret long after Little Tallchief stopped being there to love them for me. Coincidentally, my first woman lover wore her hair in braids; by then it was the late 1960s and braids were in, though not necessarily for women-loving women. Looking back on this period, I can't help but smile to myself because my lover cut off her braids and had her new short hair frizzed into an Afro as soon as we got together. She wanted to "look more like me," she claimed.

Without the benefit of actually having had the "Who Am I" assignment in middle school, I still made it into adulthood with an agenda of conscious questions. How does one arrive at a true understanding of one's identity? The ascribed and invented identities of my early adolescence either eventually gave way or became fused with the characteristics of identities already available in the adult world. How the world saw me and how I saw myself were more in sync, thanks to the movement years of the 1960s and 1970s, in which civil rights, women's rights, and gay rights conspired to make it "okay" to belong to social groups previously marginalized.

Who I am in the world today is clearly a by-product of historical developments, going back to the world in which my parents were living when I was born. The historical newspapers part of the "Who Am I" assignment would have been right on. The characteristics by which others might view me are a reflection of events happening in my external world. But what about the me that may not be known—not the secret identity of early adolescence which was more a desire to be viewed alternatively by others—but a more central, deeper version of myself which I imagine that only I can see. Is there such a thing as an identity based on an essence of "selfness" which is not a collection of the attributes that assign one to a particular social group? Is there such a thing as an essence of "selfness" which is always present within one's being from the time of birth until death? And if it is possible to discover this "essence" within one's "self," how can it be described in such a way that others can understand it, relate to it, call it, name it? Because mustn't there always be the "others" who create that "adversity" by which we ultimately define ourselves?

No one exists in a vacuum, but if it were possible to "out" the self in one's inner sanctum, perhaps the process would be somewhat similar to the way social movements impact our external selves, though possibly inversely. To get folks to see past "gay, black woman," I would have to figure out how to communicate the unique part of myself in a way that made knowing the real, more complete me more compelling than the me perceived casually. I have wanted to create an identity for myself that would have no social characteristics. I wanted to be perceived as just "person." I wanted "Little Tallchief" to become "person with no name" or even "person with many names."

I find myself going back to the idea of the names part of the "Who Am I" assignment. Again, from the stated purpose of researching the derivation of one's name, the researcher could be led to probe more deeply into the name-giving process. "Nobody Knows My Name," the work by African-American artist Charles White, which illustrates his preoccupation with the invisible status of blacks in the pre–civil rights United States, also speaks to the importance of a name as central to one's identity. What does one's name, as an ascribed attribute usually assigned (at least in Western culture) by a parent or parents, have to say about ourselves in a central or essential way? Some who have wrestled with "outing" themselves have rejected the names they received at birth and given themselves new names, sometimes making the new name their legal name. In particular, some people who have changed their gender have opted to acquire new names that would reflect the gender of their new identity. The incidents of name changes for various reasons have existed since time immemorial, but the movement years in the United States have spawned numerous new names brought forth by an insurgence of identities previously suppressed, marginalized, or made to be invisible.

If I were to come up with a new name that would encompass my new sense of self, what would this name be? I would have to evolve from my *tabula rasa* state of being "person with no name" to a state in which that unique part of myself that I want others to know is brought to the forefront. In order not to remain invisible, I have to be called something. In looking at the attributes that I would like to have reflected in a name, I find that I am taken back to my early fascination with Native American culture in which names are fitted to personal attributes that are unique to the person's self. Names like "Laughing Boy" and "Walks with the Wind" indicate both qualities central to a person's identity and expressive of how others see the person. I start by trying out various expressions on myself: "Brown-Skinned Woman" (certainly not unique, but then perhaps the uniqueness comes from how I wish to view my skin color, not as representative of an extended array of social issues, but as the essence of the color in and of itself); "Woman Who Loves Women" (also not unique, and most people who know me already know this, but then, for those who don't . . .); and how about "Dreams A Lot," "Smiles to Herself," and "Keeps a Secret."

Cycling through numerous names and attributes, I find myself back at the crossroads. I am reluctant to give up the names my parents gave me. Rejecting the names they have chosen for me feels like a rejection of them. The fact that they named me for my grandmothers seems even more significant in the light of the struggles of my extended family through generations, struggles which made it possible for me to live in a world where one has a greater chance of achieving a positive self-identity than was possible for many of my ancestors. My essence *is* my ancestry, my sexuality, *and* a kernel of special attributes that I always expect to have to discover and to share. This time, the crossroads do not materialize as an either/or proposition. Rather, I find that I am happy to stand at the vortex while others come and go, seeing around me in all directions, but also seeing only me. I answer to the names my parents named me, names that I will keep and cherish, and which I will always be proud to state as my official names. But I also answer to a burgeoning extended form of those names, for anyone who may be interested . . . *Brown-skinned daughter of Margaret's daughter dreaming woman who loves women dreaming while smiling to herself in secret . . .*

Perhaps the Santa Monica middle school teachers were ahead of me. Perhaps the real purpose of the "Who Am I" assignment is to get the students to react to the notion that who we are has something to do with how the world sees us or with what is happening in the world around us. This reaction could ultimately lead to a deeper understanding of self.

Thieves, Pimps, and Holy Prostitutes— My World

Renate Stendhal

Growing up in Germany after the Second World War was an experience of shame and mourning. In twelve years of masterfully orchestrated genocide, Germany had also succeeded in the massacre of its own culture, and nobody was talking about it. The pressures of "good behavior" and moral "cleanliness" were turning the Germans into Herr und Frau Saubermann—Mr. and Mrs. Clean. Everyone was busily sweeping the dirty past under the rug of a newly rich, respectable nation (a "washing powder nation," as I liked to call it). The group of young intellectuals I allied myself with found it hard to breathe in this clean air. Sex was not clean; it could not be mentioned. Homosexuality was a crime. Any woman who did not properly long for family and motherhood was perverse.

My perverse journey started when I was fourteen, when a friend handed me books that had just made their way into the country—books by Sartre, Camus, and Jean Genet. My childish notions of "normal" love and family life were shattered like a glass. I was in a trance reading Genet's *Notre Dame des Fleurs* (the book was censored in Germany shortly afterward) with its intense beauty of love between men, between thieves and murderers. Like any good German girl, I had been raised on the original grim version of Grimm's fairy tales: Genet's cruel eros, his romantic obsession with violence, did not deter me. I remember running to my mother who was still my confidante at that age: "*Mutti,* you have to read this—this is my world!" My poor mother read Jean Genet. Looking back, I think she never quite recovered from the shock, while I never recovered from the revelation.

Thieves and murderers, "my world"? What touched me to the core was the romance, the passion of one man for another. The idea of such

Identity Envy—Wanting to Be Who We Are Not
Published by The Haworth Press, Inc., 2007. All rights reserved.
doi:10.1300/5641_24

a passion seemed unthinkable in the German climate of the time—a passion as dirty as it was holy, transcending all laws and limitations ("The Eternal passed by in the form of a pimp"). The chord that was struck in me by imaginatively following this poetic ecstasy of deadly love foreshadowed my sexual awakening. I had never thought of, or heard of, homosexuality, but now I longed for it and dreamed of it as if my sexual awakening would be that of a boy.

I never uttered a word about my revelation after my mother's pained reaction. I protected my experience like something sacred, a mystery. Whenever the occasion arose, however, I would jump to the defense and argue for homosexuals because of the tenderness I felt for the love between men, and because of my deep conviction that homosexuality was a law of nature, as natural and normal as the sun rising in the east. Perhaps this love was even superior to the so-called normal love because it was outlaw love, chosen against convention. It was an act of individual rebellion, a breaking of taboos, an act of freedom, and it implied some notion of sameness and equality that already appealed to me.

Secretly I began looking for these men who were my "familiars." I had no guidance or gay education, but I found and recognized *Schwule,* gay men, at the theater, the ballet, in the streets of Hamburg where I would sometimes shyly follow them, just to be in their presence for a while. I felt that, as a woman, I was sadly excluded from "my world." I yearned to have a life companion straight from the transvestite prostitutes of *Notre Dame des Fleurs.* "There is a boy at the university," I confessed to my diary when I was nineteen, "who is my daily delight. A young homosexual. Thick hair, freshly washed, soft-silky curls, tastefully cut without layering. His face is silky-soft as well, with a smile as if angels were crossing his forehead. He is Divine or even still a young Culafroy. It is angel-like to smile in such a way just because one's mouth is determined to do so... He tightly wraps his hips (so narrow they can't possibly hold more than half the entrails!) in black corduroy pants and, for the sake of the game, tucks a black corduroy shirt into these pants. It is a graceful game because he is beautiful. One tends to forgive beautiful and gentle people any caprice, doesn't one? The looks he attracts, the scornful, biting remarks, no, even more the amused ones, hurt me deeply. He is my daily delight and my longing to cry."

Eager to find signs of the forbidden love, I used my studies of literature to uncover the cultural presence of gay writers. Thomas Mann, for example, who was scorned by my group of intellectual friends as a "bourgeois" author, became an inadmissible ally when I read "Wälsungenblut," his taboo-breaking Wagnerian story about brother-sister incest, and discovered his homosexual leanings in *Death in Venice*. One might expect from these beginnings the making of an exemplary "fag hag," but this it not where my desire led me. Even when I knew I was a lesbian, my sense of intimate connection and mysterious belonging to the world of gay men did not change. I felt recognized, was touched, and turned on by gay men because part of me was convinced that I was one myself.

At the same time that I was following gay men in the street, it dawned on me that women, too, could be "like that" and that my feelings for a girl my age were perhaps "like that." There was at first no name for "that" between women, and I got nowhere when I tried to stare at certain women in order to decipher their secret. I never found myself following a woman or two women in the theater or in the streets. Around me, I only perceived the usual heterosexual hunt that took every woman for a prey. And I, who felt like a stranger in this game, was stamped as a prize prey because I fit the archetype of the cool blonde "iceberg" who would not be touched or caught. In all the years of my growing up in Germany, not a single (detectable) lesbian crossed my path. In my alienation, for a brief period in my early twenties, I allowed myself to get caught and experience the physical and emotional devastation of "normality." The brief relationship that taught me the reality of "a woman's lot" was to become the palpable proof of all my intuitions about "my world."

During that unhappy period I decided to drop out of the university and, instead, focus on my body and its inhibitions. Using my body as an instrument of work and self-expression, I hoped I would be able to liberate myself. My parents had done ballroom dancing as a sport; I had been passionate about ballet since childhood and taken a few classes as a teenager. The image of the ballerina fascinated me, but I did not yet recognize that the weightless, almost disembodied grace of the female dancer was the fulfillment of my wish to transcend my body or not to have a female body at all. I went to Paris to seriously study dance, but was puzzled by the fact that I didn't fit the image of the soulful butterfly. My body did not produce the necessary long back and narrow waist that creates the perfect line of the ballerina. Instead, I had broad shoulders, flat hips, long legs, big hands, and never managed to look disembodied. I had started too late to be any good "on point." I was better at the steps and leaps the boys did. After three years of obsessive work I toured the German ballet companies to seek an engagement. When the Berlin Opera took me on in spite of my imperfections, I felt it was because the director was a *"homo,"* that we had instantly recognized each other for our shared otherness. My magical belief inspired me to outdo myself in the try-out performance for him, but my skills should not have been enough to qualify me for the opera ballet. I was convinced Herr Reinhardt said yes to a young boy pretending to dance like a girl.

Before leaving for Berlin, however, I had finally spotted a real-life lesbian, a young, part-Vietnamese woman who looked and acted like a boy. I was unable to forget her. It was the end of the 1960s. I had witnessed the student revolts in Paris and Berlin and become politicized. Now I felt split between my anti-bourgeois, avant-garde intellectual affinities and my dancing on the strings of nineteenth-century Romanticism. In addition, I found that the beginning drug culture had far more liberating potential than classical ballet. I returned to France to look up the part-Vietnamese boy-woman. She was doing violently physical underground theater in Paris. We fell in love, and I readily exchanged the beauty of ballet for the beast of anti-aesthetic, drug-inspired experimental theater.

Our theater group consisted of mostly gay extroverts, high-strung, passionate women and a few men who did everything fast: think, talk, move, create, emote, and fall apart. I was in love with all of them for their radical difference from me. I was introverted and tongue-tied and overly eager to please, while they were constantly spontaneous, uncompromising, loud, brash, and always pleased to be this way. I valued being challenged in my ponderous Teutonic ways, although I was troubled by their "hysterics." I did my best to emulate my companions and pretend that I was one of them. The feminist movement taught me the word that best described what I liked about my new pals: they were androgynous.

The difference between my lover and me was striking. She was cocky and unaware of her looks, playful like a child, unafraid to be angry and aggressive, endowed with a healthy dose of narcissism and self-interest. I, by contrast, did not know how to stop smiling, how to say no, how to be spontaneous instead of perfectionist, how to stop observing myself from the outside to check my appearance, how to fight, and how to put my own interests first. My lesbian relationship cracked open my unconfessed "penis envy"—the misery of my education as a girlchild.

"Penis envy" was anathema in the newly minted feminist movement in Paris. Carried by the fiery eros of woman-loving and radical politics, Parisian feminists were convinced that women were perfect in and of themselves—if only we stopped behaving like the "colonized" half of humanity, like female impersonators. The new mandate was to rediscover and integrate our repressed and crippled masculinity: if we could turn into perfect androgynes (or "gynandros"), there was nothing on earth we would have to envy.

It was a tidal wave of heroic romantic idealism that inspired me—although it seemed to me that a larger humanitarian vision demanded that everyone, women and men, reintegrate their split-off opposite-sex half (following Plato's myth of the origin of gender) in order to fulfill their human potential. In fact, I thought that a small segment of human beings was already pretty close to the ideal—the decadent, boyish young men who celebrated their ambiguous beauty in front of everybody as the sexual revolution made gayness a fashion. From my new feminist viewpoint I found that French men, Parisian men, were surprisingly ambiguous. Their culture seemed to give them permission to be feminine without reducing their power—to be refined and elegant, sensitive and emotional, and even hysterical, as Gertrude Stein had discovered many years earlier when she wrote in *Paris France:* "A Frenchman always breaks down when his mother dies."

The same cultural permission for androgyny seemed to exist for French women. I met a number of cultivated, brilliant Parisian feminists who embodied what I wanted to be. They were bold thinkers, easy and elegant talkers; they were sexually liberated and promiscuous, and they were ambitious and unafraid to compete with men. The fast juggling with intellectual forms and the verbal virtuosity cultivated by the French appealed to me as a light-heartedness that I linked to the south, to plenty of sun, to boisterous street cafés, to a *joie de vivre* that I had never known. I embraced it as a spirit of playfulness that (in the best cases) was linked to another virtue I longed for: self-humor.

What disturbed me most during this first feminist awakening was that the fire of anger, aggression, and desire had been almost extinguished in a "feminine" woman like myself. No matter how furious and jealous I felt that my lover could flirt and make out with another woman—or worse, with a woman I had an eye on myself—I was tied up in my corset. No matter how tormented I was by desire, I could not muster the courage to take the first step, reach out and touch another body.

Fortunately for me, the high erotic energies that ran through the movement were creating an atmosphere of free love. Every woman in Paris suddenly appeared to be a possible object of desire for every other woman. The constant parties, orgies, couple-sharing, couples inviting friends or strangers into triangles, turned life into an irresistible "exercise class." The boyish women I fell in love with instructed me through their example and through the natural osmosis of close encounters. I began to determine the sexual tasks I needed to accomplish: "I am not going to leave this party before I have kissed this woman. If the woman's partner is jealous I am going to kiss her, too. I am not going to drive her home unless I manage to seduce her in the car. I am not going to shy away from playing out the secret fantasies that I can read in this woman's eyes. I won't turn my eyes away from the embarrassing sex scene on the floor of this party. I will be a witness to everything I want to run from. I am not going to stop doing anything I desire because someone is watching . . ."

After a few years of "training" in this way, I felt that I was changing from the inside out. There was a new sense of balance in my body. I realized that as a dancer/actor my strongest suit was balance, and that balance was a spiritual and psychological theme of my life. Balance between yin and yang, masculine and feminine, north and south, between the introverted, heavy soil of my German homeland and the extroverted, playful, Mediterranean City of Light. I fell in love again with Paris and took to walking through the city by day and by night. I was thin and muscular from my theater training and very short-haired, always wearing jeans and a rough jeans jacket. The baker woman or the café waiter would greet me with "Bonjour, Monsieur." The way men started looking at me in the streets told me I was taken for a pretty young man. I was surprised and amused. I like---d it. I tried flirting with gay men in the street or in the Metro, holding their gaze and sometimes letting one of them follow me for a while. I loved the way women now looked at me, startled, confused for a moment, intrigued and sometimes turned on. I was obsessed with movies that dressed women up like men, like *Victor/Victoria* or Ulrike Ottinger's cult movie *Dorian Grey im Spiegel der Boulevardpresse (The Image of Dorian Grey in the Yellow Press)* with Veruschka von Lehndorff in the title role. I studied how gender was fabricated, disguised, and changed. Sure of my long, boyish step, my determined jaw, my big hands with short nails, my theatrically lowered voice, I continued to advance my education by going to pornographic movies. I walked around the red light districts of Pigalle or Strasbourg-St. Denis, observed the traffic of streetwalkers, johns, and pimps, exchanged long glances with the women and smiles when they called out to me.

One day, on an excursion through Algerian slum streets near Belleville, I came upon a group of men who had gathered excitedly at the huge coach door of a shabby building. They were taking turns peeping through a hole in the door. I went in line behind them. When my turn came, I peeked through the loophole into a dilapidated court-yard where fat, worn-out prostitutes were sitting on chairs or leaning against walls. Some men went over to an ordinary side door to talk to an old woman with blue tattoos on her face and a strident voice. I got the sense that they were bargaining over the fees. Most of the two dozen men in line were only there to peek, like me. None of them paid any attention to me. Nobody questioned my being there.

In a multimedia show ("In the Beginning...of the End"), which I wrote and created with a new lover, I staged a fantasy image of the androgynous on film: I split a dance costume for myself and another actress down the center. One side of the costume was a slim white evening gown, the other side a white tuxedo. Our heads and faces were also split — one side made up like a woman, the other like a man. (This image turned out to be the archetypal image of the 1970s, invented and reinvented by countless artists and designers.) I choreographed the dance to Sibelius's romantic "Valse Triste." While the fast whirl of the waltz reflected the fluidity of male and female aspects of the dancers, I used the slow, yearning parts of the music to present either the girl-to-girl side of the couple to the audience or emphasize the boy-to-boy profile in seductive closeness.

I went to see a psychic at that time to have my past lives read. She claimed that I had almost always been a man in the past. My present incarnation, according to her, had to be understood as a crash-course in femininity. This made sense to me. I certainly had had enough femininity for one lifetime. In moments of euphoria, my transformation felt like alchemy, a magical process that had restored my completeness to the point where, in moments of sexual excitement, I was able to physically "remember" the male body, down to the male genitals, of my past incarnations. But I never felt that I was in the wrong body. Instead, there seemed to be a memory-body in addition to my woman's body. Perhaps this was the reason, when I was fourteen, for my spontaneous feelings of familiarity with gay men?

For the first time in my life I experienced myself as "complete." I stopped desiring women who were more masculine than myself. They now seemed out of balance—the androgynous balance that was my ideal—and any shared intimacy with them would have threatened my own balance. I had had to work hard at my "completeness" and would not to let a "dyke" lover push me back onto the "feminine" (i.e., less powerful) side. I was determined to embody as much as possible my ideal gay "boy." The label "boy" still stood for the man with the elegance and sensitive beauty of a woman, the man with the promise never to grow up into a patriarchally defined, hardened, and toughened "man." When I thought of attractive men or looked at certain men and noticed my sexual attraction, invariably a gender shift would occur in me and I would no longer be a woman: I became a man looking at and desiring a man.

In my mid-thirties, I did not believe that I would ever find a lover who would be neither more nor less androgynous than me. Could there possibly be anyone with the same gender balance who would allow me to be my fluid self without effort or self-consciousness? Would another woman ever be able to dance the same dance in the same rhythm with me—like the couple I had invented in my fantasy scene of the waltz? When this soul mate did materialize, we were both surprised to discover that we shared the same passion for the ideal boy, the same fascination with Thomas Mann, and with cultural images of female/male two-sidedness in men. We were equally touched by the personification of this ideal in dancers like Nijinsky and Rudolf Nureyev; actors like James Dean; Alain Delon and

Helmut Berger in Visconti's films; Rupert Everett and Colin Firth in
Another Country; Anthony Andrews in *Brideshead Revisited;* Hugh
Grant, James Wilby, and Rupert Graves in *Maurice;* Jude Law in
Wilde; or *lieder* singer Ian Bostridge on the concert stage. We even
shared the mysterious sense of reincarnation that in our lovemaking
sometimes allowed us to embody and experience each other as two
boys having sex with each other.

And we also shared a sense of envy—an envy that now had no personal, but a cultural sting. The grand feminist vision of women
changing the world seemed to have reached its zenith. Even before
the backlash started, I felt confused and heartbroken to see so many of
my dreams unrealized. Yes, many revolutionary, paradigm-changing
books had been written; the existence of matriarchy had been established; there were country and even city collectives of women
witches. But the dream of a gender-free language and the creation of a
counterculture by women had barely begun before feminism became
a curse, the infamous "F-word." The deeply ingrained woman hatred
of our culture swept back in; the ideal of equality, of androgynous
sameness between women, collapsed into strife over our differences.
Fashion had allowed us the brief reprieve of broad shoulders and flat
shoes before the feminine mystique returned with a vengeance. Many
feminists I knew returned to men; many lesbians I knew retreated to
the one safe place available—the private nest of relationships with
sometimes conventional role divisions—while a younger, radical
fringe of women set out to become men.

Untouched by politics, however, and unaltered by changes in fashion, there was always the cultivated, refined, sophisticated gay man,
the archetypal "dandy" in his contemporary guises. In the first book I
published with Kim Chernin, my partner, in 1989, I expressed the
envy that we shared. I set the scene at a costume ball. Disguised as a
man, lesbian Alma Runau, my protagonist, is watching two young
men, kissing.

"They were standing at the piano in a niche of the room. Two
equally tall, beautiful boys, both dressed in *Great Gatsby* suits, long
jackets, pleated pants, body-tight vests, all in sand color, only the
shirts snow-white. The simplicity and elegance of the outfit, doubled

in this perfect twin look, made it a costume. They were wearing the same narrow leopard mask.

"The boy leaning against the piano had darker skin. His hair had the thick, silky quality of Asian hair. It was razor-cut over the ears and neck, stood up on top of his head like a thick calligraphy brush. A shock of it fell longer onto his forehead, off-white. There was a padded softness to his face, an almost girlish delicacy around his mouth, chin, and nose.

"The brown hair of the other was tightened back into a short braid. He had pale skin and a strongly marked face. The skin was tight over his bones, the cheeks hollow, his mouth finely drawn, driven. His face had the heightened nobility of someone who hasn't slept for days because of passion. He appeared to be the older of the two, the guide. He was gently assailing the other, pressing and nestling against him. He whispered into the soft one's ear, wandered down his neck with little kisses. He took him by the chin, smiling, then kissed his lips, took a bit of his tongue. As if to catch his breath, he leaned his face against the other's face and, in devotion, rested there. He moved back to look at him, spoke insistent lover's words, shamelessly breaking the rule of the night. The soft boy answered, his eyes glittering. They talked, their faces close, until the wanton lover fell silent, again approaching the other's skin. The Eurasian boy never made the slightest movement toward him. He gave in with a note of hesitation, surrendered, again and again seduced.

"I've no idea how long I watched them, seduced myself and envious. Peers, I thought. Beauty that is neither masculine nor feminine. Two boys loving each other with the knowledge and emotional fervor I believed only women could have. Only we. I marveled at the refinement of their touch, at their persistent fire. Was there anything they could envy women?

"Fascination is always mixed with envy. With the fruitless longing for identification. The longing to take part. Such boys carry a dream for me. The dream of an elegance that has cast aside the adored beauty of woman and replaced it with itself. Their self-assurance and ease is carried by a whole male culture and is secretly worshiped. They do not only embody themselves. They strive for a godly image, old as the world and eternally in fashion: the hermaphrodite. The female embodied in the male.

"Where is my own godly image, I wondered. The archetypal cultural image I could embody in one of its endless, glorious variations? A female image of human completeness and self-sufficiency? A painful void. I dream about those beautiful, decadent boys who have each other and the world at their feet. I train myself to play their role, I try to copy them. I put on their costume. I fantasize being one of them."*

Sex and Other Sacred Games, by Kim Chernin and Renate Stendhal (Times Books, 1989).

Tales of a Male Lesbian

Andrew Ramer

I was never called a sissy when I was growing up, back in the 1950s on Long Island. While I envied my girl cousins the range of emotions they were allowed, I didn't do girl things. Not that I did boy things either. I remember sitting beneath a tree in the elementary school playground, talking about the books we were reading with a handful of other misfits, Albert, Lenny, Peter, and Linda. We'd watch the other boys play softball with the same incomprehension we felt about the rest of the girls jumping rope and singing jump rope songs.

I came out in 1973, during my senior year at UC Berkeley. My first male lover and I were members of a gay men's rap group that met in the damp basement of a local church. Each week twenty or so of us would sit in a circle and bare our souls. I remember how much pain my lover's having sex with other men caused me. "You're just a reactionary heterosexist pig," one man snapped at me, when I talked about it, in tears. Another man looked at me like I was an insect under a magnifying glass and said, "Honey, you're a gay man, not a gay woman. Get over it." But I had no gay women friends, and didn't know what he was talking about.

In 1974 I left my lover and moved back to New York City, to live with my father and stepmother. I tried to fit into the gay world I found there, but I don't like opera and ballet, or bars and bathhouses either, although I forced myself to spend time in both, trying to make myself "normal" (normal for a gay man). The bars were smoke filled and noisy, and I don't drink much. The baths were dark and dank and didn't work for me either. I've never been able to separate sex and love, and as with cruising, there seemed to be all sorts of rules that I could never figure out. Colored hanky? In which pocket? Is he looking at me because he likes me, or because I'm about to be gay bashed?

Identity Envy—Wanting to Be Who We Are Not
Published by The Haworth Press, Inc., 2007. All rights reserved.
doi:10.1300/5641_25

When I moved out on my own after a year, it wasn't down to the Village, which was still the heartland of gay male culture, but across the river to Park Slope, in Brooklyn, which was more affordable. I got a job in the neighborhood bookstore, and it was there that I met my first lesbian friends, one of whom called the neighborhood Dyke Heaven. Within a short time I had a large circle of women friends, many of them former separatists. Back in the days when the official lesbian uniform was cropped hair, a T-shirt, overalls, and Birkenstocks, I did try to pass for a gay man, and wore flannel shirts and jeans and grew the right kind of mustache. But in that mythic pre-AIDS time of sex and drugs, I was always in bed by midnight, never once went to a disco, and vacationed in Fire Island every year with my lesbian friends, *after* Labor Day. I never visited the meat rack, never went to a tea dance, never did coke or any other drugs, and never had sex with anyone whose name I didn't know, who I hadn't at least shared a meal with first, usually two or three. And like a character from the classic lesbian joke, I fell in love quickly and, if I'd ever learned to drive, I too would have brought along a U-Haul on our second date.

Among my friends were women who founded one of the first lesbian presses in the world, and I remember occasions when I was the only man at parties where June Jordan, Audre Lorde, and other now-gone, now-famous writers were sitting around talking about poetry, the Goddess, and the radical transformation of the world by women. It's not that I didn't have a gay male life, but it was lived on the side, in an almost closety fashion. I always had a male lover, who I met at work or through a friend, and who was almost always exasperated by my monogamous inclinations, which seemed unnatural to many gay men back then. I envied my lesbian friends. They had a sense of community, solidarity, and an interest in spirituality. They weren't bitchy or competitive like so many of the gay men I met, and they were also conscious of racism, classism, and the ageism I found so prevalent in gay male culture.

I did have a small circle of gay male friends, who all lived in Manhattan. But while they were reading *Christopher Street*, a long-gone literate gay magazine, I was reading things like Sally Gearhardt's essay "The Death and Resurrection of a Hallelujah Dyke." One year, my gay buddies invited me to join them on a shopping expedition for wigs and gowns and makeup for a Halloween party one of them was having. I'd never done drag and had no interest in it. My friends accused me of being judgmental, repressed, and out of touch with my female side. "I don't think so," I answered, after giving it some thought. "It's just that my inner female is more butch than I am. She isn't Marilyn Monroe. She's Joan of Arc, thundering across a battlefield on a great big horse, wearing a suit of armor, and swinging a huge battleaxe."

My hero in those days was the newly out lesbian novelist and poet May Sarton. A fan letter to her lead to an infrequent but regular exchange of letters. In 1977 she wrote to tell me that she'd be speaking in New York at Barnard College, and invited me to come and finally meet her. The auditorium was packed, with hundreds of women and all of four men. I slid down in my seat when a woman in front of me snarled, "Why did they let *them* in?" Sarton was warm and inspiring when she spoke. At the end, women were pouring down from their seats toward her, and I remember the shock and anger that went through the crowd when the first person Sarton greeted, with an enormous embrace, was a gray-haired man who'd been sitting in the front row. "She comes from a different generation," I remember one woman saying to another, in a tone of pity, contempt, radical disappointment, and forced tolerance. And when I introduced myself to her, the smile and hug she gave me caused an equally strong reaction in the women clustered around her, waiting to greet her. Many of them didn't want me to be there, but I felt right at home. Why couldn't they see that I was one of them?

Once I read an interview with Anne Rice, the author of all those vampire books. The reporter asked her why her work was so homoerotic. Her answer was, "I'm a gay man living in a woman's body." If I were attracted to women it would make sense for me to say that I was a lesbian living in a man's body. But my insides and outsides don't match up neatly. I'm queer in more ways than one. I'm a man who loves men but whose sensibilities are those of a lesbian from the mid-1970s. My best relationship was with another Jewish man who loved Sweet Honey in the Rock concerts and Adrienne Rich poems. (She sometimes came to those Park Slope parties, but she was famous already and I was always too scared to talk to her.) These new lesbians, and bois, and boy dykes, with tattoos, piercings, strap-on dildos, and habits far more puzzling than lipstick, don't make sense to me at all. I'm a relic from a different time. (On the other hand, of my four closest remaining Brooklyn lesbian friends, one is married to a man, one is about to marry a man, and one is involved with a man she'd like to marry but he's already married to another woman.)

Maybe I had too many past lives as a straight woman, or maybe it was having a womanizing father who designed showrooms for women's clothing manufacturers, who read the fashion section of *The New York Times* first, then the entertainment section, and only then the sports section. Or maybe it was being raised for many years after he left by a single mother who'd been raised from age five by a single mother, who was herself raised by a single mother, from the time that she was seven. I was nurtured by strong, independent women. I remember my long-single grandmother reading to me, not children's books but stories from Dickens, Twain, Zola, and De Maupassant. We always sat on her little brocade love seat, beneath a large reproduction of nineteenth-century French artist Rosa Bonheur's painting "The Horse Fair." Bonheur, I later learned, was given permission by the French government to wear trousers, because of her vocation. And my own favorite painting, which I loved to visit at the Metropolitan Museum of Art, was Jules Bastien-Lepage's "Joan of Arc." A copy of it sits on my meditation altar.

If you look at my bookshelves you'll find all of Jane Austen, all of Virginia Woolf's fiction, some of her essays, her one play, and a few biographies of her. You'll find Gertrude Stein, lots of Collette, Emily Dickinson, and books by May Sarton (none of them signed, alas, although I still have all of her letters), and the work of my favorite poet, Louise Bogan, who Sarton turned me on to, several of whose poems I can recite from memory. Between those books you'll find a few volumes by male authors my grandmother turned me on to. But in my will I put down that the only thing I want read at my funeral is Bogan's poem "The Dragonfly."

Once, many years ago, when we were standing in my friend Joan's kitchen, she, a poet and publisher, picked up a large fat wooden spoon whose handle was almost a yard long, and tapped me on both shoulders with it, dubbing me an honorary lesbian. At my progressive and largely LGBT synagogue, I'm always the one lobbying for more prayers that use female God language in Hebrew. I'm good with power tools, and I like cats. But a man with pretty eyes and good politics can still turn my head like nothing else. So what kind of lesbian does that make me?

The Perfect Space Family

Jim Tushinski

When I was eight, I wanted desperately to travel to the stars. I built space vessels out of Lego blocks and imagined myself whisked away into the unknown. I read comic books about Space Family Robinson and the Legion of Super Heroes. I watched hours of science fiction movies on television—*Forbidden Planet* and *Destination Moon, This Island Earth* and *Rocketship X-M*—and once a week I sat mesmerized by my favorite television show in which Will Robinson was the son in a space family who traveled on the Jupiter 2 spaceship. Sometimes Will's family ended up marooned on an alien planet and sometimes they wandered around the universe without a starchart to their name. They were Lost in Space.

Will Robinson was smart and curious and brilliant, too, but he was still a kid and, just like me, still shackled to the whims of his parents and siblings.

"Will," Mother Maureen Robinson would say, "I don't want you going outside the force field tonight."

"How come?" asks Will Robinson.

"Because I said so," Mom replies, looking stern but a little saddened that her own son would even have to ask for a reason.

Will Robinson could fix things, such as the family's deadpan robot or the solar coils. He was always getting into trouble, sometimes being rescued by his handsome father or Major Don West, the pilot, and sometimes rescuing himself and others. He was only eight or nine but carried himself with confidence. I watched him in awe. I wished I could be Will Robinson, of course, but more than anything I wished I could have his family. They were all smart and trim and so nice looking. No one ever shouted, even when things were bad, and they hugged each other like they meant it. They faced the unknown and no one ever complained, except the treacherous and effeminate stow-

Identity Envy—Wanting to Be Who We Are Not
Published by The Haworth Press, Inc., 2007. All rights reserved.
doi:10.1300/5641_26

away Dr. Smith. He wasn't family, though. He was like the awful neighbor that you had to try and get along with even if he purposefully sprayed poison on his lawn and made sure some of it landed in your own backyard where your dog could eat it.

The previews of *Lost in Space* began appearing in the summer of 1965 on the walnut console black and white TV that sat on stout brass-tipped legs in the family room. I could barely contain my excitement. There were saucer-shaped spacecraft and one-eyed giants throwing boulders and ray guns and weird desert landscapes. After the show premiered, I watched each weekly episode faithfully, sitting bolt upright as close to the TV as my parents would allow. It wasn't just the adventures in outer space that fascinated me. There was something about the worried look on Mother Robinson's face when Will or his sister Penny disappeared once again into the alien night or the handsome, stoic face of Father John Robinson as he blasted some mutant to rescue his daughter Judy. These faces held me rapt. The series was an escape for me to be sure, but looking back I know it was more than just a diversion. Television took me away from my terrestrial family.

At eight years old, and probably well before then, I realized I was bound to my family by the sole fact that I was related to them. I don't remember feeling much affection or closeness for them. I was one of three children—the middle child between a sister three years my senior and a brother eighteen months younger. I knew from television and books that I was supposed to feel love for these people, that my parents were supposed to be stern, but caring, that I was supposed to pal around with my younger brother and affectionately tease my sister. Instead, I looked at these people who shared the same house that I did and wondered what I had in common with them. There were some physical resemblances, but our affection seemed ritualized to me— the kiss on the cheek before bedtime from my mother, my father's insistence on taking "the boys" fishing or to baseball games, the manic Christmas mornings full of gifts we had listed out carefully in advance. I saw moments of genuine emotions from my parents and siblings, but these took the form of shouting, tears, and pouting.

I was happiest alone in my bedroom reading or sitting inside on a sunny day watching *The Deadly Mantis* or *Them!* on TV. In our suburban neighborhood in Lombard, Illinois, there was nothing that needed exploring, no woods to get lost in, no need to venture outside except to walk to school or go to the DuPage Theater for Saturday matinees. I stayed inside myself like the Robinson Family stayed within the protection of their force field and spaceship. I was a mystery to my parents and the rest of my family—quiet, but capable of screaming rages if my father dictated that he watch a hockey game instead of my regular Saturday night ritual of Creature Features. As I looked at my family with puzzlement and irritation, I'm sure they looked at me as if I were one of those blond children from *Village of the Damned*—a cuckoo raised in a starling's nest. I filled pages with strange drawings and jottings. I dreamed of monsters and jungles and older boys rescuing me.

For a long time, we were a family with a station wagon. It was a vehicle for road trips during which my brother and I could spread out in the back with blankets and comic books, lying flat and watching billboards whiz by upside down. It felt like we were flying, just like on the Jupiter 2, or that we were rambling along in the futuristic tank-tread Chariot that the Robinsons used to explore their desert planet home. Of course, eventually one of us kids started to pick on or irritate one of the others, which led to crying or tattling. My parents would yell at us, threaten to stop the car and spank the offending party. I knew Father and Mother Robinson wouldn't have reacted that way, but then Will and Penny responded well to reason. My brother and sister and I were raised by a father whose favorite quotation was "children should be seen and not heard" and a mother who was so browbeaten by her husband that her first response to our conflicts was an outpouring of pent-up frustration. We would never have survived being lost in space.

We took road trips to visit relatives who lived on farms in Northern Wisconsin where I fit in even less than at home. I tried to approach these visits like a space explorer meeting new species. First I approached my cousins optimistically, hand extended in peace. But when it was clear the boys only wanted to play football on the yard or chase us around the barn with severed chicken feet, I retreated to the attic to read and avoided contact. My mother called me "stuck up" and said everyone thought I was odd. My brother ran shouting with the other boys. My sister baked cookies and helped clean up with the other girls. My father played cards on folding tables and smoked cigars with the men.

Occasionally one of my aunts would try to relate to me. Aunt Evelyn lived in Oshkosh and was educated. She had an Original Cast Album of *My Fair Lady,* which impressed me so much that I would look at it over and over again during the boring hours of "visiting" we had to endure on trips to the relatives. She asked what I wanted to be when I grew up and I said a writer. She didn't laugh. She just said, "Maybe someday you'll put me in one of your books." I wanted to write a book about a space family going to the moon and tried to picture Aunt Evelyn as one of the passengers, but couldn't. She wouldn't look right in the shiny silver jumpsuit with her glasses and unfuturistic hair. No one in my space family had a Wisconsin accent either. I would make sure of that.

I'm on the Jupiter 2 with my real family. It must be a nightmare. I would never have wanted this.

"Goddamnit!" my father shouts from the ship's lower level. He's down there trying to fix the atomic drive, which overheated when my brother left his space suit covering the vents. I hear my father bump his head and it reverberates throughout the spaceship's walls. "Shit!" he screams. I'm sitting at the ship's controls, looking out at the galaxies, pretending I'm piloting the ship. I don't touch the controls because I know I'll get spanked if I do.

Mom is trying to finish the laundry, but the hyper-washer is broken as well, so she has to drag wet clothes up on the elevator from the galley sink and hang them on clothesline strung across the suspended animation tubes. She looks tired and worried.

"Are you all right down there?" she calls.

"If you damn kids would do as you're told," Dad shouts, "this never would have happened."

"I didn't do anything," my brother says from his bedroom pod downstairs. "Jim took my spacesuit and probably left it on the vents."

"Mom," my sister yells from her pod, the sound of tears in her voice, "the boys looked in my diary. The key wasn't where I left it."

"Did you look in her diary?" Mom says, her tone telling me she already knows I did.

"It was Donnie," I said. "He told me he did it."

"Did not!" my brother screams.

"Shut up," Dad shouts. "You goddamn kids! Which one of you took the atomic wrench? It was right here and now it's gone. I told you to keep your goddamn hands off my tools!"

"Did you read her dairy?" Mom asks again.

I look longingly at the suspended animation tubes.

"Did you?"

Something inside me snaps. "I said I didn't do it." I shout so loud that Dad stops hammering on the atomic drive. I fling myself down the metal rung ladder connecting the two levels of the spaceship. "I hate you all," I shout. "Leave me alone." I run into my bedroom pod and hit the Close button hard. The door slides shut with a whoosh.

"You get out here right now," Dad says. It's a threat. "Right now."

"No," I shout. I'm crying now, crying so hard it feels like I'm going to break open. Outside my porthole, the universe expands. We're a tiny speck in it. There's no chance of meeting another spaceship for years and years, no planet to land on, nowhere to go. I cry and cry as my dad beats his fists against the heavy metal door, cry until the tears are gone and all I can do is heave and pant.

I wanted to think I'd fit in with the Robinsons, but I wasn't so sure. My first reaction to conflict was to run away and hide. I daydreamed too much to be attentive to chores, like caring for the hydroponic garden or helping Penny gather edible plants. I couldn't help fix the power module with Father Robinson and Will. I'd probably end up being manipulated into betraying everyone by Dr. Smith or spending hours talking to the robot about what Earth was like. I'd fantasize about ways of getting into danger so handsome, cocky Major Don West could rescue me. Judy—Don West's girlfriend and the oldest Robinson daughter—would think I was weird. She'd understand why I looked at Major West the way I did, even if it wasn't completely clear to me, and she'd tell him that I frightened her and make him pull her closer.

In one episode of *Lost in Space,* Father Robinson and Major West are checking on a remote weather station, which warns them that a devastating winter storm is approaching. Before they can get back to the Jupiter 2, load everyone into the Chariot, and escape to warmer climes on the other side of the Southern Sea, a one-eyed giant blocks their way. It throws boulders at them and pins them inside a shallow cave. Meanwhile, Will Robinson is in the spaceship fixing the radio telescope. As he makes the last adjustment, he looks into the eyepiece and sees the giant. He calls to his mom, who takes one look and knows her husband is in danger. She has that worried, far away look that she often gets—being the mom in a space family and in constant danger. Before anyone has time to tell him not to, Will grabs one of the ray guns and runs to help his father. He climbs a mountain in freezing cold without a fur-lined jacket, takes aims, and kills the giant. When Father Robinson and Major West emerge from the cave in response to Will's shouts, the first thing Father does is get on his knees and embrace Will. Then he holds Will an arms length away and says in his sternest voice, "Promise me you'll never leave your mother and sisters alone again."

"I promise," Will Robinson says. His father embraces him once more and Major West ruffles Will's hair. Father Robinson takes off his fur-lined coat and drapes it around his son.

"Here," Father says. "Now let's get going."

"Yes, sir," Will says with a big smile.

And off they go to pack up the Chariot.

There are so many things I don't remember about being a child. I don't remember much happiness or affection, though it probably was there in small doses. I don't remember my first day at school or the day we moved to Cincinnati. But I remember sitting in the family room watching that episode of *Lost in Space.*

The one-eyed giant excited me and I bounced up and down in anticipation as Father Robinson and Major West were trapped. I rooted for Will to save the day. My dad was sitting in his easy chair behind me, asleep. Mom was in the kitchen, cleaning up from dinner with my sister. My brother lay on his stomach next to me, watching the TV as intently as I was. When the hug came, I glanced behind me. Like Father Robinson, my dad was a tall, powerfully built man. He had the same dark, wavy hair that he kept combed back out of his eyes. Instead of a fur-lined coat, V-necked space sweater, and form-fitting stretch pants, Dad wore a white sleeveless T-shirt. He snored. His mouth hung open.

Back on the TV, the family was climbing into the Chariot, as if getting ready to visit relatives on the other side of the Southern Sea. Mother Robinson ran around shouting for Penny, who had been riding on the giant tortoise and was now nowhere to be found. With the temperature plunging, Father Robinson straps on his jet pack and flies off in search of his wayward daughter. If he's not back before the temperature reaches minus 15, they are to leave without him or risk death from freezing. Major West nods. Father can count on him to do what's needed.

My brother kicks me. He knows Dad is asleep and that I'm watching my favorite show. He knows he can get away with it.

"Quit it," I hiss at him.

"What?" he says.

Father Robinson circles around weird desert rock formations, searching for Penny. In the Chariot, Mother and Judy look about, sick with worry. My brother kicks me again. Dad snorts, still asleep.

"Quit it," I say a little louder.

"Quit what?"

There's Penny, freezing, lost among some weird plants with her pet Debbie, a mutated chimp. She sees her father flying to her rescue and waves. "Oh, Daddy," she cries.

"You and Debbie get up on the jet pack and hold on," Father Robinson says as he embraces Penny. He doesn't scold her. He's just happy she's still alive. One more kick from my brother. I kick him back.

"Mom," my brother shouts, "Jim's kicking me."

Dad wakes up and throws his shoe at us.

"Stop bickering or you'll both get the belt," my dad says.

"He started it," my brother says, pointing at me.

"Did not."

When Father Robinson arrives with Penny, Mother's face lights up. She wasn't going to leave without her husband and daughter. She kisses Father and hugs Penny so tight it looks like she'll never let go.

Farmer Boy

Al Cho

My father came to Illinois to study agriculture, but he never intended to put down roots. Like many Koreans in the 1970s, he arrived
with a simple plan: to obtain a degree in the United States and return
to the motherland, where a diploma from a middling state university
would turn magically into a ticket to a prestigious and stable future. A
hard-nosed, economical people, Koreans risked the precious cur-
rency of their lives en masse, buying cheap and selling dear as they
exported themselves to the land of opportunity for a couple of years
to bring home the valuable technological knowledge of the West.
This, not the technocratic narratives of Harvard economists, is the
real story of the East Asian miracle.

But this is not a story about my father, and in any case he broke the
rules. When he landed in Champaign-Urbana, Illinois, a land of bio-
technologically sweetened corn and sweet, corn-fed people, my father met my mother, and other seeds were sown. First my sister developed, a melon-like protrusion on my mother's slight Korean frame,
and then I appeared on the scene: fat and round like a suckling pig.
When strangers passed my sister on the street, they beamed, exclaim-
ing "What a beautiful baby!" As I trundled along behind her, the inev-
itable pause; then, "And he certainly looks like a boy."

None of us could have known, back in those days of falling maple
leaves, wild alliums, and fenceless backyards, that Korea would become a distant memory for my parents. None of us could have predicted what would grow in the fertile ground we leased for the six
years it took my father to get his PhD, because we were never meant
to stay. When my father first arrived in the United States, border con-

Identity Envy—Wanting to Be Who We Are Not
Published by The Haworth Press, Inc., 2007. All rights reserved.
doi:10.1300/5641_27

trol officers ransacked his luggage, checking for contraband—drugs and weapons, of course, but above all seeds, for the government was as concerned about plant invasive species as it was about aliens of the human kind. We were potted plants, never destined to naturalize or flourish in the space we temporarily inhabited. My family simply waited for the signal—my father's commencement—that would transplant us from this odd Midwestern climate back to our native soil.

Twenty years later, of course, we are still in America. My family's desire to put down roots proved incapable of containment, and my parents became naturalized citizens. In the mid-1980s, America's face turned toward the sun, and people from all walks of life joined a phototropic exodus to the Southwest in search of work, new lives, and warmth. My father landed a job as a soil scientist at an agronomic research facility near Phoenix, so we joined the masses abandoning the Midwest for towns that sprouted overnight like desert wildflowers from Arizona's crusted earth. Counting cacti to entertain ourselves during the six-day drive through the vast and featureless terrain, we finally settled in the arid, searing Valley of the Sun: as hostile an environment as possible for people accustomed to the misty greenery of mountainous Korea and then to the crisp winters of Champaign-Urbana, Illinois. Despite the climatic shock, we stayed and survived; still, my life in Arizona always seemed incidental and incongruous, shaped by circumstances rather than nature.

One of the starkest ironies of Tempe, Arizona—a desert city if there ever was one—is that deciduous trees from rainier places are spread liberally through its irrigated yards. Each year, millions of gallons of water are spilled upon these alien flora, whose leaves drop dead and yellow each fall in an ironic mockery of autumn foliage. At the height of the summer, the blazing sun wilts adult trees even as gardeners, themselves transplants from more agreeable climates, desperately flood their roots with water the desert can ill afford to give. Opportunistic nurseries sell the same lush and thirsty plants as their counterparts in wetter regions, exploiting new arrivals' desperate yearning for yards as soft and verdant as the ones they left behind. Gardening in Arizona is a tragic and futile enterprise, revealing the lengths to which people will go to pretend they do not dwell in the desert.

Tragic and futile—but also romantic, even heroic. There is something magical about the way gardening enables people to invent spaces and identities, miniature webs of life. For many new Arizonans, gardening became a way to reconstruct in miniature the worlds they abandoned in New Jersey, Ohio, or Illinois. Some efforts were more ambitious than others; on College Avenue in Tempe, there is a house rendered almost invisible, obscured by a forest of richly irrigated bamboo, this next to a squat, adobe cube surrounded by crushed granite, ocotillos, and an olive tree. In the narrow strip of backyard behind our modest, ranch-style house on Del Rio Drive, a bedroom community of lower-middle-class, cookie-cutter homes, my family planted a bizarre assortment of trees to declare our arrival: grapefruit, lemon, peach, apricot, and the spectacularly unsuccessful *daechoo,* a variety of Korean plum. These trees joined an already motley community of orange, mulberry, aloe, and agave, populating an orchard nature never envisioned. Despite the assiduous work of our sprinklers, Arizonan summers took their toll; the young *daechoos* withered and died, and the bark of the apricot tree split in the heat, leaking buboes of blood-orange resin that dripped in clumps onto the scorched earth below.

In this eerie and mismatched garden, plants became a palette of raw materials for my imagination: a way to fashion an external universe that suited me better than the world my parents had built. I found the blueprint for this world in books I discovered in my older sister's bedroom. At the age of eight, my favorite book was *Farmer Boy* by Laura Ingalls Wilder, the story of her husband's childhood in the farmlands of New York. I devoured the book, reading about Almanzo's colts, his milk-fed pumpkin, and the gruesome process of making head cheese, over and over until the dog-eared copy broke its spine in our minivan, the resin of its binding liquefied by sunshine intensified in the miniature greenhouse effect that transforms cars into furnaces during the Arizona summer.

Even in the dusty confines of our narrow, oppressively hot backyard, it was easy to imagine myself as a young Almanzo, growing up in the prairies of mid-nineteenth-century America. Like Laura's eventual husband, I had a bossy and overbearing sister. Though my parents couldn't afford livestock, and we had no room for horses, I had two pet ducks, hatched in my third-grade classroom at Meyer Elementary. Both females, named Donald and Daffy, they wandered aimlessly around the confines of our yard, encircled by cinderblock walls too high for their clipped wings to ascend. Snowy white, with greenish-black feathers on their backs and tails, they contrasted sharply with the dun brown mallards that populated the algae-strewn artificial lakes of suburban Phoenix's planned communities. Stranded in a desert they should never have been forced to inhabit, they made the best of their lot in life, instinctively pantomiming duck baths, frenzied wings beating uselessly against the ochre earth of our backyard and laying scores of sterile, unfertilized eggs that lay inert, putrefying in the warmth of the Arizona summer.

During sweltering summer days, I stayed inside and read; as the thermometer fell in the long, golden evenings, I emerged into the garden and became someone new. Equipped with lesbian waterfowl (but no water), seeds stolen from Home Depot, and an imagination capable of surmounting inconvenient details. I stripped bark from branches torn from the mulberry tree that bravely fought for life in our backyard, braiding whips to motivate horses that existed only in my mind. Wasting hundreds of gallons of water, I coaxed unwilling vegetables into existence in our backyard, trying by sheer force of desire to grow plants that had no business sprouting in the desert and that I didn't like much anyway: beets, lettuce, spinach, chard. Each night, as the air cooled and the twilight colored the world in preternatural hues, I was transformed into a bona fide American prairie farmer boy, circa 1870.

The person I cultivated in my scrappy backyard garden, of course, lived only in my imagination. In the real world, I was an accident of fate: an Asian boy in a desert city where people were either white, Mexican, or strange. At Meyer Elementary School, Mike Hale, a skinny, freckled boy with bad teeth, would corner me in the bathroom and make me watch as he stretched his eyelids to mimic mine, chanting: *Chinese, Japanese, look at my dirty knees.* Being Korean wasn't even a choice—but in another sense, how I wished it were. In those years, I would have renounced my family in an instant had the Wilders come looking for their long-lost son. Already a voracious reader, I had devoured a canon of literature populated by people who looked and behaved nothing like my family, and I began to wish that I, too, could claim our enterprising, agrarian pioneers as my ancestors. In school we sang songs about America, this amber grain-waving land where my fathers died, except mine hadn't. My family's fathers lay buried in grassy mounds in Korean cemeteries, hillocks stretching into the craggy mountains in the mist, obscured from view and from my comprehension. This land was your land; I wished it were mine. But no matter how many bulbs and seedlings I forced into the powdery dust in the corner of our yard, I could gain no purchase upon this place I had come, by a strange twist of history, to call home.

So in this desert city that garbed itself in borrowed greenery, I began to cultivate a new identity, grafting American competences, habits, and norms onto the stubby Asian rootstock I longed to make disappear. I consciously weeded out traces of difference, refusing to go to Korean language school on Saturdays, to attend Korean church on Sundays, or to invite friends home for dinner because I knew there would be embarrassing food on the table. In a Korean creation myth, a giant bear is promised transfiguration into human form if he can subsist for thirty days and thirty nights on nothing but garlic and wormwood, a narrative that explains not only the genesis of the first Korean king, but also his country's enduring predilection for aggressively pungent food. I found the tastes and smells of my ethnic identity mortifying, an olfactory reminder of the cultural firmament in which I felt inescapably entrapped, and I longed for the comparative simplicity of the American food I had encountered in the books I loved. Stacked pancakes with maple syrup, baked beans, even head cheese sounded incomparably better than the reeking, mismatched bowls of Korean food my family slurped while wordlessly watching television at the dinner table. My parents, who had grown up in abject poverty, foraging for mountain vegetables in the aftermath of the Korean War, delighted in the ready availability of foods like mackerel that had been impossibly expensive delicacies in their youth. I gagged and held my nose each time the oily, fishy fumes filled the house, inhaling only after I had retreated into the dry, clear air outdoors, where orange blossoms laced the evening with their delicate perfume.

At first, my agronomist father supported my budding interest in all things agricultural. On some weekends, he would drive me out past Phoenix's sprawling perimeter, through stretches of desert not yet terraformed by nostalgic, homesick gardeners, to the experimental fields of the University of Arizona's agronomic research center in the ramshackle town of Maricopa. There were expansive fields lined with neat rows of cotton, green and supple in spring, turned brown and brittle by winter, bearing countless fuzzy tufts that made it look as though snow had finally come to the desert. Foraging among the rows, I harvested cotton into gallon-sized Ziploc bags, mentally inhabiting *Gone with the Wind*. There were endless rows of scientifically enhanced carrots and onions; the rust-colored soil lay studded with root vegetables, their dusty and wilting tops concealing the improbably swollen, bulbous treasures that separated from the ground with a satisfying ripping sound, as though the earth were fighting to defend its most valuable possessions. Driving home, I would sit silent but triumphant, twirling cotton strands into a coarse yarn as I reveled in the experience of having been, for even one afternoon, a farmer boy.

But when my father lost his job—due to racial discrimination, he insisted—he also lost interest in indulging my agrarian fantasies. Uprooted from the career around which he had structured his life's work, he wilted and withered like crop residue in the desert sun. My parents declared bankruptcy, and my father took up a job maintaining the building that housed the nursing home where my mother worked, repairing roofs and fixing subterranean cracks in antique sprinkler systems. His skin grew brown and coarse like the rinds of kiwifruit. Where he had once encouraged my backyard imagination, my father now warned me away from agriculture, and his own, ambitious garden, full of rosebushes, birds of paradise, daffodils, began to die from neglect.

There is another Korean myth, a story of two brothers named Hyungbu and Nolbu. Hyungbu, the impoverished but kindly younger brother, happens upon an injured swallow and nurses it back to health. The swallow flies away to the celestial kingdom of birds and returns with magic seeds that yield enormous gourds that ripen and disgorge a new house full of riches beyond imagination. Hyungbu's wicked older brother, consumed by jealousy, captures another swallow, breaks its leg, carelessly splints it, and throws it into flight in the hope that it will bring him a similar fortune. The canny swallow returns with seeds that the wicked man plants with relish and anticipation. When his prodigious gourds are ripe, however, they release pests, snakes, and a tidal wave that sweeps away his home, leaving his family utterly destitute. A primitive solution to the question of theodicy—one simply reaps what one sows.

As my father's spirit shriveled like a raisin, I thought about what his supervisors had called his "inability to acclimate" to his working environment. I decided that like Nolbu, my father must have reaped what he had sown. It was not difficult to find fault; I blamed him for his stubborn foreignness, for the thick and inflected accent that must have made him difficult to work with, and for the awkward formality and social distance he maintained with his hearty, middle-American colleagues. I felt nothing but contempt for my strange, distant father, comparing him unfavorably to the robust, independent, congenial men of the American frontier: men like Almanzo's father, whose strength and savvy called forth the earth's bounty and commanded the respect of their peers. Untroubled by the broader incoherence of theodicy, I committed myself anew to cultivation and acculturation, filling our backyard with plants from the British *Herb Book:* rosemary, lavender, bergamot, anointing myself with the sophistication of English gardens to mask the traces of my troubling ethnic origins: seeking transfiguration in the healing power of herbs.

My new identity spread like bamboo in the desert: improbable, but cultivated diligently until it grew to conceal what lay beneath. As I grew ever more distant from my family, my father's shame drove him ever farther from his. He no longer had any interest in visiting his native soil, where he would face awkward questions about his career; everyone still thought he had made it big in the United States. The branches of our family tree, whose roots spanned the Pacific Ocean, atrophied until my cousins faded into names and spidery snippets of narrative, like the airborne wisps of cotton that stuck to our wheels as my father and I left the fields of Maricopa for the last time.

And so I developed into a grotesque human topiary, rigorously trained into ever more improbable shapes. At Meyer, I developed a facility with words—not their usage, but their spelling. As I triumphed in spelling bee after spelling bee, my English teachers set aside entire class periods to help me learn ever larger, more abstrusely complicated words. By eighth grade, I had won the state spelling bee by correctly enunciating each letter of the word *purlieu,* an outlying or neighboring area: a word that left me victorious, but still at the margins of the world I was so desperately trying to penetrate. Trophies crowned with olive wreaths accumulated in our living room, a fossil record of triumphs—Future Business Leaders of America competitions, a state debate championship, two state speech championships, admission to Harvard—fruits of the careful pruning I undertook to fashion myself into new forms, as though the plaques that sprouted from our walls like leaves could somehow cover the roots I so desperately wished to conceal.

It is raining in Seoul, and mists shroud high, grassy hills that are barely visible through the foggy windows of my cousin's Hyundai Elantra. I am twenty-one years old, en route from an internship in Washington, DC, to a job working with the U.S. government at the World Summit on Sustainable Development in Johannesburg, where world leaders will debate how to meet the needs of the present without compromising the welfare of future generations. But for the moment, I have a five-day layover in Korea, and my cousin Youngbae is taking me to see my relatives for the first time in seven years. On the drive from Inchon's new, modern airport, a greenhouse of glass and soaring steel arches, Youngbae and I try to make conversation until my inability to speak Korean becomes too much of a burden. The barely audible radio drones in a language whose cadence I recognize, but whose words I cannot understand. The raindrops beat percussively against the windshield, and the warm car smells slightly of baby powder and garlic: the comforting scent of young, fecund Koreans.

As we sail past open fields of soybeans and sorghum, my mind begins to wander. I recall a trip my family once took to the Boyce Arboretum, an expansive forest managed by the University of Arizona in the desert just south of Phoenix. After wandering across acres of arid, drought-resistant succulents, we stumbled gladly upon an oasis: an herb garden full of medicinal and culinary plants straight from the pages of *The Herb Book*. I saw lemon verbena, southernwood, and pennyroyal, plants I longed to own but never managed to find at Home Depot, and I could not control myself. Remembering from *The Herb Book* that these species can be propagated with cuttings, I disobeyed the posted signs beseeching visitors not to disturb the plants and surreptitiously snapped off sprigs from each, stuffing them into my coat pocket. Once home, I would place them in plastic cups of water and wait for new roots to appear. But the path through the forest meandered widely, the sun blazed overhead, and the drive in a hot car from Superior to Tempe took longer than expected. By the time I fished them out of my pocket, the cuttings had wilted; they were inert, incapable of generating new life.

Korea is the land where every single one of my ancestors, for generations traceable back six centuries, now lies buried and forgotten, at least by me. On this, my first visit to Korea as an adult, I view my surroundings with a numbing sense of detachment. I wish there were some affective feeling of connection, a primal, innate sense of recognition rising uncontrollably within my psyche, like Argos recognizing his master after a twenty-year odyssey. But the scenery is merely pretty; this land belongs to my parents, to another people.

We reach the outskirts of Seoul, and Youngbae takes me to the apartment where his mother, the wife of my deceased uncle, lives alone. It feels like the closing scene from *The Joy Luck Club;* she embraces me passionately and welcomes me into her home, which is already infused with the pungent, delicious smells of *kimchi* and *bulgogi.* For the next three days, Big Mama, as she is known to me in Korean, rearranges her life to accommodate my wishes. One afternoon, she takes me to a bookstore in downtown Seoul—an arduous trip that takes at least an hour under favorable circumstances—just because I tell her I like to read. We return the next day, despite torrential rains, and she introduces me to a section of Seoul I have never seen before—Insadong, the cultural and artistic capital of the city. Her unstinting generosity and warmth, offered to a nearly total stranger on the basis of blood ties attenuated by marriage, make me feel slightly guilty, unworthy, and grateful.

Between treks, we sit in a restaurant, eating from steaming bowls of piquant, delicious Korean food. Big Mama hands me a Korean dictionary she has purchased for me at the bookstore, and with its assistance we begin to talk. I tell her about my work, about biodiversity loss, deforestation, global trade, sustainable development. She looks bored and asks me when I am going to get married. I look down, then tell her that I am too young, and far too busy to be dating anyone anyway.

She asks me what I plan to do with my life, and I tell her that someday, after I save the world, I want to be a farmer, and maybe a beekeeper. She begins to laugh.

"Why you laugh?" I ask in broken Korean.

"Because you are so much like your father," she says. "All of this—the enormous dreams, the bees, this farming nonsense. Just like your father." Smiling, she shakes her head and slurps some more soup. Tired of leafing through the dictionary to scrabble for words, we lapse into a warm, comfortable silence.

Shiksa in My Living Room

Lori Horvitz

To tame my thick mass of dark curly hair, I used expensive conditioners and spent hours blow-drying it, section by section. Every so often I paid my sister fifty cents to iron my mane, flattening the frizz for a few hours before it coiled back into its usual rat's nest appearance.

Similar to my out-of-control hair, I felt ashamed by my unruly family. In restaurants, my father often screamed for a waitress from across the room: "Waitress, could you bring me a slab of onion?" My mother, living as if she were a Holocaust victim, stuffed her purse with sugar packets, jelly and butter sachets, and leftover bread. From the corner of my eye, I enviously gazed at happy blonde families (my father referred to them as "The Christians") who ate meals quietly, spoke in hushed tones, had napkins on their laps and graciously used them to wipe crumbs from the corners of their mouths.

I grew up in a Long Island suburb, a middle-class neighborhood with a predominantly Jewish population. Although I looked like any other Jewish kid with Eastern immigrant grandparents, by second grade, I had already been marked as an outsider, a misfit. Just as a vicious German shepherd could sense fear, my classmates sensed my vulnerability and attacked. Even Robin Greenblatt, the obese, almost-blind daughter of the local orthodontist, taunted me. One afternoon, she put her leg up on the last remaining bus seat and told me I wasn't welcome to sit down: "You've got pepper in your underpants, Smelly." When I got off the bus, I ran home and cried to my mother. "She's just jealous of you," my mother said, "because you're pretty and she's ugly." I wiped the tears from my eyes and nodded my head in agreement.

In our living room, on the never-tuned grand piano, a two-faced plastic picture frame held a Bar Mitzvah family pose on one side, and

Identity Envy—Wanting to Be Who We Are Not
Published by The Haworth Press, Inc., 2007. All rights reserved.
doi:10.1300/5641_28

on the other, a mock photo of a blonde-haired, blue-eyed, busty skier—a picture included in the frame at the time of purchase. Years went by; still, her retouched blue eyes stared me down—when I ran to answer the telephone, when I walked in from a lonely day at junior high. Through dusty glare-proof glass, her Aryan nose pointed toward my mother's screams when the greasy chuck-steak caught on fire. A decade later, with maroon earmuffs neatly arranged upon her wind-blown hair, her rosy glow endured, even when our poodle died of a heart attack in her sleep. This woman became my surrogate sister, my quiet, comforting, blonde-haired role model. The *shiksa* in my living room.

During summers, I found consolation at a local day camp where no one knew me, a free program for county residents. Because most of the Jewish kids attended other summer camps, a good portion of the kids at my camp were non-Jews. Along with reinventing myself each summer, I reunited with my best camp friend, Ellen Winfrey. Now I was the jaw-breaker-in-mouth, captain's first choice for the softball team. I had the dodge ball strong arm, won Field Day ribbons, and starred in camp plays. Ellen and I stood side-by-side, barbecuing marshmallows, grouting tile ashtrays, weaving baskets, and sharing Razzles.

But by fall, I transformed back into a long-faced, frizzy-haired, painfully shy tomboy. I did have two misfit friends while in junior high band—quiet Christian kids who lived on "the other side of the train tracks." Helen was dark and Greek, and Regina was gawky and looked like a man. The three of us played clarinet. Right before playing the themes from *MASH* and *Rocky*, we'd get all worked up and say, "Yes!"

Once we went on a band exchange trip to another school thirty miles away, a WASPy town that had a main street, a general store, and big houses on huge plots of land. Each band member stayed with a host family, and I stayed with the family of another clarinetist my age, Nancy. Together we talked about our schools and our towns and our ambitions. She told me she wanted to be a social worker. I told her I wanted to be a photographer. "I want to travel," I said. "To see the world." Nancy showed me a photo album from Disney World and Bermuda. I flipped through the pages, admiring the smiling faces, thinking *why can't I have a normal family and live in a normal town and go on normal vacations?* Instead, my parents and sister and two brothers crammed into an Impala station wagon and drove to historic villages like Williamburg, Virginia, where people wore scary old costumes and worked on spinning wheels and hammered iron nails and blew glass. For me, vacations meant going to boring museums, getting carsick, and throwing up at the side of the road.

At Nancy's dinner table, her parents and brother passed around huge platters of roast beef and fresh green beans and peach cobbler, unlike my family, where we fought over chicken parts, had creamed-corn and baked beans poured right onto our plates from the can, and the only desserts we could hope for were Ring Dings or Yodels. And unlike the loud, mean, gum-snapping competitive Jewish kids I grew up with, Nancy spoke in a soft voice and seemed interested in everything I said. Although the idea of church and Jesus Christ nailed to a crucifix frightened me, Nancy confirmed that not only did I grow up in the wrong town, I grew up in the wrong religion. After all, my only fond memory of Sunday school is riding on back of Mr. Wilkomersky's motorcycle. He took each student on a ride, and when it was my turn I wrapped my arms around his waist and shut my eyes and felt the wind whip against my face and thought, maybe this is what it means to be a Jew. But Mr. Wilkomersky got fired for endangering our lives.

And then I thought Jewish meant chanting prayers in a language I didn't understand, worrying if I had enough friends to invite to my Bat Mitzvah, and sitting through three-hour long Passover Seders led by my military officer/rabbi grandfather. Jewish meant my father dragging me by my hair to attend high holy day services and having to fast for one of those days. Jewish meant Florida-tanned high school girls snapping Dentyne and bragging about SAT scores.

I was ashamed of my last name—Horvitz. It was so damn Jewish. When I'd say my name, I cringed; I might as well have been saying Lori Yes-I'm-Jewish-Horvitz. And people couldn't get it right anyway. They'd say Lori *Horowitz*. I made a pact with myself that I'd marry a man with a pleasing last name, like Flower. Lori Flower. Or a cool-sounding name like Ferrari. Anything but Horvitz.

By fourteen, I'd already given up on my town, on making friends, knowing that the only way to find happiness was to get away. I took classes during the summer so I could graduate early from high school. I wrote notes to myself and hid them in back of my underwear drawer: *By the time you find this, I hope you're happier and that you have bigger breasts.* Mean boys asked in passing, "Where's your tits?" I walked with my head down, holding my books in such a way to cover up my flat chest. Yet I always found solace in the shiksa in my living room, her cheery expression, her windblown hair, her ski poles pointing upward.

To my dismay, my breasts remained petite. At the local library, I hid among the bookshelves, reading about breast enlargements and silicone implants, studying before and after operations. I thought, *all I need is straight hair and larger breasts and a Christian last name. Then I'd be set.*

The wallpaper in my bedroom displayed long-haired hippie men sitting in Buddha position, flashing the peace sign. My father adhered it the day Nixon resigned. Surrounded by these walls, I learned how to play Peter Frampton and Cat Stevens songs on the guitar. I composed songs about my poodle. I listened to the first album by the trio America—three hippie guys who sang songs about horses with no names and the free wind of Ventura Highway. When asked by my sister which of the three guys I liked best, I pointed to the blonde guy wearing gold wire-rim glasses on the cover. "That's the kind of guy I want to marry," I said. Another of my favorite albums, Fleetwood Mac's *Rumours*, spun around and around on my record player. One day, while listening to Stevie Nicks singing "Gold Dust Woman," I stared at her photo on the back album cover and took note of her tight silk gown and her blonde hair and for a second, I felt a strange pang in my heart, a pang of lust. *What's going on? Why am I feeling this way about a woman?* Without delay, I slipped *Rumours* back into its sleeve and put on Bob Segar's *Night Moves.* But I couldn't shake that scary feeling. For twenty minutes, I sat in the corner of my closet, holding my knees against my chest, chanting over and over, "I'm not like that, I'm not like that."

Between my junior and senior years of college, I chopped vegetables and hoed weeds and mopped floors on a kibbutz in Israel. For the first week, I hung around with a handful of Jewish students from America, but when a group of European hippies arrived, my alliances shifted. Now every night I partied with the blonde-haired Danes, the Brit from Manchester, the Germans. We drank brandy and White Russians and on my guitar, I played Joni Mitchell and Bonnie Raitt songs. I managed to get to work by 7 a.m., but some of the Europeans showed up late, if at all. One of the Danes, Maria, challenged the kibbutz manager when he gave her the task of picking peas out of pods. "Why do the men have the good jobs outside?" she asked. "Why do they get to use dynamite and blow up mines?"

"This is our home and you are our guest. If you don't like your job, you can leave," he said.

Maria left. The other Europeans followed behind. A few days later, the manager, one of the German-Jewish Holocaust survivors who founded the kibbutz, called me into his office. "We judge a person by who they choose as their friends," he said. "You're a nice Jewish girl. You need to think about who you associate with."

At the artsy state college I attended, I hung around with long-haired, intellectual hippie boys from upstate New York, and Dead-head hippie girls who obsessed about the hippie boys. With my friends, I saw the Grateful Dead in Maine, in Philadelphia, in Ithaca, in New York City. I liked the music. I liked the community. I took pride in associating with the freaks and rebels, but I never felt like a *real* Deadhead. I was an observer, an imposter. I didn't feel comfortable wearing Indian skirts and gauzy tops. I felt like an idiot if I tried to dance like the hippies with my arms flailing above my head.

I walked out of the kibbutz manager's office with my head down. But it was an act. I missed my European friends. A week later, I boarded a ship to Haifa, en route to Crete where I had planned to meet Maria. On the ship, I played guitar and sang the blues and met a beautiful blonde Dutchman who set his sleeping bag next to mine on the deck. By nightfall, we embarked on a romance. He followed me to Crete. He carried my guitar. I was a long way away from my hometown where girls made fun of me for wearing T-shirts and jeans, and nasty boys in souped-up Cameros screamed out their windows, "Hey, Ugly!" Now I was a rock star.

Three years later, while traveling on the Trans-Siberian Railway heading toward China, I found myself yearning for a soft-spoken, blonde-haired British woman. When she wasn't by my side, I longed for her. And I thought, *what the hell is going on with me? I'm not that way, am I? Wouldn't I already know?* After all, I had gone to college where the largest organization on campus was the gay and lesbian union. Yet, unlike the lesbians I knew, I wasn't tough, didn't dye my hair blue, or look like a nun. I was just a shy Jewish girl from Long Island with masses of frizzy hair that I spent hours on end trying to blow-dry straight.

I'm straight. And the train continued to chug on. *I'm not like that.* And with each passing stop I became more attracted to the Brit, her accent, her sexy smirk, the way she rolled her eyes when she laughed. Finally I gave in. *Maybe I like girls.* Scared to look each other in the eye, we talked about our ex-boyfriends. We walked along the Great Wall. When I visited her in England, we kissed. And unlike most of the boys I'd been with, something felt real, felt right; I didn't have to convince myself that this was something I ought to be doing.

Back in the States, I had a fling with another blonde-haired, blue-eyed woman. And four years later, a week after visiting Auschwitz— the darkened barracks, the final set of train tracks where thousands stepped from crammed freight cars full of lice and trepidation—I met Anna, a law student from Frankfurt. Both of us were enrolled in a Spanish course just north of Madrid. A robust, blonde woman who spoke eight languages, an avid skier who lodged in Swiss chalets, Anna *was* the shiksa in my living room.

The day after my trip to Auschwitz, I reconsidered what it meant to be a Jew. I woke up in a snarled-sheet sweat and reached for my curls, relieved to find them firmly rooted, unsnipped. I obsessed about the Holocaust, how it could have happened. I couldn't stop thinking about Third Reich atrocities, even while studying past and future and subjective conjugations during my month-long Spanish class. I interviewed German students. I held up my tiny Walkman microphone and asked them questions: *What did you learn in school about the Holocaust? What do you think about it? Do you think something like this could happen again?* Most agreed it was a black period of German history, that Hitler offered the Germans a way out of a sinking economy, that the German citizens had no idea what was happening.

Anna and I sat with each other in the cafeteria, and instead of eating the food, we'd shape it into characters and color-coordinate it and make up surreal stories about the potatoes and chocolate pudding and beef stew. Eventually we started tossing food at each other from

across the table. Anna asked me about New York and talked about To-
lstoy and Thomas Mann and Nabokov and Italian operas, and this
alone made my heart quiver.

And then I turned on my tape recorder and asked Anna what she
thought about Hitler. "I don't know what to make of him," she said,
clutching Shakespeare's sonnets (German on one side, English on the
other). "My grandfather tells me Hitler was a good man. He saved the
economy. He built the Autobahn. But my teachers say he was a bad
man." Anna folded her arms, sighed. "To tell the truth, I'm sick to
death of talking about it." She shook her head from side to side, then
placed her forehead in her hand as if just learning about the death of a
loved one. "I don't want to speak anymore about this subject."

I turned my tape recorder off.

Anna and I continued to flirt, yet neither of us could figure out if
the other was interested in women. When the course ended, Anna invited me to travel with her in Portugal. Finally, we kissed in a Portu-
guese cornfield. During the next ten days, we held each other, slept on
beaches, ate elaborate meals, talked about poetry. Before returning to
New York, Anna plucked a white hair from my head and put it in her
wallet. And there I was, falling in love with a woman who talked
about wine and art and literature with great ease but refused to talk
about the Holocaust and wasn't sure if Adolf Hitler was such a bad
man after all.

For the next year, Anna and I continued our romance from across
the Atlantic. We spoke by phone, wrote love letters, and when we had
time off, visited each other. During that year, I read every book I
could find on the Holocaust. One night I read a book by a Jewish
Hungarian doctor—Dr. Mengele's assistant—whose job was to perform autopsies on gas victims. The Hungarian doctor spoke about a
fifteen-year-old girl who survived the gassing and was led to him afterward, wrapped in a blanket, shaking, scared and confused. The
doctor gave her a bowl of soup, tried to talk to her, wanted to save her.
But after three days, the girl was led back to the chambers. "She'd
talk," said Dr. Mengele. "She knows too much." I put the book down.
I gave up on trying to read about and make sense of the Holocaust.

Soon after, Anna visited New York for the last time. She broke up
with me on Gay Pride Day. Still struggling to establish myself in a career, Anna said she didn't have the time to wait around for my success.

Before Anna's departure, we met up with a German friend of hers, also visiting New York. "Are you one hundred percent Jewish?" her friend asked.

"Yes," I said, with the zeal and ebullience of that ten-year-old girl riding atop Mr. Wilkomersky's motorcycle, swerving and vrooming and roaring through the synagogue parking lot.

Connections

Daniel M. Jaffe

My obsession with Soviet Jews began while studying politics and Russian at Princeton University in the mid-1970s. These were my people, after all. Was it not my duty to understand and help them? Of course it was. But what I did not at first appreciate was the underlying fact that my admiration for these people, my envy of their insistence upon living as they chose, had as much to do with my suffering as a closeted gay man in a homophobic society as with their sufferings as Jews in an anti-Semitic one.

For me, a teenager from the suburbs entering college in 1974, homosexuality seemed an aberration. I'd heard nothing about the Stonewall riots of 1969 and other growing efforts by gay activists to assert our rights and our humanity, but I'd sure heard about electric shock treatments and lobotomies designed to "cure" us. No amount of prayer helped reduce the frequency or intensity of my teenage fantasies about every single man I met/spotted/conjured in my imagination; still, I clung fervently to the notion that—as a good Jewish boy—I would outgrow the unfortunate Freudian developmental phase in which I was temporarily stuck. In the meantime, why not do something constructive, concentrate on my studies and earn grades sufficient for admission to law school? Right? Of course right!

I studied hard. During the fall of freshman year, on the Friday evening before my first Russian language midterm exam, my three roommates were hovering around our three-room suite—music, conversations, telephone calls. It was impossible to study there, so I searched for a quiet place on campus, starting with Firestone Library. I hunted all six floors, but every single carrel and chair were occupied with other pre-midterm crammers. This was late October in New Jersey—too cold to sit outside. Yet I had to study. But where?

Identity Envy—Wanting to Be Who We Are Not
Published by The Haworth Press, Inc., 2007. All rights reserved.
doi:10.1300/5641_29

I was not yet familiar enough with the campus to know of other, smaller libraries, and I didn't realize that many classroom buildings remained unlocked in the evenings. But I did think of Princeton's tiny train station, the Dinky Station as it was known, a stop on a spur line taking passengers to the main Amtrak route between Philadelphia and New York. When not wanting to compete with my three roommates for our one telephone—cell phones did not yet exist—I had occasionally used the public telephone at the Dinky Station, a short amble from our dormitory. So, from Firestone Library I set off across campus, shoving out of my head the vague rumor I had heard—I can't for the life of me recall where—that, after dark, the Dinky Station turned into a trysting place for men.

I was going there to study, for no other reason.

When I reached the station, I stepped inside the stone-facaded building into its fluorescent-lit, single large room, and sat on the single wooden bench facing huge windows. Not another soul in the place; perfect for study. I unzipped my pile-lined Mighty Mac coat, opened my purple-covered Russian grammar book to "Unit 4—Gender in Russian (Introductory)."

While moving my lips to recite the three different gender endings for the adjective "new"—masculine, feminine, neuter—I thought I noticed movement outside. I looked up and out the windows and saw in the shadows a man wearing a coat not terribly dissimilar to my own (mine was brown, his was forest green). He was walking back and forth on the platform. No trains departed from the station in the evening, nor did any arrive, so what was he doing here?

Refusing to acknowledge what I understood, I looked back down at the grammar book open on my lap. However, I could no longer make out a single Russian word, the Cyrillic letters suddenly having switched into Egyptian hieroglyphs. I looked up again. The man was now staring through the window at me. Thin, my height, with a bushy brown beard. Considerably older than my seventeen years; he was at least twenty-five. Our eyes met, and I felt a charge in my stomach, a churning that nearly flipped me into a somersault of panic and excitement. I watched him step to the doors and into the building.

I stared down at my book. Down at my book. Down at my book. If I stared hard enough down at my book, he'd go away. But if I stared hard enough down at my book, he'd go away. So, I looked up.

He walked over, stood directly in front of me, rocked back and forth, his crotch mere inches from my face. This was it. This was what I had longed for and dreaded. This. I stared at his crotch as he continued to rock back and forth. What was I supposed to do? Lunge forward and bite the worn black jeans covering his bulge? Reach out with my hand? Jump up and run away before plunging off the cliff that separated good Jewish boys from the abyss of heathen, perverse, golden-calf worshippers?

I shut my purple Russian grammar book and set it on the bench beside me, on my left. The man sat on the bench at my right, pressed his thigh against mine. "What ya up to?" he asked.

"Studying Russian." (Thinking back, I can't imagine how he repressed laughter at the absurdity of my reply. I suppose he was completely focused on his objective.)

He reached over to my crotch and squeezed. "Want some?"

"Sure," I said, not believing what I just heard myself say, not believing what was happening, what I knew was about to happen.

"The men's room entrance is outside and that's too cold," he said, this fellow of experience and obvious wisdom. "But we can use the women's room—the entrance is over there, inside the station."

Leaving my purple Russian grammar book on the bench, I followed him into the women's room. Into a women's room for the first time in my life. I was going to have sex in a women's room? Did that, *ipso facto,* make me a woman? (Being a college freshman enrolled in both psychology and literature courses, symbolism was everything.) Apparently, there was no limit to my taboo-breaching.

The women's room was dark, except for thin moonlight. "We can't turn on the lights," he explained with meticulous logic, "because the police might see and investigate."

The Police? *The Police?*

He led me into a stall for furtive sex beside a toilet. How disgusting, I thought, how shameful.

He yanked down his jeans and mine. To all appearances, my body was ready, but inside, I could think only, "If the police come and arrest me, I'll be expelled and will never become a lawyer and Mom and Dad will be mortified and Dad will never be able to hold his head up in synagogue again."

At my half-hearted fumbles—what on earth was I supposed to do?—the man guided me, now trying to pleasure me, now showing me how to pleasure him. I did not, back then, fully appreciate how extraordinarily kind and gentle he was, how annoyed and irritated he could have become at my utter lack of sensuality or driving desire. I was, however, grateful that he smelled of Dial soap, a familiar scent of cleanliness that I clung to in that moment while feeling gutterfilthy.

I suppose he soon recognized that my mind was less between our legs than within my own head, and that my enthusiasm, initially dubious at best, had quickly waned. He finished himself off, asked if I wanted a similar helping hand. "I'm okay," I said, wishing to bring the fiasco to an immediate end.

"Can I see you again?" he asked. Boy, he must have been desperate.

"I don't know," I said.

"That's what all you students say."

All us students?

We pulled up our jeans and zipped. "Let me check if the coast is clear," he said, poking his head out the women's room door. "Shit! A fat lady in a red dress is coming!"

I can't recall whether I actually gasped or yelped, but something, perhaps an expression of horror on my face, elicited a hearty laugh in the man. "Just kidding," he said. "Bye." He left.

As I started to leave the women's room, I realized that I had abandoned my purple Russian grammar book on the waiting room bench. Right out there on the bench where anyone could have found it. Where anyone could have stolen it, valuable commodity that it was. If it had been stolen, I'd never be able to study for my midterm. I'd fail and they'd expel me from Princeton. I'd never become a lawyer, and Mom and Dad would be mortified, and Dad would never be able to hold up his head in synagogue again.

I dashed to the bench—phew! The book remained in place, spared by the used-Russian-grammar-book mafia.

Unable to bring myself to study further at the Dinky Station that night—would other men come lurking?—I rushed back to my dormitory. Fortunately, my roommates had left. I showered, then forced myself to continue studying, because I would not compound the disaster by failing my midterm.

Young. Fresh. Good. Hot. Future. Adjectives in Unit 6 of the grammar book did not help block out thoughts of my shameful depravity. Masculine. Feminine. Neuter. Which was I?

In the following years, I would think often of that night at the Dinky Station, sometimes horrified, sometimes proud, sometimes even longing to repeat the experience. But I never did. In fact, I routinely walked blocks out of my way to avoid passing the station, no matter that it was situated in the middle of campus. Likewise, I repressed even further any remote notion I might have had of coming out. If being gay meant spending my life haunting deserted train stations, dropping my pants in a women's room, and risking theft of irreplaceable textbooks, I wanted no part of it.

Even so, throughout the rest of my freshman year at Princeton, I would on occasion see from the corner of my eye while on my way to class, a flier posted on some campus bulletin board advertising a meeting or dance sponsored by an organization subtly named the "Gay Alliance of Princeton." The invariably pink or lavender flier would invariably be defiled with a pen-scribble of "faggot." And by the time I returned from class an hour later, intending to glance askance at that very same flier as I walked quickly past without slowing my gait—just to glance so as to see it, connect with it, fantasize about what such a dance might be like, boys dancing with boys—the flier would be gone, having been ripped off the public bulletin board while I was practicing complex Russian genitive plurals. How correct I was, in this hostile world, to remain silent.

During my sophomore year, I occasionally read in *The Daily Princetonian* about a gay activist, new to campus, who was trying to bring about gay visibility. Was he insane? I once spotted him—his photograph must have been in the paper—and followed him around campus, actually hiding behind tree trunks and building corners when he slowed down. To my surprise, he entered the dormitory entryway next to my own. Had the university dormitory lottery system somehow been rigged to create a gay ghetto? One could only dream. How wonderful-dreadful that we lived in the same building; what a relief-shame that our rooms could be reached only by separate hallway entries. For months, I kept an eye out for him every time I entered or left the dormitory, staring at him whenever I could, following at a distance. I don't know whether he ever noticed, or, if he did, whether he thought me an admirer or potential basher.

One day, while passing the backside of our dormitory building, I saw that he had hung a banner from his third-story window. Orange letters, I vaguely recall, on a black field. "Gay Alliance of Princeton" hung out for all to see. And it hung just a few windows down from my own dormitory window. I cringed and grinned at the same time. If I couldn't make such a statement, at least someone could. A comfort, in a way, to see that banner so close to my own room. I felt less alone, yet also threatened, as if being taunted to come out. I began to question my assumptions about the inevitability of remaining closeted. After all, here was this guy announcing his homosexuality, and he hadn't been expelled or arrested. And he was kind of cute, after all, slim with dark hair and large eyes. I'd observed him smiling a lot, even laughing; he didn't bear a dour expression. A happy homosexual? Was such a being possible? Come to think of it, if there was an entire organization on campus, then didn't that mean there were lots of homosexuals at Princeton? All of them getting an education? Was it really possible to come out and still be a decent, respectable, happy person?

I considered all this for several days while the banner flew outside our dormitory, until one morning I saw that the banner was gone. *The Daily Princetonian* explained what had happened—one or more drunken (of course) students had smashed down the activist's dormitory room door, trashed his room after he fled, and had ripped down the banner.

Violence in my very building. So close to my room. You come out of the closet and look what happens—they break into your home and vandalize it. You're lucky if you escape unharmed. No, I would remain quiet about the feelings that lay inside, dangerous feelings whose expression meant risk of physical harm or worse.

During the spring of the following year, as I continued to obsess about my sexual yearnings, the trashing of the gay activist's room the year before, and my increasing academic interest in the plight of Soviet Jews, I boldly went on a few dates with a woman in a last-ditch effort to find my heterosexual self, clinging, as I was, to the deep philosophy that underpinned a television spaghetti sauce commercial— "try it, you'll like it." Try it, I did; like it, I didn't, even though she was as warm and intelligent and pretty as any young lady I knew. Hopeless. I was gay and that was that. But how to come out and deal with the stigma and prejudice?

It was then, a few weeks after I stopped seeing her, that I received a fellowship to spend the summer studying in the USSR. The perfect getaway to avoid obsessing about my idiotic sexuality; oh yeah, and a great way to study Russian language and literature as well as to meet Soviet Jews *in situ*. By that time, I had already spent two summers applying my new knowledge of Russian as a volunteer interpreter helping my hometown's Jewish Family Service resettle Russian-Jewish immigrant families. I had come to know a dozen such folks, warm people appreciative of my efforts to speak with them in their own language while driving them around our suburban community to shopping malls, synagogues, the movies.

A long flight from Boston to Washington and then, with a group of sixty students from various universities, from Washington to Moscow. I quickly tired of our summer routine: a half-hour bus ride from the Ostankino Hotel to the Arbat Restaurant downtown for breakfast, a half-hour bus ride from the Arbat Restaurant downtown to school, a half-hour bus ride from school back to the Arbat Restaurant downtown for lunch, an optional bus-sight-seeing tour in the afternoon ending in a bus ride to the Arbat Restaurant downtown for supper, a half-hour bus ride from the Arbat Restaurant to the Ostankino Hotel for an evening spent staring at the hotel room ceiling or laughing at the snakes in the hotel's basement shower room. Finally—to preserve my sanity if for no other reason—I took the plunge and initiated contact with relatives of one of my émigré New Jersey friends, Boris.

Like all other Soviet Jewish émigrés at the time, Boris had been stripped of his Soviet citizenship when he emigrated, and knew that he would never be permitted to return, even for a visit. Nor were his relatives ever likely to be allowed out of the country to visit him in the United States. Most likely, he would never again see Petya, the nephew he had helped raise. Since international telephone calls were monitored and letters were censored, there could be little honest communication. A meeting with me would be as close to an actual meeting with Uncle Boris as Petya was ever likely to get.

Boris had cautioned me about the risks involved for Petya if he were to agree to meet with me: in Brezhnev's neo-Stalinist USSR, association with a Westerner, especially an American, could result in interrogation by the Soviet secret police (the KGB), demotion at work or dismissal, or even arrest, imprisonment, exile to Siberia, or incarceration in a labor camp for "anti-Soviet agitation and propaganda" or some other trumped-up charge of disloyalty to the Soviet state.

Per Boris's instructions, I did not telephone Petya from the hotel room telephone which, presumably, was bugged. Rather, I stayed downtown after dinner one evening and went to a public telephone booth to make the contact call. Just in case Petya's telephone was bugged, I had to speak in "Aesopian language," as it was called, i.e., in oblique phrases. I could say neither that I was an American nor could I specify Boris's full name.

Thanks to the rigor of my Russian language professors, two of whom had grown up in Latvia, and thanks to my obsessive study habits, I spoke Russian with a Baltic accent that was in no way suspect, given that the Soviets had invaded and annexed the Baltic during World War II. Even so . . . how to identify myself on the telephone without stating exactly who I was? After all, Petya was not expecting my call. I hoped an idea would come to me.

I dropped in my two-kopek coin and dialed.

After several rings—"Allo?" said a man's voice.

"Petya?" I asked in Russian.

"Da."

"You don't know me, but I'm a visitor to Moscow. Your uncle sent me."

A moment of silence, then Petya said, "Uncle? I have no uncle."

I understood. For all he knew, I could be a KGB provocateur trying to entrap Petya into acknowledging that he was related to someone who had dared betray the Soviet state by emigrating. How could I be more specific, yet oblique at the same time? "I come from Boris," I said. I hated mentioning Boris's first name over the telephone, but I didn't know what else to do.

"Boris?"

"Yes. I live in the same city where Boris lives, where he's lived for the past two years." I purposely let my accent slip just a little. "Where he lives with his family now. We're neighbors."

Another hesitation silence. Did Petya detect my accent? Was he putting the pieces together? "The same city?" he asked.

"Yes. The same city Boris lives in now. I'm a neighbor. From far away. Boris gave me your telephone number."

"Oh!" said Petya. "Oh!"

Bingo.

"Oh my God!" he said, then added to somebody else in the room, "A visitor from Boris!"

I heard a woman's excited "Oh!"'s, then Petya asked some indirect questions in a controlled voice. In answer, I explained that I would be in Moscow for several weeks, that I was here with a group of people.

"Can you get away?" In other words, was I under constant government surveillance?

"I can get away."

"Tomorrow for dinner?"

"Sure." Petya instructed me to take a subway from downtown to the Rizhskaya Station, to "be sure to get in the first car," to step out of the train and wait for him on the platform.

I told him just my first name and added, "I have a beard and glasses." Few men in Moscow wore beards, often regarded as symbols of forbidden religious observance or emulation of Western decadence. "And a Jewish face," I added. Russians took pride in their ability to identify members of various ethnic groups—Russians, Ukrainians, Georgians, Armenians, etc., and Jews. (This fact probably explained why I and another Jewish-looking man—beards, dark hair, narrow faces, prominent noses—had been singled out from among all sixty students for a special search and interrogation upon our arrival at Sheremetyevo Airport.)

Petya set a time and the conversation ended.

I spent the next day as usual—breakfast, class, lunch, a sightseeing tour of the Kolomenskoe estate museum. But when the bus pulled up to the Arbat Restaurant for dinner, I slipped away from my fellow Americans and lost myself among the rush-hour crowds on Kalinin Prospekt.

As I hiked the long walk to the nearest metro station, I wondered if I would somehow slip up and get Petya's family in trouble. Or myself, for that matter. But I figured that the worst the authorities would do to me for contaminating a good Soviet family with my presence would be to deport me. After all, I wasn't a businessman or journalist or government official whose arrest might bear symbolic value in the Cold War tit-for-tat needling between Moscow and Washington. I also reminded myself that my backpack was full of gifts from Boris, not goods I would be selling in violation of anti-black-market laws. I would just be giving Petya and his family gifts from Boris. There was no law against gift-giving. After slipping a five-kopek coin into the metro station turnstile, I took the escalator down deep into its marble innards and sat in the first subway car of the train.

At the Rizhskaya station, I exited and stood on the platform, looking around at the bright yellow marble pillars as I scanned face after face. The James Bond furtiveness gave me a rush—how very different from my reaction to the Dinky Station furtiveness of three years before.

Finally, someone on the platform stared back. A man in his late twenties with light brown hair and a round face. I smiled tentatively as he approached. He looked me up and down. "Danya?" I nodded, we shook hands, and he led me out of the station, around the corner, down a few blocks to an apartment complex. Glancing at my full backpack—a sign of foreignness—he said, "Please don't speak in the hallway." Heaven forbid I might make some Americanish reference or accent slip or blatant grammar mistake that might be overheard by a neighbor who would then inform the KGB.

As we entered the apartment and walked into the thick aroma of onions and garlic, a woman stepped from the kitchen—light brown hair, wide face, standard flower-print dress. Anna, carrying their two-year-old son.

It was now that the smiles began, accompanied by looks and exclamations of wonder. "Thank you, thank you. Thank you for coming." They ushered me into the living room—Persian carpet covering one wall for warmth, sofa bed and coffee table beneath it, an armchair. But unlike other living rooms I would see during the rest of my trip, this one was jammed floor-to-ceiling with stacks of cartons. I wondered, but felt that to ask would be rude.

Anna unplugged the telephone, took it into the bedroom, set it beneath a pillow. She returned, shutting the bedroom door behind her. Then, with eyes rolling upwards, she made a hand gesture I would often see that summer—an arc with her index finger, pointing from wall to ceiling to wall, indicating the possibility of bugging, particularly through telephones. "Now we can talk more freely."

"So," Petya said, "you're from Boris!"

"From over there," Anna said. "You might as well be from the moon."

I emptied my backpack of jeans and panty hose and makeup, which they examined politely then set aside. What they really wanted was news, details. How was Boris living? Was his apartment decent? Had he learned English? Had he found a job? How about his wife and daughter? Were they making friends? Did they have money for food? I answered as best I could.

"Enough," said Anna. "The man's starving."

"No, I'm okay," I said, knowing how difficult it was for an average family to obtain, let alone afford, extra food.

"Nonsense," she said, bringing out open-faced sandwich appetizers of cold cuts and cheese, "you're starving." When she added, "*Ess, ess,*" the Yiddish for "Eat, eat," I thought how borders failed to separate one group of Jews from another. And so we ate. Beet salad and boiled potatoes rolled in dill and homemade cabbage-tomato borsch with meat, a Ukrainian dish.

"Petya is from Ukraine," Anna explained.

"My mother was Jewish," said Petya, "but my father was Ukrainian, so I was allowed to put 'Ukrainian' in my official documents. When you're from a mixed-marriage, you can choose. Almost everyone chooses the non-Jewish ethnicity." I had heard about this, how the Soviet government encouraged assimilation. Even before the Russian Revolution of 1917, the Russian authorities followed a three-pronged policy for solving the "Jewish Question": expel one-third, assimilate one-third, kill one-third. Emigration, assimilation, pogroms. "Beat the kikes and save Russia," was a popular old saying.

"I have a Ukrainian face," said Petya. "At work, I hear the kike jokes. But in here," he pointed to his chest, "I'm a Jew. And my son"—he lifted the two-year-old—"I don't want him to go to school afraid of being beaten up by other kids because he's a Jew. If he's Ukrainian, he can get into any university, enter any profession. But if he's Jewish"—Petya shook his head.

Anna added, "We couldn't give him a circumcision because one day others might see."

"Besides," added Petya, "it's illegal."

Anna looked down at her lap. "This must seem strange to you, for a Jew to hide his truth. But you have to understand."

I did understand. These people felt shame for living as crypto-Jews, much as the Marranos must have in Inquisition Spain. Why feel shame when this was a question of survival in the face of oppression?

Finishing the last of the borsch, Petya set down his spoon and said, "Yes, we hide and we pass. But to hide forever?" He shook his head. "I don't want my son to grow up hiding." And then he pointed to the cartons stacked floor-to-ceiling around the living room. "Filled with half of what we own. We're ready to emigrate."

"Really?" I asked, excited for them. "When?"

He shrugged. "We have to apply for permission first."

"You haven't applied, but you've packed?" I asked.

"To apply is to admit I'm Jewish. That's okay if they eventually let me out, but if not . . ." He again shook his head. "I could be fired, and we could be kicked out of our apartment. Or they'd permit Anna to emigrate with our son, but not me." And if Petya remained unemployed too long in this Communist state, he could be branded a "social parasite" and arrested, incarcerated in a labor camp. It had happened to others.

Caught between their desire to leave and their fear of taking the necessary steps, Petya and his family had packed as many of their belongings as they could in order to be ready, but could not bring themselves actually to submit the necessary papers to start the emigration process. Petya apologized for the depressing turn the conversation had taken, and we ended the evening with shots of vodka, guaranteed to mask the sharpness of anxiety and despair.

When I took my leave, Anna extended the standard Russian declaration of hospitality, inviting me to their home again any time. Petya walked me to the corner—he would not go with me as far as the Rizhskaya station for fear of further risking being seen with an American—and shook my hand, saying, "Of course, you understand, we cannot invite you to our home again." I was taken momentarily aback, then realized: he'd been willing to risk the danger once so as to maintain contact with his beloved Uncle Boris. But every decision was one of weighing risk against reward. I felt badly that I wouldn't see Petya again; I felt an unidentifiable kinship with him, an empathy.

During my remaining weeks in Moscow, I met relatives of other émigrés I knew in New Jersey. Some, like Petya, were fearful of applying to emigrate; others chose not to leave their country because they could not bear the thought of starting a new life in a strange place. Yet others undertook all the risks and did apply to emigrate, deciding that they had at least to try to improve their lives. I met Jews who congregated weekly in front of the Moscow Choral Synagogue so as to exchange news of who had been granted permission to emigrate, who had been denied, who had emigrated, who had been arrested. These people gathered under the watchful eyes of KGB agents wearing, of all things, trench coats. These people shared their Jewishness publicly. I met Lenya, who'd been refused permission to emigrate, who'd been fired, and who now scraped together a living by teaching Hebrew to Jewish children, an illegal activity for which he could be arrested. I met Ilya, whose family had also been refused permission to emigrate and who kept being denied entrance to one university after another, but who kept applying. I met Olga, the daughter of a mixed marriage, who listed herself as Jewish on her official documents. I met scientists, dismissed from their universities for having applied to emigrate, yet who continued to conduct research and to meet with one another so as to develop their professional skills. Activists in one way or another, people forced by circumstance to reveal themselves, assert themselves, claim their right to live in ways of their own choosing.

The more I thought about Petya, the more I came to a realization: I empathized with Petya because I was so like him—all my inner baggage was packed, ready to be hauled out of the closet and transported into a new, more open existence. But I was so afraid of the process of transition and the possible consequences. Of course I understood Petya's ambivalence, his efforts to survive by hiding.

And the more I thought about Petya's and Anna's embarrassment at hiding, the more pointedly I understood. Had not part of me been ashamed that whereas the campus gay activist had been bearing the brunt of homophobia at Princeton, while he and courageous others had been standing up to bring about change that could benefit me, I had been doing nothing? I lived practically next door to the guy, but what had I done to help him and our shared cause? I couldn't even muster the courage to talk to him.

Yes, I understood Anna and Petya because I was so like them. I respected them and their choices, certainly, but I *admired* all those others I had met, the activists—Lenya and Ilya and Olga and the scientists. People of courage. Courage that I envied. I wanted to be like them.

Back at Princeton in the fall, I initiated activity on behalf of Soviet Jews. Through the campus Hillel, I organized a campaign of letter writing to Jews who had been imprisoned or exiled to Siberia because of their emigration efforts, in the hopes that publicity would discourage the Soviet authorities from killing them, if not releasing them. And I began writing my senior thesis on the Soviet Jewish emigration movement—the history of anti-Semitism in the USSR, the growth of Jewish pride despite official anti-Semitism, the public protests and letter-writing campaigns and pressure to achieve the right to emigrate abroad. My pride and admiration and envy grew.

All the while, I knew that on some not-too-far-beneath-the-surface level, my activities in support of these people were also activities in support of myself. The more I studied their risks and sufferings, the more my thinking about self went back and forth: if I were to come out, I wouldn't confront risks as severe as those faced by Petya and Anna or the others. Sure, there might well be employers who wouldn't hire me if they knew I was gay, but some might; I didn't have to state my gay identity on any official government documents, nor worry about the government informing employers before I was ready to do so, nor worry that my dorm room was bugged. But hadn't I heard about FBI infiltration of various "anti-establishment" groups during the 1960s and 1970s? Maybe if I came out I would be placed on some government blacklist circulated heaven knows where? Who could forget the Soviet-like McCarthy Era? J. Edgar Hoover? But even if the whole world found out and if I were fired from a job, I would not likely have to face time in a labor camp for having asserted myself. True, there was the very real danger of gay bashing—just look at what happened to the campus gay activist—but university administrators had disciplined the criminal basher, a sign of hope that some people in positions of authority would treat me as a human being with dignity and rights.

The bottom line was clear: whatever the risks involved in my coming out, and whether or not such risks were similar to those endured by Soviet Jews, if I admired their courage, then could not their example provide me with the courage I needed to live my own life freely? The time had come for me to transfer my admiration for them into admiration for myself so that, one day, I could walk into a synagogue or anywhere else and hold my head up in pride.

So, in January 1978, I attended a meeting of the Gay Alliance of Princeton, a meeting held in a remote part of campus. Had they purposely selected the venue far from where anyone's approach would likely be seen by friends? As I walked up to the three-story brick building, my stomach churned with the same nervous panic and excitement I'd felt in the subway on my way to meet Petya, with the same pangs I felt when that stranger's eyes linked to mine at the Dinky Station.

Up three flights of stairs, each step of mine echoing. Through a fire door and down a long, dimly lit corridor to the one classroom with an open door. The room was well lit. I quickly took in the dozen assorted men and women, recognized only the campus gay activist I used to spy upon. I took a seat behind everyone else, just as the guest speaker, Arnie Kantrowitz, a gay Jewish professor, was introduced. A room full of gay students and a gay Jewish professor. I wasn't alone.

And so began my journey out from within myself. I continued political efforts on behalf of Soviet Jews and took to working for gay rights as well. Over time I grew to appreciate the connections among oppressions, to realize that oppression anywhere is oppression everywhere, how we're all part of one world, how helping others can be a way of helping self even if we don't, at first, see the connection. And I learned that admiring another's courage might well be the first step toward seeking one's own.

ABOUT THE EDITORS

Jim Tushinski is a fiction writer and filmmaker living in southern California. His novel, *Van Allen's Ecstasy* (Harrington Park Press) was a finalist for both the Ferro-Grumley Fiction Award and the Violet Quill Award. He is the director, editor, and co-producer of the feature-length documentary, *That Man: Peter Berlin*, which had its world premiere at the 2005 Berlin International Film Festival. His short fiction has appeared in the anthologies *His 3* and *Quickies*, as well as in literary journals such as *The Blithe House Quarterly, Harrington Gay Men's Fiction Quarterly, The Lodestar Quarterly*, and *The James White Review.* For more information, you can visit his Web site at www.jimtushinski.com.

Jim Van Buskirk is co-author of *Gay by the Bay: A History of Queer Culture in the San Francisco Bay Area* and *Celluloid San Francisco: The Film Lover's Guide to Bay Area Movie Locations.* His writing has appeared in *I Do, I Don't: Queers on Marriage, Dangerous Families: Queer Writing on Surviving,* and *Contemporary Gay American Poets & Playwrights,* as well as other books, magazines, newspapers, Web sites, and radio broadcasts. He is Program Manager of the James C. Hormel Gay & Lesbian Center at the San Francisco Public Library in California. For more information, you can visit his Web site at www.jimvanbuskirk.com.

Identity Envy—Wanting to Be Who We Are Not
Published by The Haworth Press, Inc., 2007. All rights reserved.
doi:10.1300/5641_30

Contributors

In the years since her wayward adolescence, **Joan Annsfire** has managed to remain on the right side of the law. She lives in Berkeley, California, and supports her writing habit by working as a librarian. Her work includes poetry, fiction, and memoir and has appeared in the following journals: *The Harrington Lesbian Fiction Quarterly, 13th Moon, Bridges, SoMa Literary Review, Evergreen Chronicles, Sinister Wisdom,* and *Mediphors,* as well as two anthologies: *The Other Side of the Postcard,* edited by devorah major and *The Cancer Poetry Project,* edited by Karin Miller.

Darin Beasley studied writing with Tom Spanbauer. He is the cofounder of the China Collective, a writer's work lab in Portland, Oregon, where he resides. Currently, Darin is seeking publication for his novel, *Dogwood.* His essay, "Start with a Farm," is featured in the anthology *Small-Town Gay,* published in 2004. He can be reached at darin.Beasley@gmail.com.

Rosebud Ben-Oni has been a Rackham Merit Fellow, a Rudin Scholar, a Leopold Schepp Scholar, and the recipient of a Horace Goldsmith Grant, given so she could complete her first novel, *The Annex Jew,* which deals with her experiences as a Jew of mixed race who survives the bombing of the Hebrew University of Jerusalem in 2002. She is currently finishing up her novel, and has had recent poems in *Arts & Letters, The Rialto* (UK), and *The Texas Poetry Review.* Aside from writing, she loves ballet, basketball, and any excuse to go clubbing in the middle of the week.

Jay Blotcher has been involved in gay journalism and community activism since 1982. His first professional job in New York City was coproducing the 1983 gay TV talk show *Our Time,* hosted by Vito Russo. His second job was towel boy at The St. Mark's Baths. Blotcher's articles have appeared in mainstream *(The New York*

Identity Envy—Wanting to Be Who We Are Not
Published by The Haworth Press, Inc., 2007. All rights reserved.
doi:10.1300/5641_31

Times, Salon) and gay *(Advocate, Out)* media. His nonfiction has appeared in five anthologies, including the Lambda Literary Award–winning *Looking Queer* (1998). He served as media coordinator for the founding chapters of ACT UP and Queer Nation and cofounded Public Impact Media Consultants. Blotcher has coproduced three documentaries, including *Heroes,* about Boy Scout James Dale. Blotcher and husband Brook Garrett were among the same-sex couples married by New Paltz mayor Jason West in 2004.

Robert Boulanger was born in Montreal, Quebec, and quickly established himself as a popular child actor for Canadian television in the 1950s. In 1959, Robert joined the U.S. Army because he loved Americans so much. After his discharge, Robert continued to split his time between Montreal and the United States, with extended periods in San Francisco. During his time in Montreal, he was a well-known bilingual DJ for several Canadian radio stations including CHOM-FM, a popular progressive rock station of the 1970s. Robert now lives in San Francisco, where he is a celebrated painter, avid gardener, accomplished voiceover artist, and master of serendipitous spontaneity.

Poet/novelist **Perry Brass** has published thirteen books and been a finalist six times in three categories for the Lambda Literary Awards. His previous novel, *Warlock: A Novel of Possession,* won an "Ippy" Award from *Independent Publisher Magazine* in 2001. His novel *The Substance of God: A Spiritual Thriller,* a Lammy finalist in the Science Fiction/Fantasy category, asks an intriguing question: Is our often censored urge toward sex the same urge as our urge toward a higher presence, known as God? His newest book is *Carnal Sacraments: An Historical Novel of the Future,* an explosive story set at the waning of the twenty-first century when your life span will be determined by your job, privacy will seem antiquated, and homosexuality will be permitted, but only in a very controlled and sanitized form. He can be reached through his Web site, www.perrybrass.com.

Al Cho is a research analyst at the UN Millennium Project. Previously, he has worked as a consultant on international trade and investment policy at the World Resources Institute and the International Centre for Trade and Sustainable Development. He has also lived and worked in Mauritius and South Africa. Al received an

MBA with Distinction from Saïd Business School and an MSc in development economics from the University of Oxford, where he was a Rhodes Scholar and served on the university's environmental advisory panel. He graduated summa cum laude and Phi Beta Kappa from Harvard University with an AB in social studies.

Margaret Cleaver has spent most of her life in libraries. She obtained her Masters in Library Science from the University of California in 1973, after some early career explorations involving world travel. Having read books on every subject in her Los Angeles neighborhood library by the time she entered high school, she found that libraries, in the end, offered the perfect career to a generalist with an insatiable curiosity. Currently retired and living in France, Margaret has found writing to be the perfect complement to a lifetime spent in the pursuit of books and learning.

Larry Connolly writes fiction and lives in San Francisco.

John Gilgun is the author of the books *Everything That Has Been Shall Be Again: The Reincarnation Fables of John Gilgun, Music I Never Dreamed Of, The Dooley Poems, From the Inside Out, Your Buddy Misses You,* and *In the Zone: The Moby Dick Poems.* He can be reached at johnboy1@stjoelive.com. He welcomes all e-mail messages.

JDGuilford is either black and gay or gay and black, depending on the slant of his politics, or the direction of the wind, on any day. A native of Atlanta, Guilford graduated from Emory University with a BA in sociology. He will complete his MA in gifted education at Columbia University in 2009. Guilford has held several odd jobs, from fashion promoter to janitor to stock boy to Algebra teacher, all in his first year of residency in New York City. His writing has appeared in *The Gay and Lesbian Review, In the Fray,* and *Flashquake.* His first novel, *The Gentrification of Sonya Crane* (Harlequin/Kimani Tru), debuted in February 2007. Guilford lives in Harlem, USA. Visit him at www.jdguilford.com or contact him directly at JDGuilford@ JDGuilford.com.

The short stories, poetry, and personal essays of **Lori Horvitz** have appeared in a variety of literary journals, including *Hotel Amerika, 13th Moon, The Jabberwock Review,* and *Quarter After Eight.* Her writing has also appeared in many anthologies, including *Rite of Pas-*

sage: Backpacking 'Round Europe (Lonely Planet), *Love Shook My Heart 2* (Alyson), and *Boomer Girls* (University of Iowa). She has been awarded writing fellowships from Yaddo, Cottages at Hedgebrook, Virginia Center for the Creative Arts, and Blue Mountain Center. At present she is an associate professor of literature and language at University of North Carolina at Asheville.

Daniel M. Jaffe's novel, *The Limits of Pleasure,* was excerpted in *Best Gay Erotica 2003* and was a finalist for one of *ForeWord Magazine*'s Book of the Year Awards. Dan compiled and edited *With Signs and Wonders: An International Anthology of Jewish Fabulist Fiction,* and translated the Russian-Israeli novel *Here Comes the Messiah!* by Dina Rubina. An award-winning short story writer and Pushcart Prize nominee, Dan is a frequent contributor to anthologies, literary journals, and newspapers. He teaches fiction writing for UCLA Extension. Dan is also consulting editor for the literary journal *Lorraine and James.* For more information, visit his Web site at danieljaffe.tripod.com.

Deborah La Garbanza lives in the evil shadow of Oakland's Mormon Temple in a cottage with her cat, Luna. She writes fiction and memoir, and her work has appeared in *Q Zine.* Since she was a girl, she has tried out many identities before settling into an uneasy truce with her current incarnation as a high school teacher.

Robert Labelle is a graduate of the MA program in creative writing at Concordia University in Montreal, Canada. His work has appeared in anthologies such as *Quickies I* and *III, Queer View Mirror II,* as well as in *Pottersfield Portfolio* and *Fish Piss Magazine.*

Born and raised in Nairobi, Kenya, **Keguro Macharia** currently lives and studies in the Midwest. His critical and creative writing revolves around questions of queer practices, national citizenship, diaspora, and postcolonialism.

Jeff Mann's poetry, fiction, and essays have appeared in many publications, including *Rebel Yell, Prairie Schooner, Shenandoah, Laurel Review, The Gay and Lesbian Review, Bear Lust, Best Gay Erotica* 2003 and 2004, *West Branch,* and *Appalachian Heritage.* He has published three award-winning poetry chapbooks—*Bliss, Mountain Fireflies,* and *Flint Shards from Sussex*—as well as a full-length book of poetry, *Bones Washed with Wine.* A collection of essays, *Edge,* and a novella, "Devoured," included in *Masters of Midnight: Erotic Tales of the Vampire*, appeared in 2003. His most recent publications include a collection of poetry, *On the Tongue* (2006); a book of poetry and memoir, *Loving Mountains, Loving Men* (2005); and a book of short fiction, *A History of Barbed Wire* (2006). He teaches creative writing at Virginia Tech in Blacksburg, Virginia.

Mike McGinty writes humorous personal essays and fiction. His work has appeared online at Gay.com, PlanetOut, Outsports, Velvet Mafia, Silicon Mom, Suspect Thoughts, and NewYorkQNews. He has also contributed to *American Magazine, Whispers from Heaven,* and *Bookmarks Magazine,* as well as the Lambda Literary Award–winning anthology *I Do/I Don't: Queers on Marriage*. He is currently writing both a travel memoir and his first novel, the divergent plots of which he tries diligently not to confuse. As a Clio Award–winning ad copywriter in San Francisco, he writes inspirational TV commercials for useless toys and thinks up evocative brand names for the scratch-resistant coating on eyeglasses. He lives in San Francisco, and no longer shows steers, heifers, bulls, oxen, or bovine of any kind. Visit Mike's Web site at www.mikemcginty.com.

Will McNamara now lives in California and is working on a collection of personal essays based on his childhood in Iowa.

Max Pierce's debut novel is *The Master of Seacliff* (Harrington Park Press), a Gothic mystery. As a journalist, his writings on Hollywood history and gay life have appeared in such diverse publications as *Classic Images* and online for *The Advocate*. Max explored the complicated relationship with his mother as part of the anthology *Walking Higher: Gay Men Write About the Deaths of Their Mothers* (Renault Publishing, 2004). Annoyingly optimistic about his future, Max really does not like to revisit his childhood, unless paid to do so. Learn more at www.maxpierce.com.

Andrew Ramer's book *Two Flutes Playing,* a Lambda Literary Award finalist, has been called an underground gay classic. Mark Thompson interviewed him in *Gay Soul,* along with Harry Hay, James Broughton, and other elders in the gay spirituality movement. Ramer writes a regular column, "Praxis," in *White Crane Journal*. His work has appeared in *Best Gay Erotica* 1998 and 2001, *Kosher Meat, Afterwards: Real Sex from Gay Men's Diaries,* and *Found*

Tribe: Jewish Coming Out Stories. His next book, *Queering the Text: Biblical, Medieval, and Modern Jewish Stories,* is forthcoming from Suspect Thoughts Press.

Cheryl Schoonmaker recently received her MA in English from SUNY Albany where she has taught English and women's studies classes. She is currently a writing tutor at Hudson Valley Community College and hoping to soon be hired as a "Human Potential Advocate" at her local YWCA. Cheryl has also taught job and life skills to adults with developmental disabilities. One foot in academia, the other in human services, she is enjoying the wild ride. She loves and lives with Deb, an engineer who is saving the world one fuel cell at a time. Cheryl thanks her parents for their love and support of her, despite differences of opinion and some rocky patches along the way. Although her essay raises questions about their acceptance of her "lifestyle," she has never doubted their love for her.

D. Travers Scott is the author of two novels, the Lambda Literary Award–winning *One of These Things Is Not Like the Other* and *Execution, Texas: 1987.* Deemed "funny and disturbing" by David Sedaris and "halfway between Flaubert and *Straight to Hell*" by Robert Glück, Scott has appeared in venues such as "This American Life," *Harper's,* and the *Best Gay Erotica* and *Best American Gay Fiction* series. Currently he is pursuing a PhD in communications. More at www.dtraversscott.com.

Renate Stendhal, PhD, is a German-born writer, writing coach, and counselor working in Pt. Reyes Station, Berkeley, and San Francisco, California. Among her publications are *Sex and Other Sacred Games* (with Kim Chernin) and the award-winning photobiography *Gertrude Stein in Words and Pictures.* Her most recent book is *True Secrets of Lesbian Desire: Keeping Sex Alive in Long-Term Relationships.* Visit Renate's Web site at www.renatestendhal.com.

Frederic B. Tate is a psychologist in Williamsburg, Virginia. He specializes in grief and bereavement counseling with individuals who have terminal and life-threatening illnesses. In 1983, when he was a student at Southern Illinois University, he started working with gay men with HIV/AIDS—still called the "gay cancer" at that time. Frederic helped to establish Virginia's first hospice for adults with AIDS in Newport News, Virginia. When he is not writing or fantasizing about returning to Ireland, Frederic can be found sitting at his baby grand piano where he receives infinite pleasure slaughtering the classics.

Gerard Wozek is the author of the short story collection *Postcards from Heartthrob Town* (Harrington Park Press). His debut collection of poetry, *Dervish,* won the Gival Press Poetry Book Award. His poetry and short prose have appeared in various journals and anthologies, including *Bend Don't Shatter, Erotic Travel Tales, Rebel Yell 2, Queer Dog, The Road Within, Best Gay Erotica 1998, Velvet Mafia, White Crane Journal,* and *Blithe House Quarterly.* Recently, his short film "Dance of the Electric Moccasins" won first place at the 2005 Potenza Film Festival in Italy. He teaches creative writing at Robert Morris College in Chicago. Visit Gerard's Web site at www.gerardwozek.com.